Will Barker is on churchmen. Ambas he has both playe vibrant, orthodox, 1 Christians, and has also served as a superb chronicler and commentator on this community's collective life together and its mutual aspirations. Dr. Barker is a first-rate church historian, and his considerable theological skills are on open display in this welcome collection of his writings. His generous spirit, powerful mind and pastoral heart are productive of theological discourse that is a model, in both tone and content, for reformed ministers and scholars as we engage with a hostile postmodern culture.

J. Ligon Duncan III
Senior Minister, First Presbyterian Church, Jackson, Mississippi
Past Moderator, General Assembly of the
Presbyterian Church in America

'A gathering of writings from different places and eras of a person's life can sometimes be eclectic, disjointed and discordant; but not so this particular collection. The writings of Professor William Barker, a respected church historian in the Reformed tradition and expert on Puritanism and the Westminster Assembly, weave together a stimulating and attractive tapestry of studies which show the centrality of the Word of God to all the works of God in history. Reading them is no dry, academic exercise, but a valuable lesson in how practical a study of church history can be. And this is not merely a re-visiting of familiar ground; there is information here on some of the lesser-known, yet equally important figures in church history. We all have much to learn from the past, and Professor Barker is a helpful guide in that enterprise.

Iain D. Campbell
Back Free Church of Scotland,
Isle of Lewis

'The publication of *Word to the World: The Collected Writings of William S. Barker* is a cause for rejoicing. Serving for most of one's academic career in the posts of seminary president and academic dean is not usually conducive to writing, yet Will Barker has been able to do both—and he has done them well. Besides producing books, he has penned the articles, essays, and addresses that are gathered together in this volume.

The book is marked by both variety and constancy. Its three parts cover matters pertaining to the role of the church in society, the Westminster Standards, and the Scriptures. The chapter topics also range widely, focusing on everything from the assurance of salvation and Christians' cultural engagement to Charles Hodge's views on slavery, from Christian missions and a heresy case to inerrancy, Puritans, the days of creation, theonomy, Thomas Watson, and more.

Running through all this variety, though, are certain constants: good writing; a combination of forthrightness and fairness; prudence and much wise counsel; a reverent, even worshipful, tone; and above all, the fruitfulness of a mind and heart devoted to the Bible. Indeed, Will Barker's attitude toward and use of the Bible in this collection makes one think of the good old biblical name that we used to use for the Word of God—the Holy Scriptures (2 Tim 3:15).'

Robert A. Peterson,
Professor of Systematic Theology,
Covenant Theological Seminary, St Louis, Missouri

Word to the World

The Collected Writings of William S. Barker

MENTOR

Copyright © William S. Barker 2005

10 9 8 7 6 5 4 3 2 1

ISBN 1-84550-050-4

Published in 2005
in the
Mentor Imprint
By
Christian Focus Publications,
Geanies House, Fearn, Ross-shire,
IV20 1TW, Scotland

www.christianfocus.com

Cover design by Alister MacInnes

Printed and bound by
Bell & Bain, Glasgow

All rights reserved. No part of this publication may be reproduced, stored in a retrieval system, or transmitted, in any form, by any means, electronic, mechanical, photocopying, recording or otherwise without the prior permission of the publisher or a license permitting restricted copying. In the U.K. such licenses are issued by the Copyright Licensing Agency, 90 Tottenham Court Road, London W1P 9HE.

Contents

Preface 7

Part 1: The Christian Church in Society

1. The Lordship of Jesus and the Preparation of His Servants 11

2. Puritans and the Purity of the Church 19

3. The Rediscovery of the Gospel:
   The Reformation, the Westminster Divines, and Missions............ 35

4. The Gospel and Human Relations.. 47

5. The Social Views of Charles Hodge (1797–1878):
   A Study in Nineteenth-Century Calvinism and Conservatism..... 73

6. America and the Coming King 107

7. A History of Church and State Relations in
   Western Christianity 123

8. Theonomy, Pluralism, and the Bible 131

Part 2: The Westminster Confession of Faith

9. Profiles in Puritanism 153

10. A Body of Divinity by Thomas Watson 193

11. System Subscription 207

12. The Samuel Hemphill Heresy Case (1735)
    and the Historic Method of Subscribing to
    the Westminster Standards 229

13. The Westminster Assembly on the Days of Creation:
    A Reply to David W. Hall 259

Part 3: The Word of God

14. Inerrancy and the Role of the Bible's Authority:
    A Review Article 273

15. The Authority of Scripture and Assurance of Salvation 293

William S. Barker (Ph.D., Vanderbilt University) was until his retirement Professor of Church History at Westminster Theological Seminary (Philadelphia). With other degrees from Princeton University, Cornell University and Covenant Theological Seminary he has taught at Covenant College and continues as Adjunct Professor of Church History at Covenant Theological Seminary. He was editor of the *Presbyterian Journal* and has contributed to the *Dictionary of Christianity in America*.

Preface

Re-reading one's writings produced over more than thirty years, one is struck with gratitude for sound teaching received from abundant sources by the grace of God. Insofar as these articles and lectures may be beneficial, they reflect the influence upon me, first, of godly parents (Theodore R. and Nancy Edwards Barker) and of brothers, both older (Edward T. Barker, M.D.) and younger (Nicholas P. Barker, Ph.D.). Then there were teachers, such as E. Harris Harbison at Princeton and T. E. Mommsen at Cornell; but especially formative were the Covenant Seminary faculty: Wilber B. Wallis, R. Laird Harris, Robert G. Rayburn, J. Oliver Buswell, Jr., and those who were my pastors as well as teachers: Elmer B. Smick, Donald J. MacNair, Francis A. Schaeffer, and pre-eminently John W. Sanderson, Jr., who was also a colleague and mentor at both Covenant College and Seminary. There are other former colleagues who still exercise a special influence upon my thought and life: Rudolph F. Schmidt, David C. Jones, and David B. Calhoun of Covenant College and Seminary and D. Clair Davis, Samuel T. Logan, Jr., Richard B. Gaffin, Jr., Sinclair B. Ferguson, William Edgar, Vern

Poythress, and Manuel Ortiz of Westminster Seminary. Former students, too, have contributed to the shaping of my thinking and ministry: Randy Nabors, Ron Lutjens (my current pastor), Philip G. Ryken, and Bryan Chapell (now President of Covenant Seminary), among many others. I am profoundly grateful to our Lord for the benefits of relationships with such servants of his. Most of all, I am thankful for my wife Gail, and daughter Anne Barker, son Matt and his wife Ginny, and our four grandchildren, Susannah, Elizabeth, Seth, and Mary. Truly, 'the lines have fallen for me in pleasant places' (Psalm 16).

If there is a unifying theme to these several articles and addresses, it is the power and authority of the Scriptures, the very written Word of God, the only infallible rule of faith and practice, as the Spirit employs them in the church, whose Confessional tradition, embodying the system of doctrine contained in the Scriptures, guides her in speaking the gospel of truth in love into the fallen and needy world. God so loved the world that he gave his only-begotten Son, and Jesus Christ loved us and gave himself for us. Now the Spirit who has brought the saving gospel to us, down through the centuries of history and across oceans and continents, impels us to convey this marvelous message of salvation through the crucified and risen King Jesus to all the world and to the generations yet to come until Jesus returns.

I wish to thank editor and friend Malcolm Maclean and all those involved at Christian Focus Publications for making it possible for me to spread my humble version of this marvelous message to still more potential readers and hearers and doers of the Word.

Will Barker

Part I

The Christian Church in Society

I

THE LORDSHIP OF JESUS AND THE PREPARATION OF HIS SERVANTS

Last month the Voyager II spacecraft was launched on what is planned to be a 1.4 billion-mile journey to Jupiter by 1979, to Saturn by 1980, and perhaps to Uranus by 1986 – it is to transmit the first live TV pictures from that far out in our solar system before plunging farther into interstellar space. One scientist has termed the spacecraft 'a bottle cast into the cosmic ocean', for it also contains a recording called 'The Sounds of Earth'. It is as though mankind were reaching out, in case we on earth should not survive, in a pathetic and noble hope that there is some other life out there somewhere.

We who believe in God the Father Almighty and in Jesus Christ His only Son our Lord, who was crucified, dead, and buried, who rose again on the third day from the dead, ascended into heaven, and is coming again to judge the living and the dead – we are firmly persuaded that there is life – divine life – 'out there,' and that the living God of Abraham, Isaac, and Jacob entered this earthly life incarnate in the historic person Jesus of Nazareth, who, having lived the only sinless human life, offered that life on the cross as the spotless Lamb of God, as the sacrifice for the sins of all who put their trust and only hope for forgiveness in Him. Our commission, as those associated with Covenant Seminary, is to prepare servants of Jesus because He is Lord of all.

Our text in Matthew 28, usually referred to as 'the Great Commission,' is ordinarily associated with world missions rather than with theological education. All of the work of the entire Church, however, is properly to be related to this commission. This is why Matthew, who begins his Gospel by linking the birth of Jesus to the historic line from Abraham through David and the Babylonian Captivity, concludes it on this note of the work of the risen Jesus going on through His servants to the end of history.

Our commission in seminary education, indeed, the commission of the entire Church, is founded on the confession that Jesus Christ is Lord, to the glory of God the Father. Jesus introduced His commission with the astounding declaration: 'All authority in heaven and earth has been given to Me.' If we do not face the implications of this claim, we cannot honestly identify ourselves as Christians.

What is the basis for such a statement and for our confession of it? Paul said in Romans 1:4 that Jesus was 'declared with power to be the Son of God by His resurrection'. It is the unique triumph over death and the sin that produces death that manifestly proclaims Jesus as Lord. Peter preached that 'salvation is found in no one else; for there is no other name under heaven given to men by which we must be saved.' Here in our text we are told that the eleven, when they saw Jesus, worshipped Him. Jewish disciples, the strength of whose monotheistic faith would regard as blasphemy the worship of one less than deity, bowed before this One, even though, as we shall note later, some doubted. And Jesus' commission includes the Trinitarian formula for baptism that joins the Son with the Father and the Spirit in the name of the one God.

All authority has been given to Jesus not only in heaven but also on earth. He is exclusively Head of His Church. Our Scottish Presbyterian tradition has emphasized the kingly prerogatives of Christ, seeking to maintain a direct conscious connection between the Christian and his Lord apart from intermediaries, be they political, ecclesiastical, or spiritual. Even the Father and Holy Spirit focus our attention on the glory of the Son as our Lord.

Jonathan Edwards, while still a young man at Yale College, meditated upon that ascription of praise to the Lord in 1 Timothy 1:17: 'Now unto the King eternal, immortal, invisible, the only wise God, be glory and honor forever and ever.' Jonathan Edwards, in the eighteenth century, recalled later how a sense of the sweetness of the sovereignty of the Lord came upon him as he meditated upon the text: 'He is the Lord.'

The name 'Covenant' was chosen for our seminary because our covenant theology views God through Scripture and history as the Sovereign who graciously initiates a covenant, a provision for our redemption from sin, our eternal life. The great commission is a statement of the Sovereign's covenant with His people. It calls for a response of commitment to the lordship of Him to whom all authority is given in heaven and earth. This is the basis for our attempting to provide theological education – Jesus is Lord and we are glad to be known as His servants, prepared to do His bidding.

The substance of Jesus' commission begins with a 'therefore'. On the basis of His authority we go and make disciples of *all* nations. His exclusive uniqueness as risen Lord means that He is the one Lord not only for individual believers but also for all the world, and everyone is to be sought for discipleship to the one Master.

This involves 'baptizing them into the name of Father, Son, and Holy Spirit'. Our spiritual union with the triune

God is of initial and essential importance. Certainly we cannot make disciples of others until we ourselves have sealed our commitment to Christ and have been sealed by Him. Our spiritual formation is of prior importance to our task of service. This requires faith, which is more than knowledge and mental assent, but that deep heart's trust that was the experience of Martin Luther after many spiritual struggles. It is that faith which can only be the gift of God's grace, for which, like Augustine, we cry out to God in the penitent humility of the abject sinner. It is that faith which, as Paul says, is a gift of God, and so we can only thankfully receive it. Baptism exhibits the grace of God who on the basis of the atonement of Christ's death on the cross seals His servants unto Himself.

Our making disciples also involves teaching: 'teaching them to obey everything I have commanded you.' Having been made disciples by God's teaching we gratefully and joyously seek to make others to be Jesus' disciples. This teaching involves obedience. Discipleship means recognition of Jesus as Master, by whose words our lives are governed. This involves all His precepts and practices. This is why we contend so earnestly for the inerrancy and infallible authority of Scripture. It is because Jesus our Lord taught it, and denial of the Bible's truthfulness is denial of our Lord. But much more than a testimony to Scripture is involved in discipleship to Jesus: we must find our very motivation for life in all the commands and example of our Lord, which represent the culmination of Scriptural revelation.

Such disciples are to be made out of all nations. Christ's lordship sweeps over all the world, cutting across all distinctions of geography, politics, culture, race, or class. Paul says in Ephesians 4 that there is one Lord, one faith, one baptism. There is only one Church for all nations. But the one Church is still the Church, defined by its commitment to the one Lord. There is that which is *not* church. There are those who speak of the *myth* of God incarnate. There are those who deny the bodily resurrection of Christ in the name of 'levelling with the public'. But the early testimony of Christian faith is as follows: 'If Christ has not been raised, our preaching is useless and so is your faith. If Christ has not been raised, your faith is futile. You are still in your sins' (1 Cor. 15:14, 17). This was Paul, who could say to King Agrippa, within living memory of the empty tomb, that these things were not done in a corner. The unity of the Church depends upon the purity of the Church as the faithful Bride of Christ.

Peter at the end of John 6 gives a testimony that brings home this point. Christ had just spoken of the need for eating His body and drinking His blood. On hearing this saying, many who followed Him said: 'This is a hard teaching. Who can accept it?' 'Does this offend you?' asked Jesus. 'What if you see the Son of Man ascend to where he was before? The Spirit gives life; the flesh counts for nothing. The words I have spoken to you, they are Spirit and they are life, yet there are some of you who do not believe.' Then He asked the Twelve: 'Do you want to leave too?' Simon Peter answered Him: 'Lord, to whom shall we go? You have the words of eternal life. We believe and know that you are the Holy One of God.' It is on that basis that we go and make disciples, because Jesus is Lord and the only Lord for all the nations!

Knowing our frame, Jesus concludes His commission with these words of comfort: 'And surely I will be with you always, to the very end of the age.' To accomplish our task, the one body must be filled with the one Spirit, the Holy Spirit, who is also called the Spirit of Christ. I say to those who profess Jesus as Lord: we must also manifest His Spirit if we are to be His servants. 'All men will know that you are my disciples if you love one another.'

We noticed earlier that although the eleven worshipped, it is recorded that some doubted. Could Thomas still doubt, who upon viewing the risen Lord with the nailprints in His hands had exclaimed: 'My Lord and my God'? Could Andrew or Philip or Matthew himself, or Peter, James, or John? Yes, they could still doubt, because seeing and hearing are not believing – we must admit we feel that ambivalent pull: 'Lord, I believe; help thou mine unbelief.' Faith does come by the hearing of the Word of God – but it requires the Spirit's effectual calling as well. Our spirit may be willing, but our flesh, our fallen human nature, is so weak. We need the Spirit of Christ! It is time that we recognized that our skepticism is not so much a product of our modern, enlightened culture that tends to dissociate the reality of God from what we experience as history and science. Rather our modern skepticism is a product of our fallen human nature, which only the Spirit can overcome.

Jesus assures us of His presence to the very end of the age. Our Lord has said to His servants, 'I shall never leave you nor forsake you' (Heb. 13:5; Deut. 31; Josh. 1). That is our need, that is our confidence. His lordship is our authority, His presence is our power. What a standing we have as servants of such a Lord!

As I meditated upon my calling, I was reminded by one the trustees yesterday of Joshua. Another one reminded me of the Abrahamic promises. 'God will be our God and we shall be His people' is echoed all the way through the Bible. I have been reflecting also upon Moses as he said to the Lord, 'If thy presence does not go with us, do not lead us up from here.' We dare not go unless the Spirit of Christ fills us, goes with us, and leads us.

What kind of theological education is called for to carry out this great commission? It must be in the name of Jesus, because He is Lord of all. There must be worship of and commitment to Him as the only Lord. There must be scholarly learning of all that He has taught and disciplined obedience to Him as Master. There must be a dependence on the presence of His Spirit, which will manifest itself in the same kind of loving self-sacrifice that was the life of our Lord Jesus. 'As the Father has sent me,' He said, 'so send I you.' Be it ever our highest joy to be faithful servants of Jesus Christ. May we enter into blessing with his words, 'Well done, good and faithful servant,' on that great and final day when every knee shall bow and every tongue confess that Jesus Christ is Lord, to the glory of God the Father. Amen.

2

PURITANS AND THE PURITY OF THE CHURCH

Puritans in the mid-seventeenth century gained their opportunity, both in Old and New England, to show the world what the church thoroughly reformed should be. But in both instances they failed – in the divisions and rigors of the Parliamentary and Cromwellian regimes in England and in the eventual compromises of the New England Way. Was there some fatal flaw in the Puritan program? Or was such a program necessarily best cast as an opposition party, on the outside of power and having its influence by prodding those on the inside toward further reform, its own innocence destined to be lost if ever it came into possession of power?

There have been many explanations for this probably inevitable failure, and no doubt several of these have a certain validity in their contexts. Within the context of the Puritans' own program, however, the program sought basically for a more thoroughly reformed church that would operate according to the sovereign authority of God as expressed in the Scriptures, I believe that the fatal flaw is to be found in their concept of the church.

The problem lies essentially in making the church coextensive with the community, thus supporting an established religion – a concept that was shared by all of mainline Protestantism in the sixteenth century, including Calvinism. But the Reformed tradition's stress upon the purity of the church made it especially ironical that it was blind to this point. The Puritans, indeed, came closest to seeing the point that the Anabaptists saw, perhaps unavoidably because of persecution from both Catholic and Protestant, the point that Christianity was not meant to be supported and fostered by the state. But this was a point that very few saw in the sixteenth century, and it would take the American environment and two more centuries to make it evident to many more.

What the Protestant Reformation did with the medieval concept of Christendom was to turn it to a profitable use. Martin Luther, when he could not achieve reform of the church through ecclesiastical channels, called on the nobility of Germany to take reform of the church into their own hands. In the Swiss Reformation, Zurich and Geneva and the other city-states had been won to the cause of reform through disputation before the civil authorities. England's case, of Henry VIII's becoming head of the church rather than the pope, was all the more blatant. After all, it was assumed, if much of Europe had become nominally Christian through such means as Charlemagne's conquering and baptizing Saxons, then the state can be God's legitimate instrument for accomplishing His ends. But such means would hardly accord with a concept of a pure church of 'visible saints'. Nevertheless, even those who grew weary of tarrying for the magistrate, or who were forced to flee to Holland, even they tended to tie citizenship to church membership, and membership in *their* church, when they gained control of the community. It wasn't simply, as John Milton would say, that new presbyter was but old priest writ large, because new congregationalists could be that, too.

The problem also was not just one of difficulty in transforming Reformed polity from Geneva to England and America. While it is true that the political and social environments of Geneva or of Scotland might make it easier to put Reformed ecclesiology into effect than in England, and that the wilderness environment of New England might encourage certain forms of implementation, it is nevertheless true that there was an inherent inconsistency between the doctrine of a pure church and the practice of an established religion.

1. *The Purity of the Church*

With regard to their doctrine of the church, the Puritans were essentially in accord with John Calvin. Calvin stressed the need for ecclesiastical discipline to maintain the purity of the church. Too much has been made of the fact that Calvin, unlike Martin Bucer, did not make discipline a third mark of the true church after the word and the sacraments.[1] Actually this is mainly a formal difference. Although Calvin frequently refers to the two notes of the true church – the Word and the sacraments – in this briefest form, where he introduces the subject in the *Institutes*, he gives them fuller definition: 'Wherever we see the Word of God purely preached and heard, and the sacraments administered according to Christ's institution, there it is not to be doubted, a church of God exists.'[2] For the Word of God to be 'purely preached and heard' and for the sacraments to be administered thus faithfully to Christ's institution surely in Calvin's historical context necessarily implied the exercise of discipline. His very argument against the charge of

---

1. Edmund S. Morgan, *Visible Saints: The History of a Puritan Idea* (Ithaca, N.Y. and London: Cornell University Press, 1963), 21-24.
2. John Calvin, *Institutes of the Christian Religion*, ed. John T. McNeill, trans. Ford Lewis Battles, 2 vols., Library of Christian Classics, vols. XX and XXI (Philadelphia: Westminster Press, 1960), IV. i. 9.

schism on his part is that the Roman Church, for all her claims to the creeds and to the sacraments, is no longer a true church of Jesus Christ.[3] In his *Reply* to Cardinal Jacopo Sadoleto, written from Strassburg in 1539 when the Cardinal had challenged the Genevans with regard to the basis of their reformed church, Calvin states that 'there are three things on which the safety of the church is founded, viz., doctrine, discipline, and the sacraments...'[4]

François Wendel comments on Calvin's treatment of the marks of the true church in this way:

> One notices... that for all the vital importance that Calvin attaches to the ecclesiastical discipline he refrained from making it one of the marks of the true church. This is a point of some importance upon which he did not follow Bucer. To the two *notae ecclesiae* of the Lutherans (the preaching of the Gospel and the administration of the sacraments), the Strasbourg reformer had finally added the ecclesiastical discipline – an element he regarded as indispensable to any true church. To Calvin the discipline was no less important, but not of the very essence of the notion of a Church; it was simply a measure of the defence and a means of sanctification and, as such, it belonged to the organization and not to the definition of the Church.[5]

Discipline was important to Calvin's view of the organization of the church for three reasons: for the sake of the honor of God and of Christ, whose bride the church is; for the sake of the members of the church who may be corrupted by an offender; and for the sake of bringing the offender himself to repentance.[6]

---

3. *Institutes*, IV. ii. 2-6.
4. John Calvin, *A Reformation Debate: Sadoleto's Letter to the Genevans and Calvin's Reply*, ed. John C. Olin (New York: Harper and Row, 1966), 63.
5. François Wendel, *Calvin: The Origin and Development of His Religious Thought*, trans. Philip Mairet (London: William Collins Sons & Co., 1963), 300-01.

The Scots Confession of 1560 lists the notes of the true kirk as 'first trew preaching of the Word of God', 'secondly, the right administration of the sacraments of Christ Jesus,' and 'last, Ecclesiastical discipline uprightlie ministered, as Goddis Worde prescribes.' It would seem strange if John Knox were to be inconsistent with the spirit of Geneva, which he had experienced as 'the most perfect school of Christ that ever was in the earth since the days of the apostles'.

Even Bishop John Jewel, who had opposed Knox at Frankfurt during the Marian Exile, in writing *An Apology of the Church of England* in 1562, stressed that truth has priority over unity as a mark of the true church.[7] Thus even the spokesman for the Elizabethan settlement, when he confronts Rome, implies the need for church discipline, the very thing the Puritans were hoping for through their monarch at that time.

But it was not to come by that route. Nor was it to come by Presbyterian government, whether surreptitiously practiced in the 1580s, or parliamentarily imported in the 1640s. Nor was it to come via non-separating congregationalism, the practice of autonomous local church government by believers within the framework of the established church, as advocated by William Ames and conveyed to Massachusetts. The actual form of church government, while much discussed because of frustration with the bishops, did not matter. It was discipline according to the Word that did. Whether the view of Edmund Morgan's *Visible Saints*, that an experience of grace as a requirement for church membership in addition to profession of belief and good behavior originated with the Massachusetts Bay,

---

6. Wendel, 299-300.
7. John Jewel, *An Apology of the Church of England*, ed. J.E. Booty (Ithaca, NY: Cornell University Press, 1963), 47.

is correct or not, it is clear that discussion between John Robinson, Henry Jacob, and William Ames in the Netherlands had been mutually beneficial toward an accommodation on congregationalism that still accepted the English churches as true churches. But what the Puritans did not see – except for a few bold separatists who then tended to lose sight of the objective authority of the Word – was that purity could not really be achieved in a way consistent with biblical discipline in a church established throughout a realm.

2. Eschatology

One thing that tended to make them think that way was their eschatology, their doctrine of the end times and the hopes and expectations that this engendered. Much theological attention has been focused on eschatology in recent years, probably because of the cataclysmic events of the twentieth century. In like manner the cataclysmic events of the sixteenth and seventeenth centuries – the sudden changes from Romanism to Protestantism and sometimes back again, the discovery of a New World in America, the horror of the Thirty Years' War – sent biblical scholars scurrying to the pages of prophecy to try to understand what was happening in God's providence and how it all might end.

The eschatology of Reformed Protestantism was not uniform as to detail, but one common consequence of it was a kind of cosmic optimism based on the Lordship of Christ and tied in with the doctrine of assurance of salvation. If Christ has triumphed over the forces of evil by His crucifixion, resurrection, and ascension, and if we are assured of being His elect, then ultimately His true church will inevitably triumph in this world.

This general sort of confident hope was held by Calvin and all Calvinists on the basis of the sovereign kingship of Christ. However, among some of the Puritans and their predecessors there developed some fresh elements of eschatology that stimulated their cosmic optimism to more specific hope. Some of the continental Reformers who came to England in the reign of Edward VI triggered study of biblical prophecy. Paul Fagius improved the study of Hebrew at Cambridge after 1549, and Martin Bucer and Peter Martyr both taught an interpretation of Romans 11 that held to a literal conversion of the Jews to Christianity. Calvin did not take this view, but his successor in Geneva, Theodore Beza, did, as did the Geneva Bible, which was produced there by the English Marian exiles and which became the English Bible of the Puritans. As a result, 'the doctrine of the conversion of the Jewish people was widely diffused in England, Scotland, and New England.'[8]

The idea that the Jews as a people were yet to be converted was held by William Perkins as something that would occur near the end of the age,[9] but whether that was conceived of as near or not, belief in this yet unfulfilled prophecy filled many Puritans with a conviction of hope for glorious accomplishment by the church yet to be achieved.

Reformed theologians held various views on the millennium, or the one-thousand-year reign of Christ over the earth, mentioned in Revelation 20. Since the time of Augustine and the Council of Ephesus in 431, the chiliasm, or literal interpretation of the thousand years, of early Christians like Irenaeus had been rejected by the Western Church. Both Luther and Calvin were inclined to follow the Augustinian view that the thousand years

---

8. Peter Toon, *Puritans, the Millennium, and the Future of Israel: Puritan Eschatology 1600 to 1660* (Cambridge: James Clarke & Co., 1970), 23-24; cf. also Iain H. Murray, *The Puritan Hope: A Study in Revival and the Interpretation of Prophecy* (London: Banner of Truth, 1971), 41.
9. Murray, 45.

referred to the spiritual reign of Christ through the church in the age since the New Testament. New interest in the prospect of the conversion of the Jews, however, began to restore a more literal approach to the Bible's predictive prophecy. The writings of Thomas Brightman, fellow of Queen's College, Cambridge, were to influence John Cotton toward a millennial interpretation of Revelation 20,[10] and the millenarian writings of Johann Heinrich Alsted, a German Reformed theologian of Hesse-Nassau who attended the Synod of Dort, would further establish the credentials of such views.[11] For the most part, such Reformed eschatological writings tended to be postmillennial, that is, holding that Christ would actually return at the conclusion of the millennium. However, premillennial interpretation also appeared in the teaching of Joseph Mede (1586–1638), fellow of Christ's College, Cambridge,[12] and was held by some of the members of the Westminster Assembly, such as William Twisse, William Bridge, Jeremiah Burroughes, and Thomas Goodwin.[13]

Belief in literal and imminent fulfillment of millennial hope would be damaged by the revolutionary application of the Fifth Monarchy Men in England, just as the excesses of the Anabaptist takeover of Munster in 1534 had given chiliasm a bad name on the continent. The majority of English Puritans, however, seemed to have been characterized by an eschatological hope for greater accomplishment by the church. Iain Murray sums up the Puritan views in four categories: (1) a small number who 'continue the views held by early Reformers that

---

10. Toon, 26-32, 34.
11. Toon, 42-45, and Robert G. Clouse, 'The Influences of John Henry Alsted on English Millenarian Thought in the Seventeenth Century,' Ph.D. diss., State University of Iowa, 1963; cf. also Christopher Hill, *Antichrist in Seventeenth-Century England* (London: Oxford University Press, 1971).
12. Toon, 56.
13. Murray, 56.

the Scriptures predict no further conversion of the Jews and that the idea of a "golden age" in history is without Biblical foundation'; (2) a large number who 'held the belief of Martyr and Perkins that the conversion of the Jews would be close to the end of the world', this being 'probably the dominant view at least until the 1640s'; (3) a minority who expect 'a premillennial appearing of Christ, when Israel would be converted and Christ's kingdom established in the earth for at least a thousand years before the day of judgement', this view held in a moderate form by some of the Westminster divines and in a wilder form by the Fifth Monarchy party, but in all its forms having only a short-lived influence in the seventeenth century until more recent times; and (4) a group which, like the second, 'believed in a further conversion of Israel and opposed the idea of a millennium to be introduced by Christ's appearing and a resurrection of saints,' but, like the third group, 'regarded Romans 11 and portions of Old Testament prophecy as indicating a period of widespread blessings both attending and following the calling of the Jews.'[14]

Even for those Puritans who may not have adopted a millennial form of eschatology, however, there was still the sense of purpose and cosmic optimism that the doctrine of the kingdom of God produced. As Sidney H. Rooy in his *Theology of Missions in the Puritan Tradition* has stated, for the Puritan, 'kingdom' meant far more than church:

> The kingdom of God...had a four-fold reference. The conversion of souls, namely, Christ reigning in man's heart, was the first step. Believers gathered in church-fellowship, Christ reigning in the church, was the next. Then followed Christ's reigning in the state, when the

---

14. Murray, 52-53.

national government proclaimed God's will supreme. Finally, when there were sufficient Christian (political) kingdoms, the universal reign of Christ would be established.[15]

This attitude would be expressed in the Westminster Assembly's Larger Catechism answer to the question, What do we pray for in the second petition of the Lord's Prayer?

> In the second petition (which is, *Thy Kingdom Come*), acknowledging ourselves and all mankind to be by nature under the dominion of sin and Satan, we pray that the kingdom of sin and Satan may be destroyed, the gospel propagated throughout the world, the Jews called, the fullness of the Gentiles brought in; the church furnished with all gospel-offices and ordinances, purged from corruption, countenanced and maintained by the civil magistrate: that the ordinances of Christ may be purely dispensed, and made effectual to the converting of those that are yet in their sins, and the confirming, comforting, and building up of those that are already converted: that Christ would rule in our hearts here, and hasten the time of his second coming, and our reigning with him for ever: and that he would be pleased so to exercise the kingdom of his power in all the world, as may best conduce to these ends.[16]

The Puritans thus anticipated a worldwide rule of Christ which would yet be expressed through the church and experienced by the church. The Protestant Reformation had clearly brought to pass much of Rooy's third stage, that of Christ's reign in the state – or at least this would occur once all the potential for reform would be secured

---

15. Sidney H. Rooy, *Theology of Missions in the Puritan Tradition* (Grand Rapids, Mich.: Eerdmans, 1965), 323-24.
16. Westminster Larger Catechism, Q. 191.

by Puritan influence on the government of England, and by 1641 the Long Parliament seemed to be bringing this to pass. Worldwide rule by Christ was a part of the motivation behind Puritan colonization in America. There was an optimism about God's purpose in the world that was a major dynamic of the Puritan drive in spite of all frustrations and difficulties. This helps to explain how John Stubbs, brother-in-law of Thomas Cartwright,[17] when his right hand was cut off for writing against Elizabeth's projected French marriage, could wave his hat with his left and cry, 'God save the Queen!' Especially after the defeat of the Spanish Armada in 1588, in spite of the liberty this now gave Elizabeth to repress the Puritans, there was a sense that England was God's 'elect nation', as William Haller has declared in the title of his book on Foxe's *Book of Martyrs*.[18] There was a sense of destiny that tied God's providential purposes with Puritan hopes in England and in the New World.

It is an irony of history that those with the strongest sense of original sin and human depravity should have had such confidence and so little self-understanding. Their confidence is explained by their assurance of Christ's sovereignty and their election by God in Christ. The lack of self-understanding is evident to us who have the advantage of historical hindsight in knowing what happened in the Puritan Revolution and in New England. But the Puritans, too, had Old Testament history. Those very models for theocracy that the Bible gave them should have warned them about the fallibility of even God's Israel. I believe that a proper reading of the Scriptures on church and state could have enabled the Puritans to avoid the

---

17. Patrick Collinson, *The Elizabethan Puritan Movement* (Berkeley and Los Angeles: University of California Press, 1967), 199.
18. William Haller, *The Elect Nation: The Meaning and Relevance of Foxe's 'Books of Martyrs'* (New York: Harper & Row, 1963).

utopianism which ensnared John Milton as well as the godly preachers of the spiritual brotherhood.

3. Church and State

The relationship between church and state has been a perennial problem for Christianity, particularly since the conversion of the Emperor Constantine in the early fourth century produced a Roman state sympathetic to the cause of the church. Prior to that time there had been no danger of confusion of the interests of church and state and of identification of one with the other. Coming in the midst of the most intense persecution of the church, that of Diocletian, Constantine's conversion was welcomed by Christians as manifestly a miracle of God's providence. The resulting situation, evident at the Council of Nicaea in 325, of the Emperor dominating the church's decisions like a thirteenth apostle, has been aptly termed caesaropapism.

Although the Protestant Reformers retained the mentality of a Christendom at least coterminous with Europe and the territories Europe controlled, they did not adhere to caesaropapism. Both Calvin and Knox eventually developed theories of resistance to civil authority when it went counter to God's commands in Scripture, such resistance being active in Calvin's scheme if led by the lesser magistracy and in Knox's if adopted by the people as a corporate body. Even Thomas Cranmer finally overcame his scruples about royal authority when he recanted his recantations and showed his ultimate allegiance to God by allowing that right hand that had penned those recantations to be the first part of his body burned at the stake.

The Reformers also did not adhere to the theocratic, or perhaps better, ecclesiocratic, position that characterized the medieval church from the Investiture Controversy of the time of Pope Gregory VII in the 1070s, through the height of papal power of Innocent III around 1200 to the most blatant claims of papal supremacy of Boniface VIII around 1300. The church was not to dominate the secular power, which also was ordained by God.

The Reformers' viewpoint was rather that of the two swords, the temporal and the spiritual, working together to accomplish God's ends in society. This had received its classic expression by Pope Gelasius in the 490s and was exemplified in Augustine's handling of the Donatist problem. According to this view, the church determines spiritual policy but looks to the state to support it and ultimately to enforce it.

It is not surprising that this view should have been adopted by the Puritans. It was congruous with the last twelve centuries of European experience, it had Old Testament models for it, and it seemed not inconsistent with New Testament principle. After all, the English Reformation had been begun as an act of state and genuine reform had been forwarded by that second Josiah, King Edward VI.

But the very persecutions of the reign of Mary and the frustrations under Elizabeth should have given pause to more than just a few Separatists. Christ's parable of the tenants of the vineyard in Matthew 21:33-46, along with the development of the New Testament church among the Gentiles, should have taught them that theocracy on the model of Israel was ended. Likewise the answer of Christ to the question of the Herodians and Pharisees concerning payment of the taxes to Caesar in Matthew 22:15-22 should have taught them that it was not the duty of the state to support the true religion. The denarius with its image of the emperor as a deity would not even be touched by Zealots among the Jews of Jesus' day, but He asks His challengers to produce it and acknowledge its proper use in the functioning of the state: 'Render unto Caesar the things that are Caesar's.'

It is true that some of the spiritual descendants of the Puritans in more recent times have gone too far in the other direction, making so sharp a distinction between church and state that Christianity is prevented from providing a critique and corrective for wickedness in government. These people, like the Herodians, those Jewish cronies of the Roman regime, need to hear the other and weightier half of Christ's word: 'Render unto God the things that are God's.' All governmental power, even Pilate's to have Christ crucified, is subject to the will of God and therefore deserves the moral scrutiny of God's people who would be responsible citizens.

But too sharp a division between church and state was not the Puritans' problem. Rather it was the tendency to blur this distinction in making the church coextensive with the community that produced the excessive expectations of the Puritan Rebellion and that resulted in the New England compromising of the purity of the church in the Half-Way Covenant of 1662. The problem was not really in the covenant concept, nor in the use of the sacraments, but in the failure to separate church and state, at least in the sense that the church should not employ the state's collective power. America's eventual contribution to this issue may not be an ideal solution to every aspect of the problem of church and state, but toleration of various religious beliefs does allow the Protestant principle of salvation through individual commitment to be achieved. It is just the sort of principle, of justification by faith through the preaching of the Word, for which the Puritans contended. As David Little's book, *Religion, Order, and Law: A Study in Pre-Revolutionary England*, has shown, the ecclesiology of Calvin, Cartwright, and Perkins conceived of the church as a new order of true believers in organic union with each other and functioning on the basis of voluntary obedience to Christ.[19] Such a pure church of visible saints, called of God and gathered together on a voluntary basis, could only be achieved where the church was recognized as independent of the state and found its support only from the Spirit of God. Failure to realize this was, I believe, the fatal flaw of Puritanism in the fulfilling of its own program.

We can hope that there are still spiritual descendants of the Puritans, and also that they are appreciative enough of the Puritans' piety and theology to learn as well from their history. For their history demonstrates the truth of one of their own convictions: that while the Scriptures are the infallible Word of God, man's understanding of the Scriptures is progressive. The understanding of even godly men is fallible. The Puritans had learned much of God's ways, but there is still much more to be learned. As an early motto of the Reformed church says, *Ecclesia reformata, semper reformanda* – the church reformed must always be reforming, and must constantly be reforming itself.

---

19. David Little, *Religion, Order, and Law: A Study in Pre-Revolutionary England* (New York, Evanston, and London: Harper & Row, 1969).

3

THE REDISCOVERY OF THE GOSPEL: THE REFORMATION, THE WESTMINSTER DIVINES, AND MISSIONS

It is sometimes claimed that the Protestant Reformation in the sixteenth century did not stimulate missions. From one perspective this appears plausible. Luther concluded that the Great Commission had been fulfilled in the Apostolic age. He offered the rediscovered gospel to the Jews in his vicinity, and when they rejected it, he decided that he should not cast pearls before swine. Meanwhile, the Jesuits were sending Francis Xavier all the way to Japan.

We should remember, however, that it was a struggle just for Protestantism to survive. The defeat of the Spanish Armada in 1588, just seventy years after Luther's posting of the Ninety-Five Theses in 1517, kept Protestantism from being destroyed in England by the resurgent Counter-Reformation. Calvin did encourage a colony in Brazil, but it was not successful. The Puritan propagators of the Reformed faith in Great Britain did gain control briefly in the 1640s to produce our Westminster Confession of Faith and Catechisms. While their clear exposition of biblical doctrine is appreciated, it is not often recognized what an evangelistic and missionary spirit they had. I would like to demonstrate that spirit in several of the Westminster divines, and make application to the evangelical church of our own day.

1. John White (1574–1648)[1]

At the very beginning of the Westminster Assembly, after a day of fasting and prayer, the members proceeded to elect two Assessors, who could take the place of the Prolocutor (presiding officer) in case of absence or infirmity. One of these two Assessors so chosen was John White.

He was called 'Patriarch White' or 'the Patriarch of Dorchester', where he was rector for forty-two years (from 1606). He was among the older members of the Assembly, being sixty-eight at its beginning. Thomas Fuller comments on White's ministry in Dorchester: '… he absolutely commanded his own passions, and the purses of his parishioners, whom he could wind up to whatever height he pleased on important occasions.' He was a 'good governor, by whose wisdom the town of Dorchester was much enriched, knowledge causing piety, piety breeding industry, and industry procuring plenty unto it. A beggar was not to be seen in the town, all able poor being set on work, and the impotent maintained by the profit of a public brew-house, and other collections.'[2]

One of the interesting things about White's enterprise is his connection with America. About 1624 he sought to organize a colony of Dorset Nonconformists in Massachusetts for the sake of religious liberty. He took

---

1. See William S. Barker, *Puritan Profiles: 54 Influential Puritans at the Time When the Westminster Confession of Faith Was Written* (Fearn, Ross-shire, Scotland: Mentor/Christian Focus, 1996), 22-24.
2. Thomas Fuller, *The Worthies of England*, 2:340, quoted in James Reid, *Memoirs of the Westminster Divines*, 2 vols. in 1 (1811, 1815; reprint, Edinburgh and Carlisle, PA: Banner of Truth, 1981), 1:102; ibid., 1:100-01; see also Barker, 23.

a lead in seeking a charter and raising funds for the Massachusetts Company, holding a service for John Winthrop before he set sail for America in 1629. White is regarded as the author of the *Planter's Plea*, published in London in 1630, one of the earliest accounts of the planting of the colony. A nephew, James White, became a wealthy merchant in Boston, and Governor Winthrop corresponded with John White in 1632 and 1636, urging him to visit the colony. With the outbreak of the Civil War in 1642 and the beginning of the Westminster Assembly in 1643, he was never able to do that. In fact in 1644 Prince Rupert's cavalry had burst into White's house in Dorchester, while he was in London, and carried off his library. Although the burdens of being Assessor became too great by 1646, he continued to take an interest in the American mission to the Indians down to his death in 1648.

2. Thomas Hill (c. 1602–1653)[3]

The evangelistic spirit of the Westminster divines is seen in one of its outstanding preachers and scholars, Thomas Hill. A product of Emmanuel College, Cambridge, from which many of the Westminster Puritans came, he lived for a time with John Cotton, pastor in Boston, Lincolnshire, the largest church in England outside of London. As a Fellow at Emmanuel College, Hill gained a reputation as an effective tutor, but also for preaching that was 'plain, powerful, spiritual, frequent, and laborious'.[4] In a Fast Day sermon in 1642, 'The Trade of Truth Advanced,' he challenged the House of Commons: 'Would you have a flourishing Kingdome, advance the Kingdome of Christ in it. Let the State maintaine Religion, and Religion will

---

3. Barker, 140-44.
4. Ibid., 141, quoting J. T. Cliffe, *The Puritan Gentry: The Great Puritan Families of Early Stuart England* (London: Routledge and Kegan Paul, 1984), 180.

blesse the State.'[5] His message took on an evangelistic, even a missionary cast:

> Improve your power to help forward the word of truth, that it may run and be glorified throughout the land: 1st, Provide that every congregation may have an able trumpet of truth; 2d, especially that great towns may have lectures – markets of truth; 3d, afford any faithful Paul and Barnabas encouragement, yea power, if Sergius Paulus desire to hear the word of God, to go and preach, though Elymas the sorceror should be unwilling. Such ambulatory exercises have brought both light and heat into dark and cold corners; 4th, What if there be some evangelical itinerant preachers sent abroad upon a public stock to enlighten dark countries?[6]

Hill's remaining years were involved with Cambridge University, where he served for a time as Vice-Chancellor. He continued very active in preaching, and did so on a regular basis in several locations. His evangelistic zeal inspired a corresponding zeal in his converts. One student, John Machin, entered Cambridge in 1646 'without any view to the ministry'; however, he

> had a gracious change effected in him, chiefly by the preaching of Dr. Hill; and that of Dr. [John] Arrowsmith [also a member of the Westminster Assembly] was much to his comfort and edification. No sooner did he find this blessed change in his heart, than his friends found it by his letters; by which together with his exemplary conversation afterward, he was the means of converting his three sisters, and there was room to hope, both his parents....[7]

---

5. Barker, 141, quoting John F. Wilson, *Pulpit in Parliament* (Princeton, NJ: Princeton University Press, 1969), 173.
6. Barker, 141-42, quoting Alexander Mitchell, *The Westminster Assembly: Its History and Standards*, 2nd ed. (Philadelphia: Presbyterian Board of Publication, 1897), 102-03, n1.
7. Barker, 143, quoting Reid, 2:41.

3. Anthony Tuckney (1599–1670)[8]

Anthony Tuckney is credited with being the major contributor to the production of the Shorter Catechism by the Westminster Assembly. He also contributed the wording for the very full exposition of the Ten Commandments in the Larger Catechism. His cousin's husband, John Cotton, was Vicar of St. Botolph's Church in Boston, Lincolnshire, and when Cotton resigned in 1633 to emigrate to America, Tuckney was chosen to succeed him. Having served as Master of Emmanuel College, after the Westminster Assembly, he was for a time Vice-Chancellor of Cambridge University.

Active in both church and academia, he corresponded with John Cotton in New England, being concerned for the conversion of the Indians there and raising contributions at the University for the propagation of the gospel in America. A notable preacher himself, he criticized the standard Puritan style of preaching, 'by doctrine, reason, and use,' as too constraining and advocated a freer style.[9] His own sermons were 'warm-hearted, practical, and strongly Biblical in character'.[10] In contrast to the church-and-state arrangements prevalent in that time, he wrote against propagating religion by the sword.

4. Edmund Calamy (1601–1666),[11] William Gouge (1578–1653),[12] and Herbert Palmer (1601–1647)[13]

These three were all key leaders of the Westminster

---

8. Barker, 175-79.
9. Ibid., 178, quoting Robert S. Paul, *The Assembly of the Lord* (Edinburgh: T. &T. Clark, 1985), 364.
10. Barker, 178, quoting John H. Leith, *Assembly at Westminster: Reformed Theology in the Making* (Richmond, VA: John Knox Press, 1973), 46-47.
11. Barker, 208-18; see also James A. DeJong, *As the Waters Cover the Sea: Millennial Expectations in the Rise of Anglo-American Missions, 1640–1810* (Kampen, The Netherlands: J. H. Kok, 1970), 48, 53, 72; Iain H. Murray, *The Puritan Hope: A Study in Revival and the Interpretation of Prophecy* (Edinburgh and Carlisle, PA: Banner of Truth, 1971), 20.
12. Barker, 35-38; DeJong, 28-29, 48, 49-50; Murray, 20.
13. Barker, 31-35.

Assembly, and all maintained an interest in the American mission to the Indians. Edmund Calamy was the main leader of the Presbyterians among the London clergy and was one of the 'Smectymnuans', who produced literature against the prelacy of Episcopacy that led up to the calling of the Westminster Assembly. Dr. William Gouge was known as 'the father of the London ministers', being one of the oldest of the Westminster divines, yet he was one of the most faithful attenders of the Assembly and served as an Assessor at the end of its proceedings. Both Calamy and Gouge addressed their concerns to Parliament for the efforts to convert the Indians in New England.

Herbert Palmer also served as an Assessor, being one of the most respected members of the Assembly. He differed from most of the Assembly in that he came from an upper-class background and remained unmarried. He learned French as a child, and this proved useful when he was serving as a pastor in Canterbury, for the minister of the French church there appreciated his gifts and had him to preach on several occasions. Short of stature and of youthful appearance, Palmer startled an elderly French lady upon his first visit to the church, who said in a loud voice, 'Alas! what shall this child say to us?' But after hearing him pray and preach with fervency and vigor, she lifted up her hands to heaven, praising God for what she had heard.[14] Palmer's preaching was characterized by plainness and simplicity, designed to reach the ordinary people. Having a sizable estate and never marrying, he was charitable in giving Bibles to the poor who could read and for giving money for instruction in reading to those who could not. Although not among the older members of the Assembly, he died

---

14. Ibid., 32, quoting Reid, 2:102.

before it had finished the Catechisms, to which he had especially contributed. Exhausted from his labors, in his last illness Palmer prayed,

> ...for himself, that God would heal the sinfulness of his nature, pardon all his transgressions, deliver him from an evil heart of unbelief, and from temptation; – teach him to improve all providences, and to live upon Christ and the promises. He also prayed much for the nation, for the church of God, and for all with whom he stood connected. He prayed particularly for Scotland, the churches in France, New England, and foreign plantations.[15]

He died in 1647, at the age of only forty-six.

5. Thomas Hooker (1586?–1647)[16] and John Eliot (1604–1690)[17]

One thing not often recognized about the Westminster Assembly is its connection with America. There were three American Puritans who had previously had significant ministry in England who were invited by Parliament to be members of the Assembly, but they were not able to attend. These were John Cotton of Boston, John Davenport of New Haven, and Thomas Hooker of Connecticut. Hooker was known for his fiery style of preaching in England, where he was also skilled in resolving cases of conscience and in leading people to assurance of their salvation. Because of his effective ministry, he was especially targeted for persecution by Archbishop William Laud. After fleeing for a time to the Netherlands, he returned to England in 1633 before embarking for America. Cotton Mather tells of a narrow escape from Laud's agents:

---

15. Barker, 34-35, quoting Reid, 2:114-15.
16. Barker, 266-72.
17. Ibid., 268; DeJong, 44-47, 75-76; Murray, 93-94.

Returning into England in order to a further voyage, he was quickly scented by the pursevants, who at length got so far up with him as to knock at the door of that very chamber where he was now discoursing with Mr. Stone, who was now become his designed companion and assistant for the New English enterprize. Mr. Stone was at that instant smoking of *tobacco*, for which Mr. Hooker had been reproving him, as being then used by few persons of sobriety; being also of a sudden and pleasant wit, he stept unto the door, with his pipe in his mouth, and such an air of speech and look, as gave him some credit with the officer. The officer demanded, Whether Mr. Hooker were not there? Mr. Stone replied with a braving sort of confidence, 'What Hooker? Do you mean Hooker that lived once at Chelmsford!' The officer answered, 'Yes, he!' Mr. Stone immediately, with a diversion like that which once helped Athanasius, made this true answer, 'If it be he you look for, I saw him about an hour ago, at such an house in the town; you had best hasten thither after him.' The officer took this for a sufficient account, and went his way; but Mr. Hooker, upon this intimation, concealed himself more carefully and securely, till he went on board at the Downs, in the year 1633, the ship which brought him, and Mr. Cotton, and Mr. Stone to New England: where none but Mr. Stone was owned for a preacher, at their first coming aboard; the other two delaying to take their turns in the publick worship of the ship, till they were got so far into the main ocean, that they might with safety discover who they were.[18]

Earlier in his ministry, in the late 1620s, Hooker had opened a grammar school in Little Baddow near Chelmsford in Essex with the young John Eliot as his assistant. Eliot would later become the outstanding missionary to the

---

18. Barker, 269, quoting Cotton Mather, *Magnalia Christi Americana*, or *The Great Works of Ch*rist in America, 2 vols. (1852; reprint, Edinburgh and Carlisle, PA: Banner of Truth, 1967), 1:340-41.

Indians in New England. He crossed the Atlantic in 1631 and began to study the Algonquin language when over forty. At the end of his notebook on the Indian grammar he wrote, 'Prayers and pains through faith in Christ Jesus will do anything.'[19] Starting to preach to the Indians in 1646, he succeeded in establishing scores of 'praying societies' among the Indians. Wars and volatile relations between the English settlers and the Indians damaged his cause, but he did succeed in translating the Bible into the Indian language. Cotton Mather, whose biography of Eliot was published in 1702, concluded his account with these words: 'May sufficient numbers of great, wise, rich, learned, and godly men in the three kingdoms, procure well-composed *societies*, by whose united counsels the noble design of evangelizing the world may be more effectually carried on.'[20]

Conclusion

The author of those words died shortly before the revival came for which he regularly prayed. Jonathan Edwards and George Whitefield were instruments of God in bringing the Great Awakening of the eighteenth century, which in turn set the stage for the great worldwide missions movement of the nineteenth century. Thus the Protestant Reformation and the Westminster Assembly have their direct connection to missions and evangelism. The Larger Catechism's answer to Question 191, 'What do we pray for in the second petition [of the Lord's Prayer]?' shows the missionary concern of the Westminster divines:

> In the second petition (which is, *Thy kingdom come*), acknowledging ourselves and all mankind to be by

---

19. Mather, 1:562, quoted in Murray, 93.
20. Mather, 1:582, quoted in Murray, 94.

nature under the dominion of sin and Satan, we pray that the kingdom of sin and Satan may be destroyed, the gospel propagated throughout the world, the Jews called, the fullness of the Gentiles brought in; the Church furnished with all gospel officers and ordinances, purged from corruption, countenanced and maintained by the civil magistrate: that the ordinances of Christ may be purely dispensed, and made effectual to the converting of those that are yet in their sins, and the confirming, comforting, and building up of those that are already converted: that Christ would rule in our hearts here, and hasten the time of his second coming, and our reigning with him for ever: and that he would be pleased so to exercise the kingdom of his power in all the world, as may best conduce to these ends.

David J. Bosch in his *Transforming Mission: Paradigm Shifts in Theology of Mission* lists five reasons why the Protestant Reformation did not lead immediately into missions, some of which are especially instructive for us today:

> Still, in spite of what Holl, Holsten, Gensichen, Scherer, and others have identified as the fundamentally missionary thrust of the Reformers' theology, very little happened by way of a missionary outreach during the first two centuries after the Reformation. There were, undoubtedly, serious practical obstacles in this regard. To begin with, Protestants saw their principal task as that of reforming the church of their time; this consumed all their energy. Second, Protestants had no immediate contact with non-Christian peoples, whereas Spain and Portugal, both Catholic nations, already had extensive colonial empires at the time. The only remaining pagan people in Europe were the Lapps, and they were indeed evangelized by Swedish Lutherans in the sixteenth century. Third, the churches of the Reformation were involved in a battle for sheer

survival; only after the Peace of Westphalia (1648) were they able to organize themselves properly. Fourth, in abandoning monasticism the Reformers had denied themselves a very important missionary agency; it would take centuries before anything remotely as competent and effective as the monastic missionary movement would develop in Protestantism. Fifth, Protestants were themselves torn apart by internal strife and dissipated their strength in reckless zeal and in endless dissensions and disputes; little energy was left for turning to those outside the Christian fold.[21]

The main point is the need to concentrate our energies where they will do the most good for carrying out our Lord's Great Commission for his church. As we consider our situation 350 years after the Westminster Confession was produced, 480 years after Luther posted his Ninety-Five Theses, and on the brink of a new century and new millennium, what efforts and measures in God's providence have brought the gospel to us, and what efforts and measures will carry it on to our children, grandchildren, and the next generations, and to the rest of the world?

---

21. David J. Bosch, *Transforming Mission: Paradigm Shifts in Theology of Mission* (Maryknoll, NY: Orbis Books, 1991), 245.

4

THE GOSPEL AND HUMAN RELATIONS

When we gather to partake of the Lord's Supper, we have vividly exhibited for us in that symbol of the death of Jesus Christ the realities of the law and the gospel. The law required His death; though innocent, He had to be crucified, being made a curse, for your sins and mine. The gospel is that He did in fact love us and give Himself for us, that God so loved the world that He gave His one and only Son, that whoever believes in Him shall not perish but have everlasting life.

Jesus summoned His disciples to regular remembrance of His death because in the continued memory of the cross they would find the proper basis for response to the grace of God both in their relation to God and in their relations with fellow human beings. In His discourse in the upper room, recorded in John 13–16, Jesus repeatedly stressed the reciprocal connection between love and obedience: the one who has His commands and obeys them is the one who loves Him, the one loving Him does what He commands, and His commandment is

---

Dr. Barker delivered this address at a Congress sponsored by The National Presbyterian and Reformed Fellowship held at Grove City College, Grove City, Pennsylvania. July 16-21, 1979.

that we love one another (cf. especially John 13:34-35; 14:15, 21, 23-24, 31; 15:10, 12, 14, 17). Later John pursues this theme further by saying: 'We love because He first loved us' (1 John 4:19).

The gospel of our Lord Jesus Christ, therefore, is the basis for our exercise of love in human relations, which is the fulfilment of the law. When asked which was the greatest commandment in the law, Jesus replied: ' "Love the Lord God with all your heart, with all your soul, and with all your mind." This is the first and greatest commandment. And the second is like it: "Love your neighbor as yourself." All the law and the prophets hang on these two commandments' (Matt. 22:37-40). The Apostle Paul reiterated: 'The entire law is summed up in a single command: "Love your neighbor as yourself" ' (Gal. 5:14; cf. Rom. 13:8-10 and cf. also Jas. 2:8).

The second great commandment, which Jesus was quoting from Leviticus 19:18, sums up the duty that God requires of man in the area of human relations. Elsewhere in the Old Testament this duty was summarized in threefold fashion: 'He has shown you, O man, what is good. And what does the LORD require of you? To act justly and to love mercy and to walk humbly with your God' (Mic. 6:8). Rather than boasting of wisdom, strength, or riches, the godly Jew was to boast about this: ' "that he understands and knows me, that I am the LORD, who exercises kindness, justice, and righteousness on earth, for in these I delight," declares the LORD' (Jer. 9:24; cf. Zech. 7:9-10). Our Lord may have had these passages in mind when He rebuked the scribes and Pharisees for neglecting 'the more important matters of the law – justice, mercy, and faithfulness' (Matt. 23:23).

It is clear from such passages that there is an important relationship between the first and greatest commandment and the second great commandment. A theistic reference point and experience of God's grace are needed as an adequate basis for human moral values. Yet there is a proper distinction between the former, dealing with our relationship with God, and the latter, dealing with our human relationships. The Christian realizes that his ability to love his neighbor stems from his loving response to the love of God in Christ. On the other hand, one who disbelieves in God obviously cannot begin to love Him, yet such a one may furnish external demonstration of love of neighbor to a noticeable degree. The distinction of these two parts of the moral law thus is a real one and one that is recognized in the Reformed tradition (cf. *Westminster Larger Catechism*, Questions 102 and 122).

The purpose of this presentation is to focus on the second great commandment as the summation of God's will for His people in the area of human relations. There are three ways in which the gospel affects human relations. One is through regeneration and its transformation of the individual believer. A second is through reform of the corruption that sin has produced in human society, and this usually entails corporate effort to achieve justice. A third is through the model of community, which the example of the church can provide. In each of these three approaches to human relations a different aspect of the kingship of Christ may be realized.

The procedure of this presentation will be to expound portions of Romans 12–16 as an outstanding section of Scripture concerned with love in human relations, then to discuss three illustrative categories of human relations – the family and marriage, race, and class, and finally to apply the material in terms of the question, what should we expect to accomplish in this life?

A. Exposition of Romans 12–16

There are, of course, several different passages that one could examine as descriptive of Christian love in human relations. The Sermon on the Mount, 1 Corinthians 13, and Ephesians 4:25–6:9 are examples. The ethical portion of Paul's epistle to the Romans, however, provides perhaps the fullest exposition of Christian love and does so in a way that develops the three approaches to human relations already mentioned: the individual, the societal, and the ecclesiastical. This section of Scripture may be outlined as follows:

The Christian Person	individual expressions of love (ch. 12)
The Christian Citizen	relationship to government, neighbors, and contemporary culture (ch. 13)
The Christian Brother and Sister	relationships within the church (14:1–15:13)
The Christian Church	God's acceptable church within the world (15:14–16:27)

A detailed exposition is not intended herein, but rather a brief indication of what Scripture teaches is to flow forth from the gospel, the mercies of God which Paul has so thoroughly set forth in the preceding doctrinal portions of the epistle to the Romans.

1. The Christian Person (Romans 12)
Romans 12 can be termed Paul's 'love chapter' almost as readily as 1 Corinthians 13, and it also deals with the gifts of the Spirit in a similar way to 1 Corinthians 12 and 14, demonstrating that love and the exercise of the gifts are intimately related.

Paul begins his exposition of love at verse 9, but the preceding verses provide an important foundation. The pattern is parallel to that of the Ten Commandments. Verses 1 and 2 hark back to the grace of God upon which loving response is based. Verses 3 to 8 provide a proper assessment of oneself in terms of one's relation to God. If one is to love one's neighbor as oneself, it is crucial that one should have an appropriate assessment of oneself. When inclined to low self-esteem we should recall that God has dealt to each of us His gifts. When inclined to think too highly of ourselves, we should remember that the gifts are after all from the Lord (cf. 1 Cor. 4:7).

Coming to terms with one's own value in the sight of God is indispensable to loving relationships with others. Often we hold back in the thought that we have nothing worth contributing. But this very self-consciousness can be a form of self-importance that forgets that we have been crucified with Christ and are risen with Christ in order that Christ may live in us. The cross, God's mercy, enables us to offer ourselves as living sacrifices, holy and pleasing to God.

Verses 9 through 21 describe what love is, and just as in 1 Corinthians the gifts vary but love is held up before everyone as the essential work of the Spirit in the Christian, so here too love applies to every Christian. Verses 9 through 13 deal mainly with love toward those in the church, verses 14 through 16 mainly with love toward those outside the church, and verses 17 through 21 with love toward one's enemies. Among the striking things said in this section is that love must be sincere, it involves hating what is evil and clinging to what is good, and yet it involves the Christian in blessing those who persecute him. There is conformity to cultural norms that are natural and honorable (vv. 15-16a and 18), yet there is a summoning beyond what could be considered normal and natural. Leviticus 19:18's prohibition of revenge is extended beyond 'one of your people' to anyone.

Clearly what is in view here is a supernatural gift bestowed by God's grace. It is this kind of love that results from the gospel and that produces the gospel's effects. Paul's own experience as a persecutor is easily recalled as the martyr Stephen's 'Lord, do not hold this sin against them' no doubt heaped 'burning coals' of shame on the head of Saul of Tarsus. The example of the Lord Jesus Himself is always near the surface of Paul's mind as he exhorts us to 'overcome evil with good'. This is indeed what happened to us when we received the impact of Christ dying for us while we were yet sinners. Thus the individual Christian is both humbled and exalted at the cross, and in response to God's love in Christ he lives out the love of Christ to others by the gift of the Spirit.

2. *The Christian Citizen (Romans 13)*
Paul has just been talking about Christian response to persecutors. So far persecution had been instigated largely by *religious* authority. But the Roman government had crucified Christ, so the difficulty in Romans 13 lies in the apparently absolute statements of Paul in verses 3 and 4 concerning the benevolence of government. In looking at the Christian's relation to the state and society, it will be necessary to compare Scripture with Scripture in order to determine some principles for the gospel's effect on human relations in this area. Paul's thought moves from the Christian citizen's relation to the government (vv. 1 through 7) to his relation to his neighbor (vv. 8 through 10) to his relation to contemporary culture (vv. 11 through 14).

'Submit' in verse 1 involves a recognition of the Lord's authority as represented in the government, just as Ephesians 5:21 directs: 'Submit to one another out of reverence for Christ.' In a sinful world anarchy is the worst political evil that can befall a society; therefore, the Christian's first duty is to support the government in its God-intended purposes. Even the rule of weak and wicked men like Pilate and Nero is preferable to evil human nature completely unrestrained.

The seemingly absolute statements of verses 3 and 4 are explained by this fact that God is accomplishing his purposes even through wicked rulers. Whether the ruler knows it or not, he is doing what God wills to be done, even his wrongful punishment glorifying the good, as in the case of the apostles who 'left the Sanhedrin, rejoicing because they has been counted worthy of suffering disgrace for the Name' (Acts 5:41). Pilate's dealing with Jesus would be one example no doubt in Paul's mind. To Pilate's question: 'Don't you realize that I have power either to free you or to crucify you?' Jesus answered: 'You have no power over Me that was not given to you from above. Therefore the one who handed Me over to you is guilty of a greater sin' (John 19:10-11). Paul's description of the governor as 'God's servant to do you good' (v. 4) harks back to the 'good' of Romans 8:28 – namely, that which works out our salvation. The governor is perceived as God's servant whose judgements ordinarily punish wickedness and reward righteousness; however, should the governor's will conflict with the clear will of God, then 'we must obey God rather than men' (Acts 5:29).

However the absolute statements of verses 3 and 4 may be explained, it is clear from verses 5 through 7 that the Christian citizen has a positive obligation toward the government and should be glad to pay his fair share of taxes.

The main point of Romans 13:8-10 is that the Christian's obligation to love his neighbor can never fully be carried out; it ever remains as an outstanding debt. We should face each new day wondering how much of that debt we will be able to pay.

Paul's sense of timing in verses 11 through 14 does not imply that the second coming of Christ was expected momentarily, but rather that history had reached its climax in the first coming of Christ, specifically in His death, resurrection, and ascension, and that anything further in this life must relate to these climactic events. The Christian is to live as in a new age, an age characterized by light, life, and love – openness, righteousness, and goodness. Realizing that Christ may come in his lifetime, the Christian puts aside the sinful activities of contemporary culture. He is distinctly not of this world, while at the same time he is very definitely active in the world.

In relation to society the Christian who is well-pleasing to the Lord will be sensitive to the authority of the Lord. He will regard himself as a citizen of the dawning age, of the kingdom of God, who governs the powers that be. His obligations to his neighbor are fulfilled in a never paid debt of love. In these ways his union with Christ is manifested in society.

3. *The Christian Brother and Sister (Romans 14:1–15:13)*

Paul's development of Christian love moves explicitly into the realm of relations between Christians in chapter 14 and the former half of chapter 15. As the gospel had gone forth from Judea into the Mediterranean world of the Roman Empire, inevitably there were differences among Christians from various cultural backgrounds, and nowhere would such differing customs and scruples be more pronounced than in cosmopolitan Rome. Here the problems included such things as what one ate and drank (14:2, 21) and the observance of special days (14:5a). The general theme of this whole section of Scripture is to achieve unity without compromise of the liberty of the gospel. Christian liberty and Christian unity are resolved, with both upheld, only in Christian love and in the light of Christ's lordship. Here again the first and second great commandments are placed in harmonious juxtaposition: 'May the God who gives endurance and encouragement give you a spirit of unity among yourselves as you follow Christ Jesus, so that with one heart and mouth you may glorify the God and Father of our Lord Jesus Christ' (15:5-6), and 'Let us therefore make every effort to do what leads to peace and to mutual edification' (14:19). The apostle's thought may be divided as follows: Christian Liberty and the Lord (14:1-12 and 15:7-13) and Christian Liberty and Love (14:13-15:6).

Christian Liberty and the Lord (14:1-12 and 15:7-13)
The threat to peace and mutual edification evidently was coming from two directions: from the one who could eat everything and would look down on one who would abstain, and from the one who abstained and would pass judgment on the one who ate (14:3). Paul responds that neither are we to look down on those with scruples, nor are we to judge those free of scruples, but each one has an individual responsibility to live unto Christ as personal Lord. It is of the utmost importance that we see ourselves and other Christians, and bring other Christians to see themselves and us, as directly responsible to the Lord. This is a large part of what the Protestant Reformation meant by the priesthood of all believers.

In the section before us Paul speaks mainly to those he terms weak in faith, that is, those as yet without perfect knowledge of Christian doctrine or without total strength of Christian life who still feel the need of some crutches. Paul does not knock the props out from under such people, but he does seek to get them face to face with the Lord. He says to them first, about the brother who feels free to eat, 'God has accepted him' (14:3c; cf. 15:7 and 9).

Paul next develops the corollary: 'To his own master he stands or falls' (14:4b). When a convert was baptized in the early church, he confessed that Jesus the Messiah, the Son of the Living God, was his Lord. This meant that he was Christ's servant, responsible directly to Him. This is an exclusive relationship, for no one else died and rose and is thus Lord of both dead and living (14:7-8).

The conclusion Paul draws is: 'Each one should be fully convinced in his own mind' (14:5c). If, before God, there is any doubt, any question, any hesitation, then do not do what you think the Lord may disapprove. Whatever you do, do it as unto the Lord (14:6).

Christian Liberty and Love (14:13–15:6)
Having directed his remarks to those he terms 'the weak', Paul now turns his attention to 'the strong' concerning the matter of Christian liberty and love. Identifying with the strong, or the one without scruples, Paul has an immense concern for the conscience of the weaker brother, that is, the one who still adheres to some extra-biblical standard of conduct. If such a brother believes something is wrong, then he should not do it, even though it may be clear to the other brethren from Scripture that it is not wrong (14:14). The conscience is a messenger of God placed in each of us. Its voice may have been muffled or distorted, so that what we hear may be wrong; but if we go contrary to it in one matter, then it will become easy to violate it in any matter. This applies to everything we do as Christians, whether we are weak or strong (14:22-23). Conscience is the voice of personal faith; whatever we do out of accord with our personal faith is sin, because it is going contrary to what we understand to be the will of our Lord. When we consider the serious implications of this for a brother's spiritual life, then mundane matters of what we eat or drink become trivial (14:17, 20a).

'Charity' describes the kind of love Paul is describing here: it is the love of the stronger or richer giving up what he has for the sake of the weaker or poorer brother (15:1-2). The strong here are right, they have truth on their side, but it is love that renders truth palatable. 'Do not allow what you consider good to be spoken of as evil'

(14:16); your right conclusion does not justify careless application of it. Do not bring truth into disrepute by failing to clothe it in love. Love is that which finds its happiness in another's good (14:13, 15, 21); therefore, not only do we receive the weaker brother, but we receive him with his scruples. The reason we do is the example of Christ (15:3). His liberty was governed by love. His liberty was the free exercise of love.

In summary, there appear to be three main applications in Paul's teaching in Romans 14–15:13. *First*, those who are stronger in faith – that is, those whose faith allows liberty in the matters under discussion – are to bear with the failings of the weak and are not to please themselves. One does not live to himself alone, but to the Lord; but also to 'please his neighbor for his good, to build him up' (15:2). Rather than a looking down on the weaker brother, Christ's love in accepting all of us should characterize the stronger. *Second*, the weaker brother – that is, the one with scruples – is not to pass judgment on those who do not abstain, but is to follow his conscience as unto the Lord. *Third*, Paul's overriding concern is that all Christians accept one another in a unity that is characterized by peace and joy and hope. Controversy over such matters as abstaining from foods and observing of special days is to be avoided. Each person should have a clear conscience before God; and service of Christ with righteousness, peace, and joy in the Holy Spirit is pleasing to God and approved by men. What serves to produce peace and mutual edification is to prevail.

4. The Christian Church (Romans 15:14–16:27)

Much of what Paul has said concerning the Christian brother and sister applies to the corporate life of the church. The remainder of the epistle suggests more fully what the church is to be within the world. Paul makes reference to the Christian mission as the purpose of the church and to Christian people as the essence of the church.

Paul does not conceive of his own mission as merely a matter between him and people to be reached with the gospel. It is the Lord's mission: Paul speaks of 'the grace God gave me to be a minister of Christ Jesus to the Gentiles with the priestly duty of proclaiming the gospel of God, so that the Gentiles might become an offering acceptable to God, sanctified by the Holy Spirit' (15:15-16). Such a mission could only be undertaken by the Lord's own initiative. Paul never forgot his original commissioning by the Lord on the road to Damascus (cf. Acts 9:15-16; 22:14-15; 26:16-20), and he conceives of the church as the body implementing the on-going ministry of Jesus on the earth. Paul's drive was to share the blessings of Christ with others (15:29; cf. 1:11-12, 15). His current program had to do with ministering to material needs in Jerusalem (15:25-27). His future plan was to go still elsewhere with the gospel (15:23-24). The constant concern of the church is the reaching of still others with the love of Christ. One key to the accomplishing of such a mission is fellowship in prayer (15:30-32).

The concluding chapter of Romans might appear to be just a list of names, but it is much more. If Hebrews 11 is a picture gallery of Old Testament saints, this is one of New Testament believers. This chapter shows us that the Christian church is not essentially buildings, or institutions, or programs, or systems of doctrines – much as these may be needed; but it is essentially Christian people.

There may be at least five groups distinguishable at Rome (16:5a, 10b, 11b, 14, 15), yet they are all addressed in one letter, they are one church in Christ. A variety of kinds of people appears: Gentiles and Jews, slaves and their aristocratic owners. Approximately one-third of the names are those of women, who apparently were actively engaged in significant roles in the church. Paul speaks glowingly and longingly of such friends and fellow-workers as Priscilla and Aquila (16:3-4), and he includes with himself in his warm greetings his colleague Timothy and others (16:21-24). Here is a model of human community that expresses much of what the church is to be.

At verse 16 of chapter 16 it would seem that Paul had finished dictating and took up his pen to conclude with his own signature when his pastoral concern welled up and he gave one last warning: 'I urge you, brothers, to watch out for those who cause divisions...' (16:17-20). Jesus likewise had warned of deceivers, like that Serpent in Eden. There are certain tests to apply: the effect of such enemies is to cause divisions, but even more important, they are contrary to the teaching learned from Christ and the apostles, that teaching that true Christians obey. Love and unity are to characterize the church, but there is a formal priority on the part of truth and purity: the 'church' must be defined according to the doctrine of Christ.

To conclude this brief exposition of Romans 12–16, there is great need today for demonstration of the Christian person, the Christian citizen, Christian brothers and sisters, and the Christian church as Paul has discussed them here. The key to this is the reality of God as the Lord. This flows from the gospel of Jesus Christ as Paul has declared it in the former portion of this epistle, chapters 1–11: 'I beseech you, therefore, brethren, by the mercies of God, that you present your bodies a living sacrifice, holy, acceptable unto God, which is your reasonable service.' The gospel of the sovereign God is the basis for human relations that manifest love for neighbor as for oneself, whether it be between individuals, in the structures of society, or in the community which is the church.

B. Contemporary Illustrations of Human Relations to be Affected by the Gospel

Any number of contemporary illustrations of human relations could be chosen for discussion. I have chosen the following three, both because they are leading problems in our time and also because they are representative of three categories of effects of the gospel on human relations:

Family and Marriage individual relationships on the model of God's relationship to His people;
Race corporate dealing with the structures of society; and
Class the model of the church as community.

1. Family and Marriage
It is one of the remarkable things in Scripture that the relationship between Christ and the church is portrayed in terms of the relationship between husband and wife. The analogy is mutually instructive, that is, the marriage relationship helps us to understand the church's relation to her Lord, and the relationship of church and Christ helps us to understand the marriage relationship. In Ephesians 5:22-33 Paul easily slides from one to the other. In the Old Testament the people of God were also portrayed as the bride of the Lord (cf. especially Jeremiah 2 and 3 and Ezekiel 16).

It is also highly significant that the commandment, 'Honor thy father and thy mother,' serves as the bridge from that portion of the Decalogue summarized by the first great commandment and that portion summarized by the second great commandment. The family relationship is evidently intended as that which conveys to the developing person the connection between love for God and love for one's neighbor. The home is to provide the natural model for the ideal in human relations.

In light of this strategic position of the relation between husband and wife it is clear that there is something even more important than sexual purity involved here. It is a matter of faithfulness to one's word, one's covenantal pledge of trust. This is what is at the heart of our salvation – the promise of God to save those who trust in Jesus Christ and the commitment of Christians to trust in no other. And it must be what is at the heart of our marriage relations – the commitment to love and cherish one another whatever the conditions of life, 'in plenty and in want, in joy and in sorrow, in sickness and in health, as long as both live.' What if the divorce rate among Christians were to approach that of the rest of society; what if 100 per cent of our marriages were to be broken? What sort of picture would marriage as an institution then provide of the relationship between the Lord and His Bride, the church? Such an extremely drastic hypothesis serves to remind us of the importance of the analogy of faithfulness in marriage to the fidelity of our Lord to His gracious promises and the church's exclusive commitment to Him. In an age when exclusive commitments of trust are increasingly rare, what sort of model will our children and our contemporary culture find for Christ and the church if not in Christian marriage?

Paul does not deal explicitly with marriage in Romans 12–16, but it is remarkable that where he does (Eph. 5:22f.; Col. 3:18ff.), and where Peter does (1 Pet. 3:1ff.), the invariable order is to direct first that wives submit to their husbands. The priority is given to the maintenance of a proper relation in the sight of God, even in what may be a difficult situation, such as 1 Peter's marriage of a believing wife to an unbelieving husband. Then comes the direction to husbands to love their wives as Christ loved the church and gave Himself up for her. In the case of either wife or husband, the ideal that is upheld is the example of Christ – His sovereign lordship over the church and His sacrificial love for the church.

Such an ideal standard is enough to humble the most sanctified of Christians. What Christian wife does not struggle with the problem of submitting to a less-than-perfect husband? What Christian husband does not struggle with the problem of sacrificially loving a less-than-perfect wife? Even in this most blessed bond it is clear that the grace of God is required to make us all what we ought to be. Fallen human nature is inclined to violate this relationship, which God has intended as a blessing for all humankind, and to exploit it selfishly. It is clear that to approach this standard we need the power of the Holy Spirit working within us, we must be born again.

As regenerate people, however, we have the potential to conform to God's will, being conformed to the image of Jesus Christ. Children are called upon to obey their parents in the Lord, fathers emulate the Heavenly Father by not discouraging their children, and the godly management of the home becomes a criterion for governance in the church. The home is thus the laboratory for human relations, the microcosm in which the effects of one's regeneration by the Spirit are nurtured and demonstrated. One of the gifts of the Reformation to the church was the model of the minister's marriage, of the parsonage to the parish. In the context of monastic and priestly celibacy that was a most significant contribution. In our day one can scarcely think of a more crucial need than the demonstration of faithful commitment, of submission and of love, on the part of all married Christians.

2. *Race*
Race relations provide an example of an area of human relations calling for Christian concern for the structures

of society as well as for individual sanctification flowing from regeneration. In the last two decades American Christians have been compelled by racial conflict in contemporary society to face the issue of racial prejudice as it affects the church. Some of the results have been a degree of evident repentance for certain unbiblical attitudes and actions, a renewed effort to extend the gospel to people of ethnic minorities, some attempt to achieve integrated congregations, and finally a concern to see minority groups produce their own leadership and Christianized cultural forms for worship. The one thing that is obvious to anyone who has worked in the area of Christian race relations is that the problems are complex. One finds that it is necessary, nevertheless, to keep returning to certain basic points that our natural mentality tends to reject. These include that any kind of theory of racial supremacy is a contradiction of the biblical doctrines of creation, of redemption, of evangelism and missions, and of the church.

The unity of mankind is one of the clear biblical teachings that the theory of evolution has tended to obscure. In his sermon to the Athenians Paul declared that God 'from one man ... made every nation of men' (Acts 17:26), and this was simply a reiteration of the Genesis account of the creation of Adam. What we observe as racial characteristics are the result of genetic shifts over a period of time, but all people on earth are descendants of Adam and Eve and also of Noah and his wife, with certain ethnic distinctions perhaps evident even by that time deriving from the differing heritages of the wives of Shem, Ham, and Japheth. To deny the essential oneness of the human race is to deny the biblical account of the creation of Adam and Eve as the parents of all mankind.

The biblical teaching of redemption also asserts the unity of the human race. In Romans 5:15-19 Paul develops the effect of Adam's trespass as condemnation for all men. As sinners we are all in the same judgment, whatever our race may be. The only distinction to be made with regard to redemption is whether one is united to Christ or not. This is why Paul was so opposed to any Judaizing tendency in the early church: it represented a distortion of the gospel to conceive of anyone as more or less in need of redemption from sin or as more or less redeemed because of one's identity as Jew or Gentile. At stake was the basic meaning of the gospel, that all have sinned and that the only way of salvation is by grace, through faith in Jesus Christ. Any concept of racial supremacy represents denial of the biblical doctrine of redemption.

That is why racism also jeopardizes the biblical teaching and practice of evangelism and missions. All mankind sharing in the human predicament of sin and condemnation, and there being only one way of salvation, the gospel is clearly intended for all whom God calls to repentance and faith, and these are to be found among every tribe, tongue, and nation of the earth. The Great Commission in each of its forms commands the Lord's disciples to convey the gospel to all the world. To believe that the gospel that we have to convey is appropriate only for certain racial or cultural groups is either to admit that our form of the gospel is narrowed or truncated or to deny that the gospel was to be extended to all.

Any concept of racial supremacy is also a contradiction of the biblical doctrine of the church. If the gospel offered to all was to break down the barrier between Jew and Gentile (Eph. 2:11-22) – a barrier which had had genuine religious significance, then cultural and racial barriers are certainly to be abolished in the church in our day. A segregated church service is a blatant contradiction of the unity in Christ that the gospel achieves in the church of redeemed sinners. Interracial marriage – usually the final point of racist resistance – must not be prohibited by the church, even though it may be fraught with problems in the area of expediency, but only the marriage of believer to unbeliever must be forbidden as a matter of principle.

The practical application of these principles is often difficult. There is a tendency in the history of American race relations for there to be a pendulum swing on the part of minority groups from a desire to integrate and become amalgamated into the dominant culture to a desire to separate for the sake of expression of ethnic distinctiveness. Because of the fact that an ethnic group is a minority within a sin-affected culture, neither of these tendencies is likely ever to prove satisfactory to the aspirations of the minority group. The church must strive for ways in which to demonstrate the essential oneness of Christians in the Lord Jesus Christ while at the same time to appreciate the diversity of cultural expressions of Christianity as long as our cultures are being transformed by the transcendent influence of the gospel.

Because of the complexity of race relations, one might well ask why God should have allowed racial differences to come into existence. At least three possible reasons are apparent.

First, racial difference may exist in God's plan as an obstacle to be overcome by the church, hence demonstrating the power of the gospel in contrast to the ways of the world. An example of this historically would be the leadership of William Wilberforce and other Evangelicals in the nineteenth-century abolition of the slave trade and then of slavery in the British Empire.

Second, God may have allowed racial differences to exist as an occasion for the recognition of our cultural blinders. Experience of efforts at cross-cultural communication is one of the swiftest ways to come to a realization of how much cultural baggage one is transporting along with the gospel. It sharpens one's sense of what is genuinely the gospel and what is merely a cultural concomitant. This is a distinction of immense importance, because the gospel must of necessity be communicated into the culture as well as the language of the recipient, and yet the essence of the gospel must be retained.

Third, racial differences may have been allowed to exist as an opportunity for Christianity to make a contribution to justice in society. If the gospel leads Christians to proper perceptions in the area of race relations, then perhaps they can influence the society in general in ways that will recognize human rights that are being denied.

For the past few years, I have been involved in the efforts put forth by a variety of religious leaders in the St. Louis area to avoid a violent reaction to a court decision concerning further desegregation of the public schools. Both Roman Catholic and Lutheran parochial schools have announced that they will not receive transfer students who are avoiding the effects of the court's ruling. Our Reformed and evangelical Christian schools should do what they can to support the achievement of equal educational opportunity. It is encouraging to note that some of our churches in the city are banding together to start a school which will seek to serve a variety of students, including the poor and the blacks in the city. Further effort by the church is needed to modify social structures that tend to produce great inequity of opportunity.

The field of race relations provides an outstanding example of an area in which the church can aid in changing the corrupt structures of society that have been affected by the fall. The pervasive influence of sin is not only individual, but also corporate. The fact that nations and societies may be judged by God indicates that there is such a thing as corporate guilt. When sin has corrupted a society into unjust treatment of some of its members, it is a responsibility of Christians of that society – their consciences informed by the church's ministry of the Word – to do what they can to correct the situation.

3. Class

Class conflict is an area of human relations that is certainly affected by individual regeneration, and which, like race relations, may be influenced by social reform, but it may be that class distinctions are best dealt with by the development of community in the church.

It is ironic that our Lord's comment, 'The poor you will always have with you, and you can help them any time you want,' in response to Judas' comment on the anointing with precious ointment at Bethany (Mark 14:7; cf. Matt. 26:11, John 12:8), has been used as an excuse for doing nothing to help the poor. Jesus' remark was an allusion to Deuteronomy 15:11, which says: 'There will always be poor people in the land. Therefore I command you to be openhanded toward your brothers and toward the poor and needy in your land.' The Lord gave as one of the signs of his messiahship to the disciples of John the Baptist that 'the good news is preached to the poor' (Matt. 11:5). Part of his inaugural address as the Messiah was his quotation of Isaiah 61:1: 'The Spirit of the Lord is on Me, because He has anointed Me to preach good news to the poor' (Luke 4:18).

The lack of ministry to the poor on the part of our suburban evangelical churches is often a result not of intention, but of lack of exposure to the poor. Frequently we succeed in building churches of people alike in social, economic, and educational background, people whom our society puts in contact largely with people of similar characteristics. Consequently, there is often a minimal understanding of the problems of the poor and of the vicious cycle of ignorance, lack of opportunity, poverty, broken homes, illness, and crime that often confronts them. Somehow the churches need to break out of their socio-economic enclaves to experience the oneness in Christ that can supersede class differences.

Marxism has taken advantage of the situation in parts of the world where class conflict is more pronounced than it is in the United States. The producing of the kind of community that the early church experienced can anticipate much of the appeal that Marxist liberation theology has. But we need to realize that such community is really not just an option for the church, but a mandate of our Lord. Respect of persons on the basis of economic distinctions is forbidden (Jas. 2:1-4), and diaconal aid to the needy of the church is presented as a normal activity of the New Testament church along with worship and witness. In some instances today it would seem that Christians are scarcely afforded the opportunity to help the poor and needy simply because they have no meaningful contact with poor people.

A contributing factor to this situation of churches of a single class of people is the homogeneous-unit principle that has been emphasized as a key to church growth. It may well be that churches grow when they are made up of people with little diversity, but we need to examine at what cost this is done. What kind of church is it that is produced? Does it really testify to the truth of Jesus' coming to seek and to save those who are lost from whatever social background? Does it reflect the essential ingredients of a church that is like its Lord, communicating the gospel by word and by deed, speaking the truth in love? This includes a sense of community and serving, as Paul put it: 'Therefore, as we have opportunity, let us do good to all people, especially to those who belong to the family of believers' (Gal. 6:10). Thus we shall reflect our Lord Jesus, who, as Peter put it, 'went around doing good' (Acts 10:38). The church that provides a model of genuine community – brothers and sisters lovingly supporting one another in need, whether material, emotional, or spiritual – will demonstrate to a shattered society the kind of cohesion that is produced only by the gospel.

Christians of the Reformed tradition thus approach the problem areas of human relations in a threefold way. Of first importance is regeneration of the individual for whom Christ died and rose again. Only through the transforming power of the work of Christ can the believer see produced in his life the fruit of the Holy Spirit, including love of his neighbor as himself. Every society contains, however, certain evils in its very structure, and regenerate Christians can become a reforming influence to restrain the forces of evil within their society. And finally, the church itself can provide a model of community that may show to the world what real love is in action.

C. What Should We Expect To Accomplish

Differences have existed among Reformed Christians through history as to how much we can expect to accomplish in the area of human relations in this life and hence how much of our energy should be applied to such activities. While one's eschatological expectations may have an influence upon his present activities, the important thing is that we understand what it is that God has commanded us to do and that we seek to do His will out of love, responding to the love of God in Christ.

The *Westminster Shorter Catechism*, Question 102, indicates that there are several facets to our second petition in the Lord's Prayer, 'Thy kingdom come': 'That Satan's kingdom may be destroyed; and that the kingdom of grace may be advanced, ourselves and others brought into it, and kept in it; and that the kingdom of glory may be hastened.' The *Larger Catechism*, Question 191, expands on this in such a way as to show the concept of the kingdom to include the propagation of the gospel throughout the world, thus destroying the dominion of sin and Satan, and also the converting, comforting, and building up of those that are already converted and in the church, Christ ruling in our hearts, and finally also the exercise by Christ of the kingdom of His power in all the world as may best conduce to the previously mentioned ends. As our hearts breathe that concern second only to the hallowing of God's name, we are praying for several things: that the gospel go forth, that our own submission to Christ increase, and that all of Satan's dominion be thwarted, including his evil influence in the world.

If obedience to God's revealed will is the thing to be desired, then how much can be expected from the civil government in a secular, pluralistic society? Jesus' response to the Pharisees' and Herodians' question concerning the payment of taxes to Caesar shows that the government has a necessary and proper function to restrain wickedness and support righteousness among men, but that the believer should not expect such a government to maintain the true faith (Matt. 22:15-22). The prerogatives of God as given in the first great commandment will be cultivated and enforced by Himself; all that the government need ensure is freedom of religion. In the area of relations between human beings, the area of the second great commandment, the government does have responsibility. It is in this area that Christians should concern themselves as citizens and prod the government to action. To the degree that Christians are numerous in a society, and to the degree that the government is responsive to its citizens, to this extent Christianity may have an influence for good in the realm of human relations through the government.

The main effect of the church in human relations will come, however, through the obedient carrying out of the Great Commission. It should be noted, though, that making disciples of all nations includes 'teaching them to obey everything I have commanded you' (Matt. 28:20). The individual Christian and the church corporately should seek to carry out all the counsel of God in its fullness and in its proper balance.

Having begun with the cross of forgiveness, we should conclude with the towel of service and the table of fellowship. Loving Him because He first loved us and gave Himself for us, we follow His example of leadership in His washing of the feet of His disciples, and we find our identity around the Table of the Lord, where He imparts to us the nurture of His life: 'A new commandment I give you: Love one another. As I have loved you, so you must love one another. All men will know that you are My disciples if you love one another' (John 13:34-35).

5

THE SOCIAL VIEWS OF
CHARLES HODGE (1797–1878):
A STUDY IN NINETEENTH-CENTURY
CALVINISM AND CONSERVATISM

1. *Calvinism and Conservatism: Statement of the Problem*
As adherents to the Biblical faith – that faith that God has once for all entrusted to the saints – twentieth-century orthodox Calvinists have properly identified themselves theologically by means of the label 'conservative'. Properly, because there is a godly tradition – in the good sense of that word as used by the Apostle Paul in 2 Thessalonians 2:15 and 3:6 and 1 Corinthians 11:2 – to be preserved.

Unfortunately the term 'conservative' has often too easily been transferred from the area of theology, where the Scriptures provide an infallible basis for doctrines that must not be changed, to areas of social, political, and economic life, where the cultural norms may be largely influenced by Christianity in certain societies, but where we can be sure that the *status quo* shall never have arrived at the perfection that ultimately pleases God. Until Jesus comes again, there will always be room for improvement and hence for progress to which the Biblically oriented Christian should be contributing.

Scholars who have studied the connection between the various forms of Christianity and social issues have long recognized a conservative-progressive ambivalence in Calvinism with its other-worldly concern with spiritual salvation and its this-worldly concentration on serving God, its stress on individual responsibility combined with an emphasis on corporate and social activity.[1] By the nineteenth century, however, orthodox Presbyterianism has appeared to many to present only a conservative aspect, and the main example of this orthodox conservatism is usually found in the Princeton theological position as represented by Charles Hodge.[2] It is the intention of this study to examine Hodge's social thought in order to determine to what extent this interpretation is just. But before turning to Hodge it will be necessary to define with some care the word 'conservatism'.

Conservatism is a slippery term in our day. Its basic meaning is not hard to grasp, but in application it easily slides from one area to another in which its connotation may be much more or less favorable. Clinton Rossiter, in his *Conservatism in America*, breaks down his definition into four categories: temperamental, possessive, practical, and philosophical conservatism. Temperamental conservatism refers to a man's natural disposition to oppose change. Possessive conservatism 'is the attitude of the man who has something substantial to defend against change, whether it be his status, reputation, power, or, most commonly, property'. Practical conservatism is 'a sense of satisfaction and identity with the *status quo*' of one's community. Philosophical conservatism 'subscribes consciously

---

1. Cf. Ernst Troeltsch, *The Social Teaching of the Christian Churches*, trans. Olive Wyon, 2 vols. (New York: Macmillan and Glencoe, Ill.: The Free Press, 1949), II, 577, 620-21; R. H. Tawney, *Religion and the Rise of Capitalism* (Gloucester, Mass.: Peter Smith, 1962), 212; H. Richard Niebuhr, *The Social Sources of Denominationalism* (New York: Henry Holt, 1929), 43.
2. Henry F. May, *Protestant Churches and Industrial America* (New York: Octagon Books, 1963), 193; Charles Howard Hopkins, *The Rise of the Social Gospel in American Protestantism, 1865–1915* (New Haven: Yale University Press and London: Oxford University Press, 1940), 16.

to principles designed to justify the established order and guard it against careless tinkering and determined reform'.[3]

In each of these categories resistance to change and defense of the *status quo* appear as the essential characteristics of conservatism, but for different reasons, some easier to justify than others. Rossiter cherishes philosophical conservatism and recognizes value in temperamental conservatism; while he clearly dislikes conservatism of the possessive and practical varieties.[4] In America of the middle nineteenth century, the period of Charles Hodge's activity as teacher and writer, conservatism carries the basic meaning of opposition to change, but it is characteristically accompanied by an elitism, supporting an establishment of wealth and exalting the individual over society while limiting the role of government. The social thought of Charles Hodge reveals very little of – in fact, much in opposition to – the glorification of the individual over society or support of an establishment of wealth. There is not much here of a possessive conservatism. On the other hand there is much of a temperamental and philosophical conservatism in this representative of nineteenth-century Calvinism. The reasons lying behind this conservatism, however, indicate that orthodox Calvinism did not always, and need not, inhibit constructive social progress.

2. *The Significance and Personal Characteristics of Charles Hodge*

One writer extravagantly calls Charles Hodge 'the greatest theologian America has ever produced'.[5] A

---

3. Clinton Rossiter, *Conservatism in America* (New York: Alfred A. Knopf, 1955), 5-9.
4. Ibid.
5. Ralph J. Danhof, *Charles Hodge as Dogmatician* (Goes, The Netherlands, n.d. [c. 1928-34], 171-72; cited in James Ward Smith and A. Leland Jamison, *Religion in American Life*, vol. I: *The Shaping of American Religion* (Princeton, N.J.: Princeton University Press, 1961), 262.

more accurate evaluation is that 'By the time of his death he was one of the most influential exponents of old Calvinism in the English-speaking world'.[6]

Hodge taught at Princeton Seminary from 1822 until the year of his death, 1878, without interruption except for a period of study in Germany at Halle and Berlin from 1826 to 1828. During that span of more than half a century he helped to train more than three thousand men for the ministry. His three-volume, 2,000-page *Systematic Theology*, written at the climax of his career in 1871–72, became the textbook for the 'Princeton Theology', and in some Presbyterian seminaries was still being used as such down to the present decade. In his own day his influence was conveyed by the quarterly journal founded by him in 1825 and known as the *Princeton Review*. He remained as editor through 1868 and continued as joint editor through 1871, and it is estimated that his own contributions comprise more than one-fifth of the journal's pages, or about ten volumes.[7] His articles range over a wide variety of topics, from highly technical theological matters to political and economic issues and practical moral questions. The amount of controversy they stirred up indicates that they were not without influence. Each year from 1835 through 1867, with the exception of 1841, he wrote a critical review of the annual meeting of the General Assembly, the highest court of the Presbyterian Church, concerning which articles 'one of his associates said, "there is no inducement to prepare

---

6. H. Shelton Smith, Robert T. Handy, and Lefferts A. Loetscher, *American Christianity* (New York: Charles Scribner's Sons, 1963) II, 89-90.
7. 'Charles Hodge,' in *Biblical Repertory and Princeton Review*, Index Volume from 1825 to 1869 (Philadelphia: Peter Walker, 1871), 207. The journal went through a series of names: *Biblical Repertory*, 1825–1829; *The Biblical Repertory and Theological Review*, 1830–1836; *The Biblical Repertory and Princeton Review*, 1837–1871; and subsequent to Hodge's editorship, *The Presbyterian Quarterly and Princeton Review*, 1872–77. Hereafter it will be referred to as *P.R.*, for *Princeton Review*. The volume numbering will be that of the new series beginning in 1829.

a good article for the July number, because every one turns at once to that on the General Assembly, which absorbs all the interest".'[8]

The significance of Charles Hodge lies, therefore, in the widespread influence of his Calvinistic teaching and writing, particularly on many of those who occupied Presbyterian pulpits throughout America. Princeton was the stronghold of Calvinistic orthodoxy, and Hodge was the leading mind and voice of Princeton. It is possibly without exaggeration that one writer claims:

> Three thousand divinity students sat at his feet to learn their theology – more parsons, Presbyterian and otherwise, than were trained by any other American in the nineteenth century. Thousands more drank deep of his heavy *Systematic Theology*, in three volumes. Like a mighty army, preachers, teachers, and college presidents bore forth from Princeton town the somber banner of Charles Hodge, to an incalculably great part of the nation. No other alumnus of Princeton College, possibly excepting Woodrow Wilson, shaped so deeply the thought-molds of his day.[9]

What sort of man was it who exerted this influence? Two personal characteristics stand out: conservatism and moderation. The conservative, unchanging character of his nature extended to every area of his life and thought, from details of habit to the argument of doctrine. Confined by lameness to remain in his house for almost a decade, he came to use exclusively one particular chair for thirty-eight years. 'The little tailor shop he first happened to patronize in Princeton he clung to for sixty years, despite

---

8. Ibid.
9. John Oliver Nelson, 'Charles Hodge, Nester of Orthodoxy,' in Willard Thorp, ed., *The Lives of Eighteen from Princeton* (Princeton, N. J.: Princeton University Press, 1946), 192. Cf. Leonard J. Trinterud, 'Charles Hodge (1797–1878): Theology – Didactic and Polemical,' in Hugh T. Kerr, ed., *Sons of the Prophets: Leaders in Protestantism from Princeton Seminary* (Princeton University Press, 1963), 22-38.

the succession of good and bad proprietors, and the complaints of the younger Hodges.'[10]

His habits of thought were similarly unchanging. Looking back on more than forty years of the *Princeton Review* on the occasion of his retirement as editor in 1871, he could comment with satisfaction, 'Whether it be a ground of reproach or of approbation, it is believed to be true that an original idea in theology is not to be found in the pages of the Biblical Repertory and Princeton Review from the beginning until now.'[11] Similarly he stated proudly at the celebration of his semi-centennial at Princeton, 'I am not afraid to say that a new idea never originated in this Seminary.'[12]

While these statements seem in themselves to be extreme, nevertheless the other main characteristic of his life and thought was moderation. He deplored ultraism of whatever type. When engaged in controversy, although his argument was always firm and full of conviction, he characteristically found himself occupying middle ground, subject to attack from either side.

A. A. Hodge, one of his sons who eventually joined him on the faculty of Princeton Seminary, provides, in a biography remarkable for its own moderation, an explanation for this combination of conservatism and moderation in the character of Charles Hodge:

> The same qualities caused him to be both conservative and moderate. He was conservative because the truth he held was not the discovery of the progressive reason of man, but the very word of God once delivered to the saints, and therefore authoritative and irreformable; and because reverence for that word repressed in

---

10. Nelson, loc. cit., 206.
11. A. A. Hodge, *The Life of Charles Hodge* (New York: Charles Scribner's Sons, 1880), 256-57.
12. Ibid., 521

him all ambition for distinction as the discoverer of new opinions, or as the improver of the faith of the Church. The consistency with which, under all changes of times and party-combinations, he for fifty years maintained without shadow of change absolutely the same principles was very remarkable, and without any parallel in this age. He held precisely the same doctrines in his age as in the early controversies of his youth, and the same principles as to the relation of government to moral and religious questions, and as to temperance and slavery after the war as he did years before. He was always moderate also, because his loyalty to the Master made party spirit impossible, and because the amount of his knowledge and force of his logic caused him to see things in all their relations in all directions, by the aid of the sidelights as well as by the aid of those shining in the line of his direct vision.[13]

The remark about amazing consistency is certainly true. As late as 1865 Hodge was able to declare, 'With regard to slavery, both in its moral and political aspect, we stand now just where we always have stood. The doctrine advocated in this journal in 1836 is still our doctrine.'[14] As one traces his thoughts on particular issues through the *Princeton Review,* one gets the feeling of listening to a phonograph record with the needle stuck. There is no noticeable development in his thought.

Yet it is true that his thought is balanced and moderate. It characteristically sees evils at either extreme and seeks to resolve social issues for the good of the whole society. What conservatism there is in his social thought is, thus, not to be explained by an identification with a particular social class or by a glorification of the individual at the

---

13. Ibid., 253.
14. Charles Hodge, 'The Princeton Review on the State of the Country and of the Church,' *P.R.*, XXXVIII (1865), 637.

expense of society, but rather by a simple adherence to the Scriptures as an authoritative rule of life as well as faith – which is a concept with reforming and even revolutionary potential, but in the view of Charles Hodge only by moderate means. All of this will become more evident in an examination of his thought on politics and economics.

3. Politics: The Slavery Issue

Hodge's stance of moderation in politics is manifest nowhere more clearly than in his discussion of the slavery issue. In addition, this controversial subject, which was before the public all during the heart of Hodge's active life, reveals the genuine foundation of his conservatism. Throughout his writings on the slavery issue he consistently deplores the agitation of the abolitionists and also expresses his abhorrence of the evils of slavery. While aiming at some peaceful method of emancipation, he nevertheless avoids any condemnation of slaveholding as such.

A review of *Slavery*, by the abolitionist William Ellery Channing, in the *Princeton Review* in 1836 provided Hodge with the opportunity to expand his thoughts on slavery for the first time into a full article. To the sentiments expressed in this article he continually harks back in later discussions of the subject. The article was reprinted as early as 1838, was included in a collection of Hodge's essays in 1857, and was circulated essentially unchanged in a book bearing the date 1869.[15]

---

15. Charles Hodge, 'Slavery,' *P.R.*, VIII (1836), 268-305. A footnote appearing with his article 'West India Emancipation,' *P.R.*, X (1838), 609, indicates that it had been reprinted. It appears in his *Essays and Reviews* (New York: Robert Carter and Brothers, 1857), 473-511, under the title 'Slavery' and with little or no change in E. N. Elliot, ed., *Cotton is King*, 3rd ed. (Augusta, Ga.: Pritchard, Abbott and Loomis, 1860), 841-77, under the title 'The Bible Argument on Slavery.' The influence of Hodge's views on slavery within Presbyterianism, North and South, is indicated in Andrew E. Murray, *Presbyterians and the Negro – A History* (Philadelphia: Presbyterian Historical Society, 1966), 64.

In the article Hodge begins by noting the shift in attitude on the subject of slavery from a universal condemnation of it as an evil to a growing defense of it in the South. This he blames on the inflammatory methods of the abolitionists. While assuming that slavery is an evil, he clearly regards abolitionism as no solution and considers it to be a greater evil than slavery itself.

His method of dealing with the slavery issue soon is evident:

> The great question, therefore, in relation to slavery is, what is right? What are the moral principles which should control our opinions and conduct in regard to it? Before attempting an answer to this question, it is proper to remark, that we recognize no authoritative rule of truth and duty but the word of God. Plausible as may be the arguments deduced from general principles to prove a thing to be true or false, right or wrong, there is almost always room for doubt and honest diversity of opinion.... Unless we can approach the consciences of men, clothed with some more imposing authority than that of our own opinions and arguments, we shall gain little permanent influence.... It is our object, therefore, not to discuss the subject of slavery upon abstract principles, but to ascertain the scriptural rule of judgment and conduct in relation to it.[16]

Here is the method by which Hodge deals with any issue. Never is the basis of conduct found in feeling or reason, but always in the authority of the Bible, which is for Hodge the infallible word of God.

The Bible reveals that Jesus and the apostles received slave-holders into the fellowship of the New Testament church; therefore, the modern church has no grounds for excluding slaveholders from its membership. It is as

---

16. C. Hodge, 'Slavery,' *Essays and Reviews*, 479-80.

simple as that. 'We think no one will deny that the plan adopted by the Saviour and his immediate followers must be the correct plan, and therefore obligatory upon us, unless it can be shown that their circumstances were so different from ours, as to make the rule of duty different in the two cases.'[17] The possibility of a modification of the rule by circumstances is recognized, but it is only a remote possibility. The principles of the New Testament Scriptures carry over as the final authority: 'the conduct of the modern abolitionists, being directly opposed to that of the authors of our religion, must be wrong and ought to be modified or abandoned.'[18]

His method of using the Bible as the authority is further illustrated by the way in which he meets the argument that slavery must be sinful because it interferes with the inalienable rights of men. He carefully adopts as a definition of slavery that of William Paley's *Moral Philosophy*: 'I define,' he says, 'slavery to be an obligation to labor for the benefit of the master, without the contract or consent of the servant.'[19] As he later expresses it, slavery is 'involuntary servitude – that is, the obligation to render service is not conditional on the will of the servant.' It is not, by definition, what the abolitionists claim it is: 'a system which makes a man a chattel; a thing which denies to him the rights of a husband and father; which debars him from instruction and means of improvement.' If this be slavery, then all slaveholding must be a crime and no more justifiable than murder: '… no Christian can voluntarily assist in making or enforcing laws which give to involuntary servitude this character.'[20]

Having defined slavery as a state of bondage and no more, Hodge goes on to admit that this condition

---

17. Ibid., 481.
18. Ibid., 482.
19. Ibid., footnote, 484.
20. C. Hodge, 'The General Assembly,' *P.R.*, XXXI (1859), 592-93.

involves the loss of many of the rights commonly and properly called natural. 'It is, however, incumbent on those who maintain that slavery is, on that account, necessarily sinful, to show that it is criminal, under all circumstances, to deprive any set of men of a portion of their natural rights.' Hodge claims that this cannot be maintained.

> The very constitution of society supposes the forfeiture of a greater or less amount of these rights, according to its peculiar organization. That it is not only the privilege, but the duty of men to live together in a regularly organized society, is evident from the nature which God has given us; from the impossibility of every man living by and for himself, and from the express declarations of the word of God. The object of the formation of society is the promotion of human virtue and happiness; and the form in which it should be organized, is that which will best secure the attainment of that object. As, however, the condition of men is so very various, it is impossible that the same form should be equally conducive to happiness and virtue under all circumstances. No one form, therefore, is prescribed in the Bible, or is universally obligatory.[21]

This statement of Hodge's view of the limited extent of natural rights is significant for two reasons. It reveals a subordination of the rights of the individual to the promotion of human virtue and happiness of society – in contrast to the individualism of the 'possessive conservatism' that would prevail later in the nineteenth century. It also indicates that the Bible serves as authority in a negative way as well as a positive: where the Scriptures indicate a principle – as in the case of the acceptance of slaveholders into the church – that principle sets up a binding rule; but when the

---

21. C. Hodge, 'Slavery,' Essays and Reviews, 494-95.

Scriptures leave a question open – as in the question of the best form of government – then no rule is to be made obligatory.

This last point appears also in an unexpected place. Temperance was an issue emphasized by many of the Protestant groups adhering strictly to the Bible. To Hodge, however, the temperance movement is full of dangers. Total abstinence from 'ardent spirits' could not be made an absolute principle of Christianity, for Christ himself had partaken of wine. Hodge deplores the evils of drunkenness, but labels the temperance movement as an example of 'the infidelity of benevolence' and opposes it on two principles: first, that the Bible is the only rule and therefore it is the very spirit of infidelity to set up one's own opinions as to what is true or false, right or wrong; and second, that one should not do evil that good may come.[22] Hodge puts the temperance movement in the same category as abolitionism. Both direct their energies at genuine evils, but they go to an extreme in doing so. Like slavery, the use of alcohol is not a sin in itself since it is not disallowed by God and Christ in the Bible. Hodge opposes 'ultraism', which he describes as displaying a 'want of due discrimination somewhere as to the elementary principles of ethics'.[23] Here again he manifests his moderation.

The concept that there is no binding rule where the Bible is silent does not, however, open the door to change of a radical sort for Hodge. All depends on the circumstances. Referring to the patriarchal form of government in the Old Testament, Hodge declares that it would be immoral to change such government unless

---

22. C. Hodge, 'The General Assembly of 1842,' *P.R.*, XIV (1842), 485.
23. C. Hodge, 'The General Assembly of 1843,' *P.R.*, XV (1843), 463-65. Temperance and abolitionism are elsewhere linked by Hodge for their extremism in his 'Abolitionism,' *P.R.* (1844) 547, 554 and in his 'Retrospect of the History of the Princeton Review,' *P.R.*, Index Volume from 1825–1868, 15-19.

it could be shown that the great end of society was not attainable by that mode and more securely promoted by some other. If change became obviously desirable, its nature and extent would be determined by the circumstances rather than by rule of abstract right:

> It would be absurd to maintain, on the ground of the natural equality of men, that a horde of ignorant and vicious savages, should be organized as a pure democracy, if experience taught that such a form of government was destructive to themselves and others. These different modes of constituting civil society are not necessarily either just or unjust, but become the one or the other according to circumstances; and their morality is not determined by the degree in which they encroach upon the natural rights of men, but on the degree in which they promote or retard the progress of human happiness and virtue.[24]

It is interesting that Hodge's thought thus includes the idea of progress. 'The principle that social and political organizations are designed for general good,' he says, 'of course requires they should be allowed to change, as the progress of society may demand.'[25] But such progress is to take place only gradually. As Hodge states concerning the progress of society:

> Though these changes have resulted in giving the people the enjoyment of a larger portion of their rights than they formerly possessed, it is not hence to be inferred that they ought centuries ago to have been introduced suddenly or by violence. Christianity 'operates as an alternative.' It was never designed to tear up the institutions of society by the roots. It produces equality not by prostrating trees of all sizes to the ground, but

---

24. C. Hodge, 'Slavery,' *Essays and Reviews*, 496.
25. Ibid., 497.

by securing to all the opportunity of growing, and by causing all to grow, until the original disparity is no longer perceptible.²⁶

The mention of equality raises the subject of Hodge's attitude toward egalitarian democracy. It proves to be an attitude of favor on the ground not of principle but only of pragmatism – when he does favor it. In good American fashion he takes a dim view of monarchy. Writing to his wife from Paris in 1827 after having visited the palace and viewed the king, he comments, 'Although royalty always sinks upon a close inspection, yet I am very glad I went. How it is that the million can by choice consent to exalt one like themselves so much above them, I cannot conceive.'²⁷ Yet, back in America, he could complain to his brother in 1837 of 'the ascendancy of the rabble':

> If we would have a Republic with the right of suffrage restricted to householders, who can read and write, and have been at least ten years in the country, we could get along grandly. But a democracy with universal suffrage will soon be worse than an aristocracy with Queen Victoria at the head. I feel such an interest in that youthful sovereign, that I could acknowledge her authority with far more complacency than that of Martin Van Buren.²⁸

Again he writes, 'It seems that, notwithstanding all the country has suffered, the elections are going in favor of Van Buren, almost as much as ever. I do not believe we can stand it much longer. We must get rid of universal suffrage or we shall go to ruin.'²⁹ His political leanings are not hard to infer from a letter of 1844: 'In this country the Democratic party must always be the strongest, and

---

26. Ibid.
27. A. A. Hodge, *Life*, 112: C. Hodge, Paris, 10 Jan. 1827, to his wife Sarah.
28. Ibid., 233: C. Hodge, 1 Aug. 1837, to his brother, Hugh Lenox Hodge, M.D.
29. Ibid.: C. Hodge, 17 Aug. 1837, to his brother.

it is only on extraordinary occasions, and for a short period, that the Whig, the Conservative, the Federal, or by whatever name the mass of the intelligence and property of the country may be called, can get the upper hand.'[30] Another letter shows him realistically resigned to the unruliness of democracy: 'Commotion, noise, nonsense, and at times violence are the price of liberty, and on the whole are better than the stagnation of despotism.'[31] The essence of his practical political philosophy is perhaps best shown by a letter of 1852:

> It is so clear to me that liberty can exist only on the foundation of intelligence and religion, that I have no hope for France, when the intelligent part of the population have no religion and the religious part no intelligence. It seems, however, almost incredible that such a nation can submit to be so insulted, abused, and downtrodden by such a pretender as Louis Napoleon.[32]

This sampling of Hodge's more intimate thoughts on politics reveals an emphasis on liberty, rather than equality, as the great desideratum. Equality is accepted only pragmatically as the most workable means in America of securing the end of the good of society: 'We, moreover, decide that a majority of one may make laws for the whole community, no matter whether the numerical majority have more wisdom or virtue than the minority or not. Our plea for all this is, that the good of the whole is thereby most effectually promoted. This plea, if made out, justifies the case.'[33]

---

30. Ibid., 346: C. Hodge, Princeton, 15 Dec.1844, to his brother.
31. Ibid., 344: C. Hodge, Princeton, 18 June 1841, to his brother.
32. Ibid., 395: C. Hodge, Princeton, 16 Feb. 1852, to his brother.
33. C. Hodge, 'Slavery,' *Essays and Reviews*, 496-97. Other passages showing Hodge's view of equality are to be found in his *The Way of Life*, new ed. (Philadelphia: American Sunday-School Union, 1893), 302, and in his *Commentary on the Epistle to the Ephesians* (Grand Rapids, Mich.: Wm. B. Eerdmans, 1950), 369.

For all of his criticism of American democracy, Hodge nevertheless holds a high view of the United States' position in world history. In an article in 1862 deriding England for sympathizing with the South in the Civil War, he argues that the secession is essentially a rebellion of the cotton states to perpetuate and extend the slave system: 'For this end, this glorious Union – founded by God, as all good people hoped and believed, to be the home of the free, the refuge of the oppressed, the instrument in his hand for the dissemination of Christianity and civil liberty throughout the world – is to be overturned.'[34] A sense of mission ties up the future hopes of civil and religious liberty in the world with the national existence of the United States of America. In January of 1861 he proclaimed that, should the whole South secede, 'the glorious flag which has so long floated in the advance of civilization and liberty, must be furled. We lose our position as one of the foremost nations of the earth – the nation of the future – the great Protestant power, to stand up for civil and religious freedom.'[35] The providence of God has bestowed this role on America, and this heritage must be preserved: 'Our national life we have received from our fathers, we hold it in trust, and are bound to transmit it unimpaired to future generations.'[36]

This sense of the providence of God operating in history accounts more than anything else for the inherent conservatism and moderation of Hodge and of Calvinism in general. At the conclusion of his 1836 article

---

34. C. Hodge, 'England and America,' *P.R.*, XXXIV (1862), 177.
35. C. Hodge, 'The State of the Country,' *P.R.*, XXXII (1861), 33.
36. C. Hodge, 'The Church and the Country,' *P.R.* XXXIII (1861), 336. Hodge's concept of America as a Christian, and specifically Protestant, land is to be found particularly in his articles on the Sabbath and on religion in the schools, including 'The American Quarterly Review on Sunday Mails,' *P.R.*, III (1831), 85-134; 'The Education Question,' *P.R.*, XXVI (1854), 504-44; and 'Sunday Laws,' *P.R.*, XXI (1859), 733-67. John R. Bodo includes Hodge among the 'theocrats' whose patriotism he studies in *The Protestant Clergy and Public Issues, 1812–1848* (Princeton, N.J.: Princeton University Press, 1954).

on slavery Hodge summarizes his moderate position on that subject with these words:

> We cannot too frequently remember, that it is our province to do right, it is God's to overrule results. Let, then, the North remember that they are bound to follow the example of Christ in the manner of treating slavery, and the South, that they are bound to follow the precepts of Christ in their manner of treating their slaves. If both parties follow the Saviour of men, both will contribute to the promotion of human excellence and happiness, and both will have reason to rejoice in the result.[37]

This is scarcely the spirit of radical social reform, but rather the spirit of constructive conservatism. It seeks to preserve and promote that which is right and good. While it recognizes progress, it is unlikely to provide the impetus for change; but, awaiting evidence of the providence of God, it welcomes progress when it appears.

Such a patient awaiting of progress of providence characterizes the remainder of Hodge's discussion of the slavery issue. His article of 1836 has served to provide a framework on which to hang most of the salient points of his political views. As the slavery issue developed up to and into the Civil War, he further elaborated some of these points.

In 1849 he expresses disappointment at the defeat, in Kentucky, of emancipation, which he describes as a duty and a necessity. At the same time he manifests some misgivings at the thought of either amalgamation or segregation within a single society and favors expatriation for freed and civilized Negroes to Liberia.[38]

Two years later the question of whether the fugitive slave law of 1850 should be obeyed led him to produce a

---

37. C. Hodge, 'Slavery,' Essays and Reviews, 511.
38. C. Hodge, 'Emancipation,' *P.R.*, XXI (1849), 582-607, reprinted in *Essays and Reviews*, 513-38.

full statement of his views on civil government. Here he stresses the idea of government as a divine ordinance, as expressed in the thirteenth chapter of Romans. Obedience to the civil authority is thus a matter of submission to the sovereignty of God. The Bible again is the basis: '... the will of God is the ground of all moral obligation. To seek that ground either in "the reason and nature of things," or in expediency, is to banish God from the moral world, as effectively as the mechanical theory of the universe banishes him from the physical universe and from history.'[39] The Bible also supports the principle, however, that no human authority can make it obligatory to sin.[40] The decision as to the application of these diverse principles must rest with the individual's judgment: 'No human power can come between God and the conscience.'[41] There is still a place for the right of revolution, but the right of revolution on the part of the people is regarded as quite a different thing from the right of resistance on the part of the individual. The individual may conscientiously disobey the civil authority – it may sometimes be his duty to disobey; however, he may not resist the law with impunity, but must submit to the penalty. Only when the individual finds himself in the midst of the 'mass of the community' which is desirous of change of law or government may he then peacefully and legitimately exercise the right of revolution.[42] Hodge's conclusion is that the fugitive slave law must be obeyed, or the penalty for violation

---

39. C. Hodge, 'Civil Government,' *P.R.*, XXIII (1851), 139. This article also appears with little or no change in E. M. Elliot, ed., *Cotton Is King*, 809-40, under the title 'The Fugitive Slave Law.'
40. Ibid., 143.
41. Ibid., 145.
42. Ibid., 152-54. More on the right of revolution appears in 'The State of the Country,' *P.R.*, XXXIII (1861), 27; 'The Church and the Country,' *P.R.*, XXXIII (1861), 339; 'President Lincoln,' *P.R.*, XXXVII (1865), 452; and in Hodge's *Commentary on the Epistle to the Romans*, new ed. (Grand Rapids, Mich.: Wm. B. Eerdmans, 1955), 404-15, in which he disavows the doctrine of passive obedience.

accepted, until or unless it is repealed. The main point is that man and society are subject to the revealed will of God, not merely to reason and to expediency.[43]

The efforts of the Presbyterian General Assembly to produce statements on the slavery question led to controversy over the church's right to speak on political issues. Some held that the church's role is purely spiritual. Hodge disagreed. The church has nothing to do with the totally secular business of the state, he argues, but 'if Caesar undertakes to meddle with the affairs of God, then it is the duty of the church, to whom God has committed the great work of asserting and maintaining his truth and will, to protest and remonstrate. If the state ... does anything directly contrary to the law of God, the church is bound to make that law known, and set it home upon the conscience of all concerned.'[44]

By 1864 Hodge is still contending on the basis of Scripture that slavery as an institution is not necessarily wrong: 'Paul tells us that a child, so long as he is a minor, ... differs in nothing from a slave.... It is morally right that he should be restricted in the use of his liberty, so long as he is unfit to use it aright.' But by this time he is ready more clearly to denounce slavery as it existed:

> One of the saddest proofs of the injustice of the Southern laws is, that after more than a century, the vast body of the slaves of the extreme Southern states are in a condition of the greatest degradation. That this is not to be attributed to their inferiority as a race, but to the systematic effort to prevent their improvement, is clear, because it is only the 'field hands' who are thus degraded. Household servants, and those living in the cities, where they have the opportunity of learning mechanic arts, are as much improved, as intelligent

---

43. Ibid., 158.
44. C. Hodge, 'The General Assembly,' *P.R.*, XXXI (1859), 615-16.

and moral, as any other class of men of no higher advantages.⁴⁵

At the end of 1865 Hodge could look back with contentment at what he had proposed as the solution to slavery from 1836 on:

> ... the immediate repeal of all the unjust slave laws; the legal recognition of their conjugal and parental rights, their right to acquire and hold property, and their claim to a just compensation for their labour; provision for their moral, religious, and intellectual culture, and liberty at any time to acquire their freedom by the payment of a sum to be determined in each case by a public officer appointed for that purpose. In that way we believe the whole system would be gradually, peacefully, and speedily abolished, and the slaves elevated and prepared for liberty.⁴⁶

Such was the conservative, moderate approach of Charles Hodge to the slavery question. In 1849 he had said: 'The old school Presbyterians have been the great conservative body, in reference to this subject in our country. They have stood up as a wall against the flood of abolitionism, which would have overwhelmed the Church and riven asunder the State. But at the same time they have been the truest friends of the slaves and the most effectual advocates of emancipation.'⁴⁷ These were tender and noble sentiments to utter in 1849, but the trouble with them is that in the subsequent years before the Civil War little of effect was accomplished for the slaves and the state was eventually riven asunder. What can be said for the constructive conservatism of

---

45. C. Hodge, 'The General Assembly,' P.R., XXXVI (1864), 548.
46. C. Hodge, 'The Princeton Review on the State of the Country and of the Church,' P.R., XXXVII (1865), 639.
47. C. Hodge, 'Emancipation,' *Essays and Reviews*, 517.

Hodge is that it was ready to welcome and support emancipation when the tortuous course of providence finally did produce it.

4. Economics: Support of the Clergy

The thought of Charles Hodge nowhere engages itself in economic theory to the extent that it engaged in political theory. It does enter into the area of practical economics, however, in a way that brings into question some of the commonly accepted judgments on conservatism. The Calvinistic conservatism of Hodge, at least, was not guilty of a lack of concern for the poor, a neglect of the cities, or a hyper-individualistic apathy toward society, combined with a laissez-faire type acceptance of the survival of the fittest. An examination of Hodge's arguments and activities in the economic realm may reveal also that the Presbyterian Church's failure to reach the industrial masses may not be attributable to an identification with a particular class so much as to a fault in the missions system.

Hodge devoted much of his attention and energy to the subject of support of the clergy. His annual reviews of the General Assembly reflect a continued interest in the Board of Education's program for supporting candidates studying for the ministry and in the Board of Domestic Missions' and the Board of Church Extension's efforts to establish new Presbyterian churches. In 1847 he reviewed Thomas Chalmers' *An Earnest Appeal to the Free Church of Scotland, on the subject of Economics*,[48] and in the same year he preached at the General Assembly, as its retiring moderator, on 1 Corinthians 9:14: 'Even so hath God ordained, that they which preach the gospel should live of the gospel.'[49]

---

48. C. Hodge, 'Support of the Clergy,' *P.R.*, XIX (1847), 360-78. This article was reprinted in *Essays and Reviews*, 285-302.
49. C. Hodge, 'General Assembly,' *P.R.* XIX (1847), 396.

At the General Assembly of 1853 the policy of making self-sustentation – that is, self-support by each congregation – the goal for home missionary operations was presented. Hodge attacked this policy vehemently and argued strenuously for two Scriptural principles: it is evident that 'every minister devoted to his work is entitled to a competent support. It is no less clear that the duty to provide such support rests on the whole Church, and not exclusively on the particular congregation whom the minister may serve.'[50] Hodge is not asking that the income of all ministers be equal, but 'that one should not be left to starve while the others have more than they need'.[51] The evil in the self-sustentation system is not only that preaching to the poor becomes a penalty, obliging hundreds of ministers to devote one-half to two-thirds of their time to making a living, but even more important, it tends to confine the preaching of Presbyterians to a certain class of the people.

> The determination that every Presbyterian church shall sustain itself, is a determination that we shall preach the gospel only to the rich, or, at most, to those who are able to pay for it. Woe betide us, whenever any such determination shall receive the deliberate sanction of our Church. It is already our reproach, that the poor are excluded by our system from our churches; that our plan of making each congregation sustain itself, thus throwing the support of the preacher upon the hearers, shuts our church doors, even in our cities, upon thousands.[52]

Hodge had great enthusiasm for Chalmers' system, employed in the Free Church of Scotland and similar to the plans of the Prussian Church and of the Methodists,

---

50. C. Hodge, 'General Assembly,' *P.R.* XXV (1853), 499.
51. Ibid., 500.
52. Ibid., 500-01.

of a centralized church agency to make collections and to assure that each minister had a certain minimum income sufficient to support him. Almost annually he appealed in the pages of the *Princeton Review* for someone to devise such a plan and thus to become 'one of the greatest benefactors of the Church and country'.[53] By 1864 he was losing heart: 'Against this system [of self-sustentation] we have written and protested for years; and some of the best men of our church have argued and laboured to subvert it; but to no purpose.'[54] Looking back from 1866 on almost twenty years, he confessed, 'All these efforts proved powerless. They produced no sensible impression.'[55]

The only response appears to have been a resolution from some of the large city churches, reflecting annoyance at continual solicitations,[56] objections to the Chalmers system that making the pastor independent of his congregation would render him idle and that the whole system would be too expensive,[57] and a wondering if there were not already too many ministers.[58] Hodge answered:

> Can the church complain that we have too many ministers, when there are thousands and millions of our fellow-men perishing for lack of knowledge, if she fails in providing the means of sustaining them in the field? Here is the difficulty; and it is inherent in our system. We almost tremble while we write the sentence – but does not truth demand that it be written? – The Presbyterian church is not a church for preaching the gospel to the poor. She has precluded herself from that high vocation by adopting the principle that the

---

53. C. Hodge, 'The General Assembly,' *P.R.*, XXVI (1854), 577.
54. C. Hodge, 'The General Assembly,' *P.R.*, XXXVI (1864), 511.
55. C. Hodge, 'Sustenation Fund,' *P.R.*, XXXVIII (1866), 2.
56. C. Hodge, 'The General Assembly,' *P.R.*, XXXI (1859), 542.
57. C. Hodge, 'Sustenation Fund,' *P.R.*, XXXVIII (1866), 23-24.
58. C. Hodge, 'Are there too many Ministers?' *P.R.*, XXXIV (1862), 133-46.

support of the minister must be derived from the people to whom he preaches. If, therefore, the people are too few, too sparse, too poor, to sustain a minister, or too ignorant or wicked to appreciate the gospel, they must go without it.[59]

Meanwhile Hodge, always aware of the rapidly growing population in America, became increasingly concerned for the cities. He devoted the next-to-last article that he submitted to the *Princeton Review* to the subject of 'Preaching the Gospel to the Poor', in which he noted, 'We cannot deny the fact that in our cities and larger towns the poor are not in our churches. We cannot get them in. They will not occupy "free seats" set apart for their accommodation. They instinctively go with their class.'[60]

Hodge offered no real solution to the problem, but in his concern he anticipated the Social Gospel movement of the following generation. In 1872, in his final great publication, his *Systematic Theology*, he turns his attention to Communism in his consideration of the Eighth Commandment:

> If Communism is the product of materialistic Atheism, its cure is to be found in Theism; in bringing the people to know and believe that there is a God on whom they are dependent and to whom they are responsible; in teaching them that this is not the only life, that the soul is immortal, and that men will be rewarded or punished in the world to come according to their character and conduct in the present life; that consequently well-being here is not the highest end of existence; that the poor here may hereafter be far more blessed than their rich neighbours;… that it is not the rich and the noble, but the poor and the lowly, that are his special favourites; and that the right of property, the right of

---

59. Ibid, 142.
60. C. Hodge, 'Preaching the Gospel to the Poor,' *P.R.*, XLIII (1871), 92.

The Social Views of Charles Hodge (1797–1878)

> marriage, the rights of parents and magistrates, are all ordained by God, and cannot be violated without incurring his displeasure and the certain infliction of divine punishment. To imbue the minds of the mass of the people, especially in great cities, will be a slow and difficult work; but it is absolutely necessary.

These are the old conservative answers and, typically, a teaching ministry is stressed. But Hodge goes on:

> The religious training of the people, however, is only one half of the task which society has to accomplish, to secure its own existence and prosperity. The great body of the people must be rendered comfortable, or at least have the means of becoming so; and they must be treated with justice. Misery and a sense of wrong are the two great disturbing elements in the minds of the people. They are the slumbering fires which are ever ready to break into destructive conflagration.[61]

Here we see a call for social melioration – amorphous and undeveloped, to be sure; but, at the same time, compatible with and uttered in the same breath as the doctrines of Calvinistic orthodoxy.

The stress on the world to come and the statement that well-being here is not the highest end of existence show that, while concerned for the poor, Hodge, in contrast to the later Social Gospelers, was not primarily concerned to alleviate the suffering of the poor. He himself had experienced a share of suffering and thought he recognized the value of it. His mother had been widowed in the year of his birth, his father, a surgeon, having died of overwork during a yellow-fever epidemic in 1797.[62] Life had always been something of a

---

61. C. Hodge, *Systematic Theology* (Grand Rapids, Mich.: Wm. B. Eerdmans, 1952), III, 433-34.
62. Robert Hastings Nichols, 'Charles Hodge,' *Dictionary of American Biography*, IX, 98.

financial struggle, and a theology professorship did not change that situation to any great extent. Writing to his brother, he said:

> M— — (a daughter visiting her uncle) tells me that you laughed much at my sending her *two* dollars. I can remember the time, old fellow, when the sight of two dollars would have made you laugh with a very different emotion. You don't know what it is to be a Presbyterian Abbe, with seven children. Only think of seven mouths, seven pair of feet, seven empty heads, and worse than all seven pairs of knees and elbows. Don't take this for a begging letter; for Friday is the first of May, when I expect to be as rich as Croesus for a week.[63]

But beg he sometimes had to do. His brother, a successful obstetrician and professor of medicine, frequently became the provider, as shown in a correspondence that helps account for Charles' sympathy for the underpaid Presbyterian home missionaries:

> There is, financially speaking, always a shallow spot with me during the month of April. If my salary is paid, I can generally get over it; if it is not, I am very apt to stick fast. As not the half of the salary due the 1st of February last has been paid, I am in the latter predicament just now. I must either submit to the mortification of begging time – etc., or to that of borrowing from you. The latter, though something, is much the less trial of the two.
>
> I have yet to learn the art of paying without being paid. All this is a prelude to my saying that I wish you to lend me a couple of hundred dollars, or one, if convenient. If you have it not on hand, say so. For it is not a case of necessity, but of feeling. I must pay certain calls which have already come in; but I can, on

---

63. A. A. Hodge, *Life*, 344: C. Hodge, Princeton, 28 April 1840, to his brother.

an emergency, get the money from the Bank, but that I, of course, do not like.[64]

These are middle-class problems, not reflecting the misery of grinding poverty. Real suffering was involved, however, in a painful lameness affecting his right thigh that kept him practically confined to his house for ten years after 1833.

This account of his own sufferings provides background for an article on the Civil War which further explains his view of providence, which significantly affects his attitude toward poverty. Considering whether suffering is always punitive and whether 'to interpret providence on the assumption that this is the state of retribution,' Hodge declares:

> What the Scriptures plainly teach on this subject is, 1. That so far as rational creatures are concerned, where there is no sin, personal or imputed, there is no suffering. 2. That no man, no community of men, no society, church, or nation ever suffered in this life as much as their sins deserve. And, consequently, no individual or nation can ever justly complain of the dispensation of Divine providence as unmerited inflictions. 3. But thirdly, it is no less clearly taught, that the distribution of good and evil in this world to individuals, churches or nations, is not determined by the principles of justice; but according to the wise and benevolent sovereignty of God. He puts up one, and puts down another of the princes of the earth; he exalts one nation and humbles another; he gives one man prosperity and another adversity, not according to their several deserts, but according to his own good pleasure.[65]

He goes on to say that suffering may be punitive, but this is no proof that it always is so.

---

64. Ibid., 347: C. Hodge, Princeton, 4 April 1844, to his brother.
65. C. Hodge, 'The War,' *P.R.* XXXV (1863), 143.

> Such being the case, it is obviously most unscriptural, and often the manifestation of a pharisaical and censorious spirit, when men regard calamities,…as necessarily Divine judgments, and manifestations of his wrath. This is not only a fundamentally erroneous view of the Divine government as administered in this world, but it betrays an inordinate estimate of mere temporal prosperity. Happiness, abundance of the good things of this life, health, riches, and honours, are not the highest gifts of God. Poverty, suffering, the necessity of labour, disappointment and reproach are often the greatest blessings, and evidence of God's especial favour.[66]

Such views clearly put Hodge at odds with the prevailing sentiments of Victorian Liberalism, which corresponds in many points to the twentieth-century American meaning of conservatism. 'The monstrous doctrine of Carlyle, and of the modern philosophy,' Hodge continues, 'that the Weltgeschichte is the Weltgericht; that history is judicial; that the strong are always right; that those who succeed ought to succeed; that we must always take sides against the afflicted and downtrodden, is simply diabolical. It would make us the partisans of the kingdom of Satan from the beginning until now.'[67] There is no gospel of success here, no harsh judgment of poverty. Hodge summarizes his thought in this area thus:

> Are we entitled to gather up our skirts lest they should be defiled by the touch of poverty or suffering? Do not the Scriptures and all experience teach us, that God is a sovereign, that the orderings of his providence are not determined by justice, but by mysterious wisdom for the accomplishment of higher ends than were punishment or reward? We are in his hands, and we are to learn his

---

66. Ibid., 144.
67. Ibid., 145-46.

will and our duty, not from the adverse or prosperous dispensations of providence, but from his holy word.[68]

Hodge thus espouses a view that sees poverty neither as something horrible that must be alleviated nor as something horrifying that represents a judgment of God on sin. It is recognized simply as a result of the working of divine providence, whose mysteries leave one humbled and submissive to the revealed will of God. One such mystery of God's providence is why President Lincoln, whom Hodge admired tremendously, should have died suddenly and violently.[69] Hodge points out various ends that God may have in mind to accomplish by means of sufferings:

> As with individuals, so with churches and nations.... Sometimes .... he means to punish them for their sins; sometimes he designs to try their faith and patience, and to make them examples to others; sometimes he intends to develope their character, to call forth their powers, to fit them for higher degrees of usefulness; and sometimes, as our Lord said, the end of their sufferings is, 'that the works of God should be made manifest in them.'[70]

Here, in a rising scale, are the possible results of the working of God's providence – everything from a very conservative punishment for sin to a highly revolutionary working of God in man. Hodge's Calvinism appears, then, to be by implication not necessarily a conservative force.

His care to apply the statement above to churches and nations as well as to individuals helps to answer one

---

68. Ibid., 147.
69. C. Hodge, 'President Lincoln,' *P.R.*. XXXVII (1865), 435-58. See also A.A. Hodge, *Life*, 482-84.
70. C. Hodge, 'The War,' *P.R.*, XXXV (1863), 144.

other charge leveled at nineteenth-century Calvinism – the charge of an extreme individualism. It is true that Hodge stressed individual spiritual regeneration, a personal conversion to trust in Jesus Christ for salvation from sin. He himself had experienced such a conversion during a revival in 1815, in his college days.[71] In his more mature years, however, he became wary of the methods and effects of revivalism. He stressed the religious training of believers' children over the idea of sudden conversion as the normal and most effective way of inculcating the Christian faith.[72] In reviewing Horace Bushnell's *Discourses on Christian Nurture*, Hodge finds little to disagree with on the main issue: 'The leading idea of Dr. Bushnell's Discourses, is organic, as distinguished from individual life. Whatever may be thought of the expression, or whatever may be the form in which it lies in his mind, it represents a great and obvious truth; a truth, which however novel it may appear to many of our New England brethren, is as familiar to Presbyterians as household words.' Recognition of the significance of organic, corporate, or social life was nothing new to Hodge: '… we see on every hand abundant evidence that every church, nation and society, has a common life, besides the life of its individual members.'[73]

This point of contact with Bushnell is rendered all the more significant by the judgment of Charles Howard Hopkins that:

> Bushnell's *Christian Nurture* did more than any single factor to break down the extreme individualism of the old Puritanism. He insisted upon experience in theology, leveled the dividing wall between nature and

---

71. A. A. Hodge, Life, 30-34.
72. C. Hodge, 'Bushnell on Christian Nurture,' *Essays and Reviews*, 319-22. This article originally appeared in *P.R.*, XIX (1847), 502-39.
73. Ibid., 303.

the supernatural, and set Christ in the center of the Christian system. The 'new theology' that later built upon these premises provided the religious background for a social gospel movement that was rapidly nearing maturity as the century drew to its close.[74]

The only real difference between this description of Bushnell and Charles Hodge would be with regard to the leveling of the dividing wall between nature and the supernatural. For Hodge there is a distinction between nature and the supernatural but no dividing wall, for the supernatural is real and permeates through the mysterious working of providence as revealed in God's word. This view, although tending to express itself more gradually and moderately, is no less full of potential for social progress.

5. Conclusion: Charles Hodge and Social Melioration

If the social thought of Charles Hodge contained potential for social progress, why did it not produce actual results in that direction? His ideas have demonstrated that Calvinistic determinism, operating through the providence of God, need be no more a conservative force than the determinism of Karl Marx. His ideas have manifested no exaltation of the individual above social concerns, so that social development is inhibited, but instead have revealed a Christianity that is both individual and social in its emphases. His ideas have shown no identification with a particular social class to the exclusion of some other; as a matter of fact, contrary to what one might expect, he is concerned for the poor and is inclined to attack the unscrupulous businessman.[75]

The problem is that his ideas remain merely ideas. His words seem to have fallen on deaf ears. For whatever

---

74. Hopkins, *Rise of the Social Gospel*, 5.
75. C Hodge, *Systematic Theology*, III, 434-37.

reasons, the Presbyterian Church evidently lacked the practical means of implementing social change. Hodge provides much evidence for the fact that the Presbyterian Church was composed mostly of the wealthier classes, and it is true that the Presbyterian form of church government gave wealthy lay elders a prominent role. The evidence in Hodge's writings indicates, however, that the elders tended to push harder than the ministers for increased ministerial support, especially for the domestic missionaries.[76]

As unlikely a solution as Hodge's perennially proposed ministerial sustenation fund would appear to be, perhaps the mechanical flaw of self-sustenation is what effectively cut the Presbyterian Church off from the poor. After all, it was direct contact with the poor in the industrial areas that produced many of the zealots of the Social Gospel movement.

On the other hand, it must be admitted that Hodge's strict allegiance to the Bible as authoritative and his belief in providence as governing the affairs of the world result in a conservatism expressed in invariable moderation in means as opposed to any sudden or violent change. 'In firmly resisting ... unscriptural demands,' he could claim of the Presbyterian Church, 'we have preserved the integrity and unity of the Church, made it the great conservative body of truth, moderation, and liberty of conscience in our country.'[77]

This sort of Calvinistic conservatism is not incompatible with social melioration. But what must be sensed to a greater degree than Hodge sensed it is the progressive

---

76. C. Hodge, 'The General Assembly,' *P.R.*, XXVI (1854), 575-76 (elders were in heavy attendance at this General Assembly, 545); and 'The General Assembly of 1856,' *P.R.*, XXVIII (1856), 580.

77. Robert Ellis Thompson, *A History of the Presbyterian Churches in the United States* (New York: The Christian Literature Co., 1895), 383, quoting Hodge's Protest to the General Assembly of 1861.

movement of God's providence in history. To apply the social norms of Roman society in the New Testament age directly to nineteenth-century American society, as Hodge did with regard to slavery, manifests a blindness to the differences in the forms of slavery in the two societies and to the general development of civilization over the centuries of time between the two eras. With this kind of sensitivity the inherently conservative and moderate aspects of Calvinism can be balanced with the essentially reforming and socially activist aspect of that same Biblical Reformed tradition.

6

AMERICA AND THE COMING KING

Introduction
Once upon a time there was a Christian political leader who announced that he would support only the orthodox, Nicene faith and that the practice of pagan idolatry would be a capital crime. All followers of other religions than the orthodox Catholic Christianity would be branded heretics, and their conventicles would not be allowed to be called churches. Not only was this leader committed to the true faith, but he was effective in bringing peace and unity to his realm. Like most politicians, however, he had his bad moments. After a riot in which a military commander was killed, this leader reacted in a rage, his soldiers slaughtering some seven thousand in that place, regardless of guilt or innocence, age or sex. The next time he came to his Bishop's church, the Bishop confronted him in the vestibule of the church: 'How will you lift up in prayer the hands still dripping with the blood of the murdered? How will you receive with such hands the most holy body of the Lord? How will you bring to your mouth his most precious blood? Get you away, and dare not to heap crime upon crime.' When this leader appealed to King David's murder and

adultery, the Bishop replied: 'Well, if you have imitated David in sin, imitate him also in repentance.' And he did. The Roman Emperor Theodosius the Great submitted to church discipline, made public confession of his sin, and was absolved by Ambrose, Bishop of Milan, after eight months of penitence when he issued a law in 390 that a sentence of death would not be executed until thirty days after it had been pronounced.

Do we not sometimes yearn for political leaders like that – ones who are committed to the Christian faith and who will also submit to the church's discipline? The late fourth century in the Christian Roman Empire almost sounds like an ideal setting, yet that very era illustrates some of the problems of trying to establish the kingdom of God upon earth. Just two years before Ambrose's discipline of Theodosius there was a similar incident. In 388 some Christian zealots had burned down a Jewish synagogue at Callinicum on the Euphrates, and Theodosius had as a matter of justice ordered that the local Bishop make restitution in full out of church funds. Ambrose, however, refused to proceed with the Lord's Supper until the Emperor would rescind his order of restitution. Who was right in this case? I submit to you that Theodosius was closer to the principles by which our Lord expects political leaders to operate.

1. The Dream of a Christian State
There is a natural longing within each of us for an ideal political setting. We desire to see an end to all of the evils that have intruded upon human society since the expulsion from the Garden of Eden – physical violence stemming from envy and hatred, poverty and destitution stemming from greed and indolence, wars growing out of lust and ambition, lack of health and safety coming from disease and crime. We long for peace and prosperity, if not primarily for ourselves, then

for our children and grandchildren. This is a legitimate longing. The prophet Jeremiah (29:7) told the Jewish captives in Babylon to pray for the peace and prosperity of the city to which the Lord had carried them into exile. The apostle Paul urged Timothy that, first of all, prayers be made 'for kings and all those in authority, that we may live peaceful and quiet lives in all godliness and holiness' (1 Tim. 2:1-2). There is a hope in our hearts for that ruler, that king, who will reign in righteousness and justice. But we are not to expect that perfect kingdom until the King himself comes. As Paul said to Timothy, 'everyone who wants to live a godly life in Christ Jesus will be persecuted, while evil men and imposters will go from bad to worse, deceiving and being deceived' (2 Tim. 3:12). Jesus likewise told his disciples what to expect in this world:

> Then you will be handed over to be persecuted and put to death, and you will be hated by all nations because of me. At that time many will turn away from the faith and will betray and hate each other, and many false prophets will appear and deceive many people. Because of the increase of wickedness, the love of most will grow cold, but he who stands firm to the end will be saved. And this gospel of the kingdom will be preached in the whole world as a testimony to all nations, and then the end will come (Matt. 24:9-14).

Any vision of the Kingdom of God on earth is going to be premature if it is a merely political thing before the great King himself comes.

A) The Old Testament Theocracy
Sometimes the Old Testament theocracy is held up as a model. But think what things were like in the days after the conquest of the Holy Land, when the memories

of the exodus and Red Sea miracles and also the Sinai deliberations were still fresh. God raised up hero after hero among the Judges because the people repeatedly declined into sin. The time of small government was not a time of great peace and prosperity. 'In those days Israel had no king; everyone did as he saw fit' (Judg. 21:25). Samuel is one of the great spiritual leaders of Israel, but the people are scarcely ready to follow him. He paves the way, however, for the glory days of Saul, David, and Solomon. Think of Jerusalem in that era. The former Jebusite fortress is conquered by David and turned into the model for the City of God. What a celebration there is on that second occasion when the Ark of the Covenant is brought up to the city. Choirs are established to sing the Psalms of David. The man after God's own heart governs. Then Solomon, not a man of war but of peace, builds the Temple as the visible house of God. And the Lord grants him wisdom to be the marvel of the world. But not yet do we have the Kingdom of God on earth. David and Solomon are not without their sins, and the Kingdom divides in the next generation.

B) The New Testament Situation
By New Testament times the Messianic expectation of even the godliest remnant among the Jews was still a largely political one. Even after the resurrection of Jesus the disciples ask him, 'Lord, are you at this time going to restore the kingdom to Israel?' Not yet, not yet. Jesus says, 'It is not for you to know the times or dates the Father has set by his own authority. But you will receive power when the Holy Spirit comes on you; and you will be my witnesses in Jerusalem, and in all Judea and Samaria, and to the ends of the earth.' He did not deny a restoring of the kingdom in the sense the disciples anticipated, while still under Roman dominion, but that was not yet to be. Here is the temptation for the church of the time of

Theodosius the Great and Ambrose and Augustine. By the fourth century the Roman Emperor Constantine had been converted. The new capital city of Constantinople is built, like a new Jerusalem, a new City of God. The laws, which previously persecuted Christians, are made to favor them. The proportion of those who identify with the Christian church grows from c.15% in 312 to c.95% by 387. Surely now the Kingdom has come to earth. The church historian Eusebius of Constantine's day thought the millennium had begun.

Augustine, who had been converted at the age of thirty-two, partly through Ambrose's ministry just four years before the excommunication of Theodosius in 390, was spiritually astute enough to perceive that the City of God could not be identified on a one-to-one basis with either the institutional church or the Christian Roman state. No, the Heavenly City was spiritually defined, made up of those characterized, thanks to God's grace, by *amor dei*, love of God, rather than *amor sui*, love of self. Even so, when all attempts to persuade failed to bring back into the Catholic Church every one of the schismatic Christian Donatists, Augustine turned to the Christian civil magistrate to coerce them into the church. His text was Luke 14:23, 'Go out into the highways and the hedges and compel them to come in,' the very text that Bishop Bossuet would use, on the basis of Augustine's authority, to persuade Louis XIV of France to revoke the Edict of Nantes in 1685 and to persecute the Huguenots, the true spiritual descendants of Augustine.

C) The Irony of the Augustinian Tradition
What happened to Augustine would happen again in the High Middle Ages. Bernard of Clairvaux, in the twelfth century, could see it coming and warned against the growing wealth and power of the church and of the papacy in a Europe recovering from centuries

of domination by waves of Byzantine, Muslim, and barbarian incursions. The papacy led in the Crusades, mobilizing the new military power of the rising nation-states. As knowledge increased, the church sought to control the new universities, and Dominicans and Franciscans led in the development of Scholasticism. When trade revived through European control of the Mediterranean, the church tried also to control the new economy. It succeeded less here, but it nevertheless became wealthy. This was what had worried Bernard: In mastering the thriving new culture of the High Middle Ages, the church itself was being subtly mastered by the culture and was in danger of becoming thoroughly secular. If man's reason can reconcile Aristotle and the Bible, why should we need to start with God's revelation? If the pope is Christ's vicar on earth, why do we need Christ? If we have the funds to build great cathedrals and send great armies, why do we need trust in God?

Christian faith, in the Augustinian tradition of the 'spoiling of the Egyptians', taking the best of secular culture and transforming it for the uses of the City of God, need not succumb to the culture, but we need to be alert to the imminent danger. The New England experiment of the Puritans fell prey to this temptation also, making too close an identification between the state and the church, the community and the true believers of a pure church, so that groups such as Baptists and Quakers were persecuted. All such dreams of a Christian state, including John Calvin's Geneva or John Knox's Scotland, have proven to be a delusion, resulting either in hypocritical claims of 'In God We Trust' or in an impure church and often both.

2. *What Do Christians Desire in and of the State?*
If the establishment of a Christian state is part of the 'not yet', that is, the Kingdom of God will achieve its visible

political manifestation only when the King is here, what is it that we should expect of the state now?

A) Religious Freedom and Liberty of Conscience
In 1 Timothy 2, after urging that prayers be made first of all 'for kings and all those in authority, that we may live peaceful and quiet lives in all godliness and holiness', Paul goes on to say: 'This is good, and pleases God our Savior, who wants all men to be saved and to come to a knowledge of the truth. For there is one God and one mediator between God and men, the man Christ Jesus, who gave himself as a ransom for all men – the testimony given in its proper time. And for this purpose I was appointed a herald and an apostle – I am telling the truth, I am not lying – and a teacher of the true faith to the Gentiles.' Paul thus links his calling as a missionary to spread the gospel of salvation through Christ with his concern for the political situation. He wants peace and restraint of evil so that Christians will be free to make Christ known by word and by deed. The very universal character of the gospel as the way of salvation for all nations and the very exclusive uniqueness of Christ as the one mediator of this salvation make this freedom urgent. He does not expect, nor does he desire, the direct support of the state for the spread of the gospel. But he does seek freedom to persuade. He accepts the challenge of the religious pluralism of the Greco-Roman world and uses the freedom of thought and expression boldly to make known the one way of salvation that all need to hear. And because faith comes by hearing of the word, by persuasion resulting from the message being proclaimed, he does not seek coercion. George Weigel of the Ethics and Public Policy Center in Washington captures this concept in his commentary on Pope John Paul II's address to the United Nations in October of 1995:

So basic human rights are truly universal in character. They are not cultural quirks, of interest only to the West. Nor are basic human rights a benefice granted by the state. The reality of the matter works precisely the other way: any just state must recognize that inside every human being there is a sanctuary of conscience – a sanctuary of personhood, if you will – where state power may not tread. Thus religious freedom and freedom of conscience are not only the first of human rights in personal terms: they also help make pluralism and democracy possible by establishing that the state is not omnicompetent, and therefore ought not to be omnipresent.[1]

We desire from the state, then, first of all that religious freedom and liberty of conscience be preserved. Our Lord taught us to pray, 'Thy kingdom come,' and the Westminster Shorter Catechism says that in this petition 'we pray, That Satan's kingdom may be destroyed; and that the kingdom of grace may be advanced, ourselves and others brought into it, and kept in it; and that the kingdom of glory may be hastened.' We do not, however, look to the state to accomplish these ends. As the Presbyterians who founded the General Assembly of the Presbyterian Church in the United States of America said in 1788 in their 'Preliminary Principles' to the Form of Government:

> They are unanimously of opinion: (I.) That 'God alone is Lord of the conscience; and hath left it free from the doctrine and commandments of men, which are in any thing contrary to his word, or beside it in matters of faith or worship:' Therefore they consider the right of private judgment in all matters that respect religion, as universal and unalienable: they do not even wish to see any religious constitution aided by the civil power,

---

1. Georg Weigel, *American Purpose*, Vol. 9, No. 4, (Winter 1995), 7.

further than may be necessary for protection and security, and, at the same time, be equal and common to all others.

This means that we welcome a pluralistic society where religious freedom is protected. It means that open religious expression among adults is encouraged. We can enter into inter-faith dialogue with boldness – for example, with Jewish friends we can declare openly that we believe Jesus is the Messiah – and also with courtesy and graciousness because we know that faith is a result of persuasion not coercion.

B) No Establishment of False Gods
So far my comments have addressed the area of the 'free exercise' clause of the First Amendment. With regard to the 'establishment of religion' clause, not only do we not seek establishment of Christianity, or of our particular branch of it, by the state, but we stand in opposition to the establishment of any other religion, including such religions as communism, civil religion, or secular humanism. Some years ago I was spectator of a panel discussion on religion and law at which a member of a secular law-school faculty, with no particular religious identification, responded to the then popular line 'we can't legislate morality' with the comment that all law is a reflection of somebody's morality. In the absence of any conscious commitment to a deity, secular humanism is a religion. In Augustine's terms, it is as though *amor sui* has won out over *amor dei* and has gained the throne. One's ultimate value is oneself, or at best the human race. And in civil religion one's ultimate loyalty is to the country and is expressed in patriotism. However noble this may be, they are idolatries and are accompanied by their respective blasphemies. What is considered a blasphemy in a given culture is a clue as to what is its

religion. In the case of civil religion, blasphemy might be desecration of the flag or dishonor of military veterans. In our contemporary American culture blasphemy might be a racial epithet, using the 'N-word', or denying the Jewish Holocaust occurred, or perhaps wanting to censor a sexually explicit film or TV program. Pretty soon it may be discriminating in any way against homosexuals. All of these suggest that a religion of secular humanism is nearly established.

It is time that Christians register shock at the genuine blasphemies that dishonor the Lord. Jesus taught us to pray, 'Hallowed by thy name,' and the Shorter Catechism says that in that petition we pray, 'That God would enable us and others to glorify him in all that whereby he maketh himself known; and that he would dispose all things to his own glory.' We don't expect the state to require everyone to honor God, but in a pluralistic society we can expect that disrespect for God, the Bible, the church, and that which religious people regard as sacred will be restrained.

C) Commitment to Common Values

The state's role in protecting religious freedom and in prohibiting the establishment of any one religion appears to be largely negative. What positive role can we expect the state to play? The answer is that God has ordained the state to uphold what is right and wrong in the sphere of human relations. Although we do not expect the state to do more than guarantee freedom in the area of the first great commandment, 'Thou shalt love the Lord thy God with all thy heart, soul, mind, and strength,' we do expect it to use its authority in the area of the second great commandment, 'Thou shalt love thy neighbor as thyself,' which sums up the latter half of the Ten Commandments. If those from another perspective should challenge these values, we should not hesitate to say that we represent the Judeo-Christian – that is, biblical – value system that has been the foundation of this culture, and until they can offer a better foundation, the country should stick with this one. Jesus taught us to pray, 'Thy will be done in earth, as it is in heaven,' and the Shorter Catechism says that in this petition we pray, 'That God, by his grace, would make us able and willing to know, obey, and submit to his will in all things, as the angels do in heaven.' Knowing his revealed will in the Scriptures, we need to appeal to the consciences of even the unbelievers in our culture to do what they know is right. With regard to political leaders, perhaps the best we can hope for in this life is someone who has enough sensitivity to the will of God to sense the workings of his providence in the affairs of state. The best example I know of is the Second Inaugural Address of Abraham Lincoln in the latter stages of the Civil War in 1865: Listen to what Lincoln said about the North and the South:

> Both read the same Bible and pray to the same God; and each invokes His aid against the other. It may seem strange that any men should dare to ask a just God's assistance in wringing their bread from the sweat of other men's faces; but let us judge not that we be not judged. The prayers of both could not be answered; that of neither has been answered fully. The Almighty has His own purposes. 'Woe unto the world because of offences! For it must needs be that offences come; but woe to that man by whom the offence cometh!' If we shall suppose that American Slavery is one of those offences which, in the providence of God, must needs come, but which, having continued through His appointed time, He now wills to remove, and that He gives to both North and South, this terrible war, as the woe due to those by whom the offence came, shall we discern therein any departure from those divine attributes which the believers in a Living God always ascribe to

> Him? Fondly do we hope – fervently do we pray – that this mighty scourge of war may speedily pass away. Yet if God wills that it continue, until all the wealth piled by the bond-man's two hundred and fifty years of unrequited toil shall be sunk, and until every drop of blood drawn with the lash shall be paid by another drawn with the sword, as was said three thousand years ago, so still it must be said 'the judgments of the Lord, are true and righteous altogether.'
>
> With malice toward none; with charity for all; with firmness in the right, as God gives us to see the right, let us strive on to finish the work we are in; to bind up the nation's wounds; to care for him who shall have borne the battle, and for his widow, and his orphan – to do all which may achieve and cherish a just, and a lasting peace, among ourselves, and with all nations.

Whatever Lincoln's connection to the church, he knew his Bible and he had a sense of God's purposes. That is what our society needs in this time before the coming of the King.

Conclusion

Did you notice how often the response of the people of God in the Bible to an alien political situation was primarily in prayer? I would propose to you a theology of prayer, a political theology of prayer. Not only do we have Jeremiah 29 and 1 Timothy 2, but the very structure of the Lord's Prayer – beginning with 'Hallowed be thy Name; Thy Kingdom come' through 'Give us this day our daily bread' to 'Deliver us from the Evil One' – is full of political implications. It is not unusual to hear Christians in America quote, or even sing, 2 Chronicles 7:14: 'If my people, who are called by my name, will humble themselves and pray and seek my face and turn from their wicked ways, then I will hear from heaven and will forgive their sin and will heal their land.' The Israel of

King Solomon and those restored from the Babylonian captivity in the time of Chronicles were, or course, called by the name of the Lord in a way that America is not. Nevertheless, the very things Solomon prays for in 2 Chronicles 6 are the kinds of concerns we should have as we pray for our political leaders.

Concerning verses 22 and 23 – 'When a man wrongs his neighbor.... Judge between your servants, repaying the guilty.... Declare the innocent not guilty....' – one thinks of all the history of injustice done to African Americans from slavery to Jim Crow segregation, or to Native Americans from the Trail of Tears to Wounded Knee, or the Rodney King beating by police, or the Clarence Thomas–Anita Hill hearings, or the O. J. Simpson trial, or locally the Eddie Polec murder.

Concerning verses 24 and 25 – 'When your people have been defeated by an enemy because they have sinned... hear from heaven and forgive' – one thinks of the Vietnam war.

Concerning verses 26 and 27 – 'When the heavens are shut up and there is no rain.... Forgive. Teach the right way to live' – one thinks of tornadoes, hurricanes, floods, and drought.

Concerning verses 28 to 31: 'When famine or plague comes ... whatever disaster or disease.... Forgive, and deal with each man according to all he does ... so that they will fear you and walk in your ways...', or verses 32 and 33: 'As for the foreigner ... who prays ... do whatever he asks of you ... so that all the peoples on the earth may know your name and fear you,' or verses 34 and 35): 'when your people go to war ... hear their plea and uphold their cause...' – one thinks of the Gulf War of 1991, or perhaps the bombing of the U.S. Trade Center, or the Oklahoma City bombing, or the conflict in Kosovo.

'When ... in captivity ... they repent ...forgive' (vv. 36-39). All of these crisis events become occasions for prayer, repentance, and forgiveness. We have access to the King of Kings. We should be leading the way in such prayer. The pastoral prayer from the pulpit should be emphasizing these concerns. We should have prayer groups focused on those in positions of political authority; just as we have prayer groups focused on missions, so we should have prayer groups focused on political authorities, for the two are not unrelated. And we should inform the political authorities that we are praying for them. Justin Martyr wrote to the Roman Emperor Antoninus Pius and his associates in the mid-second century: 'So we worship God only, but in other matters we gladly serve you, recognizing you as emperors and rulers of men, and praying that along with your imperial power you may also be found to have a sound mind' (*First Apology*, 17).

In our increasingly secular age it is important that our praying be public as well as private. I recall the Norman Rockwell painting on a *Saturday Evening Post* cover from the 1940s or 50s with a young boy and a woman (perhaps his mother or aunt) praying over their meal in a diner, with the blue collar workers from the surrounding tables and booths staring at the curiosity.

But the Lord's summoning of us to prayer does not lead to a passive quietism. Justin Martyr could say to the Emperor:

> Those who once rejoiced in fornication now delight in continence alone; those who made use of magic arts have dedicated themselves to the good and unbegotten God; we who once took most pleasure in the means of increasing our wealth and property now bring what we have into a common fund and share with everyone in need; we who hated and killed one another and would not associate with men of different tribes because of [their different] customs, now after the manifestation

of Christ live together and pray for our enemies and try to persuade those who unjustly hate us, so that they, living according to the fair commands of Christ, may share with us the good hope of receiving the same things [that we will] from God, the master of all (*First Apology*, 14).

You see, when we engage in prayer according to the will of God, our very lives tend to become conformed to his will. Praying Christians become the best of citizens. The early church was opposed to abortion, and filled with concern for the unborn children, they became the rescuers of those children who had been born and left to die, and they adopted them to become children of the Covenant.

The Lord summons us, in 1 Timothy 2, 'first of all, that requests, prayers, intercession and thanksgiving be made for everyone – for kings and all those in authority, that we may live peaceful and quiet lives in all godliness and holiness. This is good, and pleases God our Savior, who wants all men to be saved and to come to a knowledge of the truth. For there is one God and one mediator between God and men, the man Christ Jesus, who gave himself as a ransom for all men ....' Once upon a time, in the year that good King Uzziah died, the prophet Isaiah saw the Lord seated on a throne, high and lifted up. 'Woe is me,' he cried, 'for I am a man of unclean lips, and I live among a people of unclean lips, and my eyes have seen the King, the Lord Almighty.' But when one of the angels touched a coal from the altar to his lips, he said, 'Your guilt is taken away and your sin atoned for.' And the voice of the Lord said, 'Whom shall I send? And who will go for us?' And Isaiah said, 'Here am I. Send me!'

In an interview in *Christianity Today*, African-American economist Glenn Loury was responding to questions about the problems of the inner-city. He said: 'The solution is the Christian faith: I mean the church and the community of believers engaged with these problems, and bringing the moral teachings of the church and the salvation that's available through faith to those who are in need.... I don't believe that tinkering with economic incentives can get us to where we need to go. Indeed, I think the larger society is in some difficulty and that there are various indicators that people are recognizing that the only way to respond effectively to that difficulty is through revival and evangelism in a large sense.'[2]

The City of God will not come until the King himself comes again. But until that time, you and I who know that King must bear witness by word and deed to his kingdom. Once upon a time – indeed, already – God has exalted him to the highest place and given him a name that is above every name. But once upon a time, – though we cannot know the date, or time, it is certain – he will come again, that at the name of Jesus every knee shall bow, and every tongue confess that Jesus Christ is Lord, to the glory of God the Father.

---

2. Glenn Loury, *Christianity Today* (January 8, 1996), 20.

7

A History of Church and State Relations in Western Christianity

Introduction
Western Christianity is not monolithic (like Islam: Shi'ites, Sunnis, etc.). There are Protestantism (with roots in the sixteenth-century Reformation, but claiming to go back to Biblical Christianity), Roman Catholicism, Eastern Orthodoxy, etc. Among Protestants, there are mainline liberal ecumenical denominations influenced by modern critical approaches to Scripture, and there are evangelicals who emphasize the truth of Scripture and the reality of God and the supernatural. We represent that evangelical Protestant tradition with an effort to present and defend that position with the best scholarship possible. It should also be understood that among all of these Western Christian groups there may be various views on church-state relations (like Islam: Pan-Arab, Islamicist, and no doubt other positions on how to relate to the modern, secular state and/or world). My hope is that a review of approaches to Western Christian history may be helpful in stimulating thought with regard to an

---

This chapter was a Presentation to the International Center for Dialogue Among Civilizations (ICDAC), Tehran, Iran, October, 2003

issue that confronts all religious people in the twenty-first century, and that such a review may at least contribute toward mutual understanding. After a brief account of the earliest Christian statements with regard to the state in the New Testament, I shall present four distinct approaches to church and state in Christian history, culminating with what I believe is the American position (still controversial in the United States), and then by contrast the approach of world Communism as represented by the former Soviet Union and current China or North Korea or Cuba.

1. The Position of Christianity in the New Testament

The New Testament was produced in the first century when the Jews were under the dominion of the yet-pagan Roman Empire. Just three days before he was arrested and crucified, Jesus was confronted by the Pharisees and the Herodians about whether it was lawful to pay taxes to Caesar. He said, 'Show me the coin for paying the tax,' and they produced a Roman denarius with an image of Caesar on it and an inscription saying 'Emperor Tiberius son of the deified Augustus'. Jesus asked, 'Whose image and inscription is this?' and they said, 'Caesar's.' And he said, 'Render unto Caesar what is Caesar's and to God what is God's.' We will come back to Jesus and the coin in discussing the American so-called 'separation of church and state', but for now we can see that Jesus' statement showed a certain respect for the prerogatives of the state even when pagan, and yet recognized a distinct sphere of God's prerogatives which cannot be claimed by the state. As the New Testament era unfolded, Christianity was persecuted both by Jewish authorities and by the Roman regime, yet Christianity taught obedience to the state in its legitimate sphere as ordained by God and obedience to God in whatever he has commanded (Acts 4:18-20; 5:29 ['We must obey God rather than man'], 1 Pet. 2:13-17, Rom. 13:1-7; 1 Tim. 2:1-6).

2. After Persecution: Caesaropapism

Christians experienced persecution sporadically and locally through the first three centuries of the church's existence in the Roman Empire, with the first universal persecution under Decius in the mid-third century and the most widespread and worst one under Diocletian in the beginning of the fourth century. The main issue was the Christians' refusal to worship the Emperor or to engage in pagan ritual. But then came a dramatic reversal when the Emperor Constantine was converted to Christianity. Here was an entirely new situation, seemingly not envisioned in the New Testament, of the ruler of the state now favoring the true faith as regarded by Christians. Constantine wanted to support and promote the church and even presided at the Council of Nicaea in 325, which he called to resolve doctrinal issues. He referred to himself as 'the apostle to those outside the church'. He was both *rex* and *sacerdos*, king and priest. Hence this approach became known as 'caesaropapism', the combination of headship of the church with headship of the state. This would become characteristic of the Byzantine, or Eastern Roman Empire, centered in Constantinople (Istanbul), through its long history until conquered by the Turks in 1453.

3. The 'Two Swords Theory'

The church in the Western Roman Empire of Europe, and particularly the Pope in Rome, was not ready to accept this superiority of influence by the state in the affairs of the church. Pope Gelasius I in 492 admonished the Byzantine Emperor that there are two governing elements in the Christian world, and while the secular ruler has *potestas* (power), the spiritual or ecclesiastical ruler has *auctoritas* (authority). In Roman law *auctoritas* was the higher principle, declaring the governing will, while *potestas* was the executive power to implement or enforce the governing will. This was consistent with the great North African theologian Augustine, who wrote of the 'two cities' in his *City of God*. This would be the policy of the Frankish ruler of much of Europe, Charlemagne, in the eighth and ninth centuries, a cooperation between church and state, each seeking to support the programs of the other.

4. The Theocratic State, or 'Ecclesiocracy'

Almost inevitably, however, as political power became weak in medieval Europe, there was the temptation for the ecclesiastical leadership to intrude into the political sphere. In what is known as the 'investiture controversy' in the eleventh and twelfth centuries and into the fourteenth century, the papacy, in reaction to the king's appointing of church leaders, claimed the authority not only to excommunicate kings but to depose them from their royal office. Pope Gregory VII sought to do this to Emperor Henry IV in the 1070s and Pope Boniface VIII to King Philip IV of France in the 1300s. This is the two-century period of the crusades, in the midst of which Pope Innocent III would launch a crusade against 'the Turk' which ironically ended up conquering Constantinople in 1204.

5. 'Separation of Church and State'

It is partly against this misuse of power by the papacy that the Protestant Reformation reacted in the sixteenth century. There were more basic spiritual and doctrinal issues, such as the authority of Scripture and the way of salvation to which Protestantism sought to return, but recognition of the legitimate sphere of the state was one aspect of the Protestant Reformation. At first the Reformers believed that in each nation-state there should be an established church, so that in Germany and Scandinavia it was Lutheranism, in England Anglicanism

(Episcopalian Church), in Scotland Presbyterianism, in the Netherlands and Switzerland the Reformed Church, etc. In America, where these various Protestant groups and Roman Catholics came in the seventeenth century to escape persecution and experience freedom of religion, there developed the concept of 'separation of church and state', or the non-interference of each in the sphere of the other. This is currently the prevailing view in America, although it is interpreted and understood in varying ways.

My own position is that, properly understood, it is consistent with the teaching of Jesus and the New Testament. Going back to the situation of Jesus and the coin for paying the tax to the Roman regime, we see that he was confronted by two groups of Jewish leaders, the Pharisees and the Herodians. The Pharisees' most extreme members, the Zealots, would not even touch the Roman denarius because its inscription violated the first commandment of having only one God and its image violated the second commandment that worship should be without graven images. But Jesus invites them to take up the coin and presumably he handles it when he asks, 'Whose image and inscription is this?' In other words, recognize the prerogatives of the state to mint coins, levy taxes, build roads, maintain defense and justice, but do not expect it to support and maintain the true religion. On the other hand, the climactic part of Jesus' statement falls on the Herodians, who were the political cronies of the Roman regime. Yes, there is a legitimate role for the state to play, as ordained by God, in maintaining justice among human beings. So the Herodians were told, 'But render unto God the things that are God's.' There is a higher authority than the state to which we owe obedience, and only God can tell us what we are to believe concerning him and how we are to worship him. These are not two separate and equal compartments; the authority of God is the over-arching authority over all. Jesus summed up the Ten Commandments in the two great commands: 'You shall love the Lord your God with all your heart, soul, mind, and strength; and you shall love your neighbor as yourself.' The state should guarantee freedom in the sphere of relation to God while focusing its energy on maintaining justice in the sphere of human relations.

6. The Atheistic State: Communism

The danger of an improperly understood 'separation of church and state' is a totally secular state. We see what that can be like in the former Soviet Union of Russia and in contemporary Communist states such as China, North Korea, and Cuba. Here we have the deification of the state, the absolutizing of government power in an ideology that amounts to religion in that it decrees what is to be believed and enforces how that is to be celebrated. This is not what American 'separation of church and state' was intended to be, but the religious population of America must be vigilant in safeguarding freedom of religion to keep the trends of culture from moving in an increasingly secular direction. The founding document of the United States of America, the Declaration of Independence of 1776, refers to the Creator, to the laws of nature and of nature's God, to the Supreme Judge of the world, and to providence. The founding fathers did not want to establish a specific religion, but they acknowledged a Creator-God. The U.S. Constitution of 1787 is the document to implement the principles expressed in the Declaration of Independence, and its Bill of Rights, in the 1st Amendment, declares that the U.S. Congress shall make no law regarding the establishment of religion or to prohibit the free exercise thereof. Since we believe that salvation is by grace through faith, that is, by persuasion not coercion, we cherish America's freedom of religion and look to the state to guarantee that freedom in the sphere of belief and worship while using its power to maintain justice in the sphere of human relations.

8

THEONOMY, PLURALISM, AND THE BIBLE

Ever since the late 1970s evangelical Christians in the United States have become increasingly active in politics. Particularly those who would term themselves fundamentalists have suddenly discovered what was widely held – if not always practiced – in Reformed circles; that our faith applies to all of life and thought. Of great, and evidently growing, appeal to such American Christians has been the movement in the Reformed camp known as theonomy. This movement, as represented for our purposes in the book *Theonomy in Christian Ethics*, by Greg L. Bahnsen,[1] seeks a restoration of God's law as the recognized basis for civil government. In making his appealing case for this theonomic approach to civil authority, Bahnsen admirably seeks to steer clear of some historic mistakes in church-state relations in a

---

This chapter originally appeared in William S. Barker and W. Robert Godfrey, *Theonomy: A Reformed Critique* (Grand Rapids, Mich.: Zondervan, 1990).

1. Greg L. Bahnsen, *Theonomy in Christian Ethics* (Nutley, N.J.: Craig, 1977); the expanded edition, with a seventeen-page additional preface replying to critics, otherwise has the same pagination (Phillipsburg, N.J.: Presbyterian and Reformed, 1984). See also Greg L. Bahnsen, *By This Standard: The Authority of God's Law Today* (Tyler, Tex.: Institute for Christian Economics, 1985).

chapter entitled 'Separation of Church and State' and particularly to avoid certain unwelcome connotations of the term 'theocracy' as applied to American politics.[2] His argument is that there was a separation of church and state in Old Testament Israel, and that the same kind of distinction will serve as well today in a government operating according to God's law.

At the same time, Bahnsen's advocacy of the law of God as the basis for civil government is clearly opposed to the modern concept of pluralism.[3] The term pluralism is used today in several senses. *Webster's Ninth New Collegiate Dictionary* defines pluralism as (1) 'a state of society in which members of diverse ethnic, racial, religious or social groups maintain an autonomous participation in and development of their traditional civilization' and (2) 'a concept, doctrine or policy advocating this state'.[4] In terms of civil rights for ethnic or racial minorities pluralism is so widely acknowledged in our American culture as to be accepted as common place. It is the idea of religious pluralism, however, that is of concern to Bahnsen. God's law as the basis for civil government, according to the theonomy movement, clearly militates against religious pluralism.

As this essay undertakes to answer the question 'Is pluralism biblical?' in the affirmative, it is necessary to mention one kind of pluralism that clearly is contrary to Scripture. That is the concept, which has become increasingly favored in the churches most affected by secular and ecumenical trends, of pluralism of religious belief within Christianity.[5] This is not the variety of

---

2. Bahnsen, *Theonomy*, 427-32.
3. Bahnsen, *By This Standard*, 340.
4. Springfield, Mass.: Merriam, 1983.
5. For an example, see Wilfred Cantwell Smith, *Religious Diversity: Essays by Wilfred Cantwell Smith*, ed. Willard G. Oxtoby (New York: Harper & Row, 1976). In the first essay, 'The Christian in a Religiously Plural World,' 3-21, Smith argues for what he terms the Christian value of acceptance of other people over against the

pluralism with which we are concerned here. Rather, we are concerned with the concept of the civil authority recognizing the freedom of religious belief and practice by a variety of groups – including theists, humanists, naturalists, and atheists – with no one such group established or favoured by the state.[6] It is my contention that such religious pluralism within a society is our Lord's intention for this time in history and hence is biblical. Bahnsen's advocacy of God's law as the basis for civil authority, with essentially the same kind of separation of church and state that existed in Old Testament Israel, opposes this sort of pluralism.

A brief review of the history of church-state relations since New Testament times will give us perspective on this theonomic approach.

During its first three centuries in the Roman world, Christianity obviously did not enjoy favourable relations with the civil government, frequently experiencing its persecution and having little opportunity to exercise

---

value of doctrinal truth, citing favourably the United Church of Canada's declaration in 1966 that God works creatively and redemptively in various religions, not just through knowledge of Jesus Christ.

6. For descriptions of religious pluralism in America, see Robert T. Handy, ed., *Religion in the American Experience: The Pluralistic Style* (Columbia, S.C.: University of South Carolina Press, 1972), Introduction, xiv-xvi; Franklin H. Littell, *From State Church to Pluralism: A Protestant Interpretation of Religion in American History*, new ed. (New York: Macmillan, 1971). E. Clinton Gardner, *The Church as a Prophetic Community* (Philadelphia: Westminster, 1967) comments that 'religious pluralism implies – indeed, presupposes – a secular society,' but he makes a distinction between 'secular' and 'secularist': 'A pluralist society is secular, but it is not secularist; for a secularist society is one in which secularism as an anti-theistic conception of reality has become the official world view' (p. 94). Certain dangers inherent in the American trends are described by Phillip E. Hammond, 'Pluralism and Law in the Formation of American Civil Religion,' in *America, Christian or Secular? Readings in American Christian History and Civil Religion*, ed. Jerry S. Harbert (Portland, Ore.: Multnomah, 1984), 205-29. He argues that law and the courts have replaced the church and theology as the basis of public morality with the coming of religious pluralism. Kathryn J. Pulley, 'The Constitution and Religious Pluralism Today,' in *Liberty and Law: Reflections on the Constitution in American Life and Thought*, ed. Ronald A. Wells and Thomas A. Askew (Grand Rapids: Eerdmans, 1987), 143-55, also points out such dangers; she comments on the tendency toward relativism inherent in religious pluralism.

an active positive influence. Guided by New Testament teachings such as Romans 13:1-7; 1 Timothy 2:1-7 and 1 Peter 2:13-17, the early Christians kept the laws that did not require them to go counter to the commands of the Lord and prayed for their governors as rulers ordained by God.

A new complication arose when the Roman emperor himself identified with the Christian church. Constantine's conversion in the early fourth century put the church in a favored position, bringing it relief from the immediately preceding fiercest persecution of Emperor Diocletian and also adding to its numbers many with less commitment than that of the earlier martyrs. Doctrine was consolidated in the age of great ecumenical councils, but the secular rulers themselves exercised undue influence in ecclesiastical decisions as by the late fourth century the orthodox emperor Theodosius the Great established Christianity as the state religion.

Augustine sought to sort out the relative authority and power of church and state in the new situation in what became known as the 'two swords' theory, especially as it was enunciated by Pope Gelasius I (492–496). Using a technical distinction of Roman law, Gelasius claimed that while the emperor in Constantinople had *potestas*, or power, the bishop of Rome had *auctoritas*, or authority. The church through its clergy was to declare the will of God, and the emperor and his civil magistrates were to carry it out.

The relative influence of Christian bishop and Christian king on matters of law and government ebbed and flowed through the centuries. The high tide of papal influence carried church-state relations to a new stage, however, in what might be termed the 'ecclesiocracy' of such popes of the High Middle Ages as Gregory VII (1073–85) and Innocent III (1198–1216), who claimed ability to depose secular rulers and to launch the military campaigns known as crusades.

With the coming of the sixteenth-century Reformation there was an attempt to restore balance in church-state relations. Reformers like Luther and Calvin in their movements clearly curtailed the kind of political excess that characterized the medieval papacy. They tended, however, still to think in Augustinian 'two swords' terms of an established church and were not able, as were the persecuted Anabaptists, to return to a pre-Constantinian consciousness, which more aptly suits a missionary situation. Calvin deserves credit for developing one side of church-state separation, the protection of ecclesiastical integrity against intrusion by the civil magistrate into essentially spiritual matters, such as admission to the Lord's Table. The Scottish Presbyterians likewise stressed the prerogatives of King Jesus in his church over against Erastian attempts to have the civil authority decide such matters.

It remained for American Protestantism, however, to conclude that disestablishment of the church would be in the best interests of Christianity as well as of the state. The Presbyterian Church of America expressed this sentiment in the first of the 'Preliminary Principles' attached to its new Form of Government in 1789:

> I. That 'God alone is Lord of the conscience; and hath left it free from the doctrine and commandments of men, which are in anything contrary to his word, or beside it in matters of faith and worship:' Therefore, they consider the rights of private judgment, in all matters that respect religion, as universal, and unalienable: They do not even wish to see any religious constitution aided by the civil power, further than may be necessary for protection and security, and at the same time, equal and common to all others.

It is important to be aware of this historical background in order to appreciate the need for a further distinction between church and state than that which is made by theonomy. Bahnsen does make a proper distinction, as Calvin does, between outward behaviour, as the civil magistrate's area of responsibility, and sins of the heart, which are God's concern alone.[7] He refines this distinction thus: 'While the church propagates the gospel of God's grace, the state maintains the standards of God's justice in social matters (matters of outward behaviour, but not matters of the heart, conscience, or belief).'[8] Further on he says, 'Thus the state cannot be a promoter of the gospel or personal Christian faith, and the church cannot use the sword of the state in its evangelism.'[9]

This distinction, however, is regarded as 'simply the reaffirmation and confirmation' of Old Testament separation of church and state functions. In Old Testament Israel there was a distinction of functions, but both the civil ruler and the priests were under the authority of God's law.[10] But herein lies a problem. For in the Old Testament, godly kings like David, Jehoshaphat, Hezekiah, and Josiah, while recognizing a distinction of function (see particularly Jehoshaphat's distinction in 2 Chronicles 19:11), surely were concerned, and properly so, to use their authority not just for social matters, but for the propagation of God's saving truth and the promotion of personal faith. More was expected of even the civil ruler in a nation in covenant relationship with the Lord.

A further distinction between church and state is called for in our time than that which Bahnsen makes. It is a

---

7. Bahnsen, *Theonomy*, 381-82.
8. Ibid., 386.
9. Ibid., 426.
10. Ibid., 417, 420-21. In *By This Standard*, 166, 288, 289, 330, Bahnsen describes certain discontinuities between the old and new covenants in regard to church and state.

distinction between that part of the law summed up by what Jesus termed the first and greatest commandment and that part of the law summed up by what he termed the second commandment, which is 'like it'. Love of God and love of neighbour are of course intimately related, because our Lord scarcely mentions the one without also referring to the other, and on these commandments all the Law and the Prophets hang. But unless a proper distinction is made between them, confusion of function will result. In making his point that the Old Testament holds the nations surrounding Israel responsible for keeping God's law, Bahnsen appears to make no distinction between the first great commandment and the second: 'When the Israelite, Daniel, assumed civil office in a nation which was not Jewish or located in the promised land, he apparently did not feel that the rules for leadership had changed from what God would have expected of a civil magistrate in Israel.'[11] Yet just the sort of distinction I am concerned to make was followed by Daniel. He applied the principles of God's law as it affected relations between human neighbors, and he himself was diligent in his own relations to God. But, although he bore witness to the true God, he did not use his civil authority to enforce the true religion, in the sense of belief and worship, on a pagan society. Nebuchadnezzar eventually gave his personal testimony that the Lord is 'the Most High God' (Dan. 4:2) and 'the King of heaven' (v. 37), but he said at the same time that Daniel 'is called Belteshazzer, after the name of my god, and the spirit of the holy gods is in him' (v. 8). This is clearly not an exclusive commitment. In like manner Darius decreed that 'people must fear and reverence the God of Daniel' (Dan. 6:26), but there is no evidence that these kings destroyed the other religions as the civil ruler was required to do in God's covenant nation.

---

11. *Theonomy*, 358.

This further distinction, between the first great commandment and the second, as applied to church-state relations, is implicit in Jesus' statement concerning the tribute money in Matthew 22:15-22 (with parallels in Mark 12:13-17 and Luke 20:20-26). The position that I believe this passage indicates is that (1) the civil authority is ordained by God to function in the area of the second great commandment, namely, that of human relations, and that (2) in the area of the first great commandment, namely, our relation to God, the civil authority's responsibility is not to enforce the true faith, but to maintain freedom. With complete respect for the theonomists' contention that Jesus came not to abolish the Law and the Prophets but rather to fulfil them, I seek the answer to the questions, How does our King intend for the first great commandment to be fulfilled? and, How is our righteousness to surpass that of the Pharisees and the teachers of the law with regard to church-state relations?

Picture the scene as Jesus is asked about paying tribute to Caesar. It is the Tuesday of that last week between his triumphal entry into Jerusalem and his arrest and crucifixion. The religious and political leaders among the Jews are so deeply concerned about his growing following that the Pharisees and Herodians conspire together to trap him in his words. Luke says, 'Keeping a close watch on him, they sent spies, who pretended to be honest. They hoped to catch Jesus in something he said so that they might hand him over to the power and authority of the governor' – that is, the Roman procurator Pontius Pilate.

In this sort of religio-political context, they ask a religio-political question: 'Teacher, we know you are a man of integrity and that you teach the way of God in accordance with the truth. You aren't swayed by men, because you pay no attention to who they are. Tell us then, what is your opinion? Is it right to pay taxes to Caesar or not?'

Realizing their evil intent, Jesus charges them with hypocrisy and demands, 'Show me the coin used for paying the tax.' Mark adds, 'and let me look at it.' They bring him a denarius, and he asks them, 'Whose portrait is this? And whose inscription?'

'Caesar's,' they reply.

And Jesus says, 'Give to Caesar what is Caesar's and to God what is God's.' And all three synoptic Gospels record that the crowd was amazed at his answer.

The reason for their amazement at the wisdom of Jesus becomes apparent as we grasp the full dynamics of this situation. And as we do so, we see how, although this may not be the *locus classicus* in the New Testament for church-state relations, it provides the foundation on which such passages as Romans 13 and 1 Peter 2 build. The basic principles can all be inferred from Jesus' simple but profound statement.

First, it is important to see the horns of the dilemma on which Jesus' enemies sought to trap him. His questioners included disciples of the Pharisees along with the Herodians. The two groups might themselves give different answers. The Herodians were those associated with the Herods, the Idumean-Jewish rulers who were politically allied with the Roman regime. The Pharisees, on the other hand, were zealous for the prerogatives of the Jewish religion and were sensitive to anything that might compromise one's consecration to the Lord by recognition of pagan religion. In the audience there no doubt were the most extreme in this direction politically, the Zealots, who advocated revolution against the Roman regime.[12]

---

12. For information on the Herodians, see Harold W. Hoehner, *Herod Antipas* (Cambridge: Cambridge University Press, 1972), Appendix X, 'The Herodians,' 331-42; H. H. Rowley, 'The Herodians in the Gospels,' *Journal of Theological Studies*

A yes-or-no answer was impossible. Either way, Jesus would offend some significant part of his audience. If he said no, the Herodians and those like them would have grounds for charging him with treason against the Roman government. If he said simply yes, the Zealots and many like the Pharisees would have grounds for claiming he could not be the Messiah, for he would recognize not only a pagan regime, but pagan religion.

The reason for this last point lies in the roman denarius. Many of these coins from the reigns of Augustus and of Tiberius have been found, and the images and inscriptions on them are of similar nature. Most likely the tribute money here is the silver denarius of Tiberius, which shows a bust of the emperor on the obverse with the inscription 'TI (BERIUS) CAESAR DIVI AUG(USTI) F(ILIUS) AUGUSTUS' ('Tiberius Caesar, son of the deified Augustus, and Augustus') On the reverse is a female figure, probably Tiberius' mother Livia, as Pax, with the inscription 'PONTIF(EX) MAXIM(US)' ('Highest Priest').[13] Some scrupulous Jews regarded the minting of such coins as a violation of the first commandment because of the recognition of another deity in the inscriptions and

---

41 (1940): 14-27. Concerning the Zealots in this context, see Oscar Cullmann, *The State in the New Testament* (New York: Scribner, 1956), 20, 34-37, and his book *Jesus and the Revolutionaries* (New York: Harper & Row, 1970), 45-47.

13. For pictures of the denarius of Tiberius, as well as discussion, see Stewart Perowne, *The Later Herods: The Political Background of the New Testament* (London: Hodder and Stoughton, 1958), Plate 10 (opp. p. 33); S. G. F. Brandon, *Jesus and the Zealots: A Study of the Political Factor in Primitive Christianity* (New York: Scribner, 1967), Plate 1(a) (opp. p. 144) and 45-46, 347-48; H. StJ. Hart, 'The Coin of "Render unto Caesar ..." ' in *Jesus and the Politics of His Day*, ed. Ernst Bammel and C. F. D. Moule (Cambridge: Cambridge University Press, 1984), 241-48; Ethelbert Stauffer, *Christ and the Caesars: Historical Sketches* (London: SCM, 1955), trans. K. and R. Gregor Smith from 3rd German ed. of 1952, 112-37; Herbert Loewe, *'Render under Caesar' Religion and Political Loyalty in Palestine* (Cambridge: Cambridge University Press, 1940), 97. See also J. Duncan M. Derrett, *Law in the New Testament* (London: Darton, Longman & Todd, 1970), especially chapter 14, ' "Render to Caesar ...,"' 313-38. For a contrasting point of view, see J. Spencer Kennard, Jr., *Render to God: A Study of the Tribute Passage* (New York: Oxford University Press, 1950), especially 139.

also a violation of the second commandment because of the graven image. The holiness of third-century rabbi Nahum ben Simai of Tiberia is illustrated by the fact that he never allowed his eyes to look at the portrait on a coin.[14] Bar Kochba, the revolutionary who claimed to be the Messiah in the second century, 'had the imperial *denarii* collected, the obnoxious portraits and inscriptions beaten out by hammers and replaced by Hebrew temple vessels and inscriptions.'[15] In the third century Hippolytus, a Christian, reported that some of the Essenes would not handle such a coin.[16] Ethelbert Stauffer says of Tiberius' denarius that it 'is the most official and universal sign of the apotheosis of power and the worship of the *homo imperiosus* in the time of Christ.'[17]

With such Jewish scruples concerning this Roman coin no doubt present in Jesus' audience, it is significant that Jesus requested that they show him the coin that he might look at it. At a stroke he not only embarrasses his questioners, who might have wanted to avoid being implicated with those who carried the coin by making them fetch one, but he also demonstrates that the scruple is exaggerated by taking the dime-sized coin into his own hands when he asks, 'Whose portrait is this?'

But when Jesus gives his terse response to their sheepish answer, 'Caesar's': 'Give to Caesar what is Caesar's, and to God what is God's,' the weight of his statement falls on Herodians, Pharisees, and all alike. His emphasis is clearly on the latter half of the statement, in such a fashion that the force of the recognition of Caesar's due

---

14. F. F. Bruce, 'Render to Caesar,' in *Jesus and the Politics of His Day*, ed. Ernst Bammel and C. F. D. Moule (Cambridge: Cambridge University Press, 1984), 259; Stauffer, *Christ and the Caesars*, 126.
15. Stauffer, *Christ and the Caesars*, 126.
16. Hippolytus, *Refutatio omnium haeresium*, 9:26; English translation in *Ante-Nicene Fathers*, 5:136.
17. Stauffer, *Christ and the Caesars*, 127.

in the former half is much diminished.[18] Yes, Jesus was willing to pay the tax to Caesar – who minted the coins, maintained defense, administered justice, and built the roads – because God had ordained civil government for such purposes. But no, Jesus would not render to Caesar what was God's alone, namely, worship and ultimate defence. And the significant point for our purpose here is that it was not a compromise of Jesus' commitment to the things of God to pay the tax to Caesar, even with Caesar's blasphemous religion on the coin. *In the New Testament situation, under a Gentile regime, he did not expect the civil authority to support the true religion.*

Jesus' recognition of a new political situation in the new era that was to dawn with the institution of the church is shown in the wider context of all three Synoptic Gospels. The challenge from the Pharisees and Herodians concerning the tribute money is preceded, evidently earlier on the same day, by Jesus' parable of the vineyard and its wicked tenants, which the chief priests and the Pharisees rightly understood as directed at them (Matt. 21:45; Mark 12:12, Luke 20:19). This parable is so pointed in its conclusion, 'Therefore I tell you that the kingdom of God will be taken away from you and given to a people who will produce its fruit,' that it functions as a pronouncement of the end of the Old Testament theocracy. In Luke's account the people, not just the religious leaders, respond, 'May this never be!' But Jesus looked directly at them and applied Psalm 118:22, 'The stone the builders rejected has become the capstone' (Luke 20:16-17). It is as though a curtain is being drawn down on the earlier act of God's drama of redemption, later to be raised on a stage with a new political setting as the gospel goes forth to those other people, the Gentile nations. In this new setting

---

18. Günther Bornkamm, *Jesus of Nazareth*, trans. Irene and Fraser McLuskey with James M. Robinson from 3rd German ed. of 1959 (New York: Harper and Brothers, 1960), 122.

it will not be appropriate for the civil authority to support the true religion as it was in the Old Testament theocracy.

The wider context in Matthew and Mark also provides reinforcement for the idea that Jesus' response concerning the tribute money had in view the twofold division of the law. The statement itself, referring to 'the things of Caesar' (who is, pointedly, a man) and 'the things of God', already makes such a division explicit in the minds of those involved in the debate with Jesus. Then evidently at the conclusion of the same discussions, after Jesus had silenced the Sadducees concerning the resurrection, a representative of the Pharisees (Mark 12:28 says, 'One of the teachers of the law came and heard them debating') asks him, 'Of all the commandments, which is the most important?' Jesus replies: '"Love the Lord your God with all your heart and with all your soul and with all your mind." This is the first and greatest commandment. And the second is like it: "Love your neighbour as yourself." All the Law and the Prophets hang on these two commandments.'

In the same conversation in which his teaching concerning the civil government is uttered we have also his familiar division of the law of God concerning our obligation toward the Lord and our obligation toward fellow human beings. Clearly Jesus recognized Caesar's prerogatives in the latter area of human relations, but Caesar was not to infringe on our liberty, nor was he expected to enforce the true faith and worship, in the former area of our relation to God.

If we are indeed zealous for the application of God's law in society, our first question must be, What is our King's intention? Jesus' response to the question concerning the tribute money reveals that his intention is for the civil authority to apply God's law in the area of human relations in which God has ordained him to serve. In the area of our relation to God, not only is it not legitimate for the state to enforce its false religion on us ('Give to God the things that are God's), but it is not even the proper function of the state to enforce religion ('Bring me a denarius and let me look at it') – even the true faith and worship.

This distinction became important as the gospel went forth into the Gentile nations. All that missionaries could rightly ask of the civil authority was the freedom to preach the gospel so that people might be freely persuaded by the word and by the Spirit. To have the state in any way coerce belief or worship could only compromise the free nature of the gospel and contaminate the purity of the church.

This distinction that I propose is one that was recognized in the Westminster Confession of Faith. Chapter XIX,2, says of the law of God that it 'was delivered by God upon Mount Sinai in ten commandments, and written in two tables; the first four commandments containing our duty toward God, and the other six our duty to man.' Chapter XX,2, says of Christian liberty: 'God alone is Lord of the conscience, and hath left it free from the doctrines and commandments of men which are in any thing contrary to his word, or beside it, in matters of faith or worship.' Here we have two categories of human doctrines and commandments that must not infringe on our liberty: (1) those that are contrary to God's Word in any area and (2) those that are even just beside God's Word – that is, alongside it – in the areas of faith or worship. Faith and worship, the area of our relationship to God and of his unique prerogatives, are not to have any doctrines or commandments laid on our consciences apart from God's own Word. In other areas the requirement is only that such doctrines and commandments not be contrary to God's word; and, as Romans 13:5 tells us, we are conscience-bound to obey the civil magistrate in such matters so long as they are not contrary to God's word.

Yet theonomy seems not to recognize such a distinction in its claims that the civil authority is responsible to carry out all of the law of God (although an important distinction is properly made between crime and sin). In the context of Old Testament Israel as the nation in covenant with the Lord, the civil ruler was responsible to exterminate false religion and support the worship of God. But with the close of the Old Testament theocracy and the spread of the gospel among the Gentile nations this is evidently no longer our Lord's intent for the civil authority. Bahnsen seeks to make a distinction between, on the one hand, outward behavior and justice in social matters and, on the other hand, matters of the heart, conscience or belief; but his position of applying the whole law of God in the state, as in the Old Testament, does not provide sufficient basis for his own distinction and thus protect the liberty of conscience and belief of non-Christians under a Christian government or of Christians under an unbelieving government.

How would this distinction apply to some of the issues of our time? Abortion and pornography, for example, as violations of the sixth and seventh commandments and hence in the area of the second great commandment, would be proper concerns for the civil government to deal with. It is appropriate for Christians to address the conscience of unbelievers in such matters and to seek through the legitimate channels of government to restrain wickedness in outward behaviour by law and its enforcement.

The kind of distinction I am making, however, would oppose the requirement of prayer or acts of worship in the public schools. This would be enforcing a matter in the area of relations to God by means of civil authority.[19]

---

19. Here I am essentially in agreement with Paul Woolley, *Family, State and Church – God's Institutions* (Grand Rapids: Baker, 1965), 21-25, 26-29; and with Edmund P. Clowney, *The Doctrine of the Church* (Philadelphia: Presbyterian and Reformed, 1969), 33-34.

On the other hand, we should contend for the freedom to have theistic perspective, as on the question of human origins, included with other possible perspectives in the teaching of the public schools, so that a specifically antitheistic doctrine is not forced on the children of our society.

A matter such as Sabbath observance raises even more complex questions since there are clearly issues related to the fourth commandment that fall under the second great commandment as well as the first. In a society that includes substantial numbers of Jews and Muslims, as well as Christians with different understandings of the Sabbath, what we should expect from the civil authority is a measure of freedom for people to observe their one day of the week for religious practices.

We can well ask about such a position as I outline, What standard is there, if not the law of God, for the secular government? The answer is that the law of God does function here, in the area of the second great commandment, explicitly for the unbeliever, whose conscience does to some degree – as Paul indicates in Romans 2:14-15 – witness to him. Our responsibility as Christians is to have *our* consciences so well informed by the word of God that we live and testify in such a way that will influence the unbelieving society toward righteousness. Knowing that obedience to this second great commandment can flow ultimately only from obedience to the first great commandment, we cherish the freedom to appeal, as did Paul in the Roman Empire, to the God who raised Jesus from the dead as the one whose 'eternal power and divine nature' people have no excuse for denying since the creation of the world (Rom. 1:18-20). If it is indeed not our King's intention for the civil authority to enforce the first great commandment, then among the five alternatives that Bahnsen offers as possible standards for civil law, natural revelation as indeed 'a sin-obscured edition of the same law of God' 'suppressed in unrighteousness by the sinner'[20] is that to which we must appeal – on the basis of our own knowledge of special revelation and with the intent of bringing more of the unbelieving population to repentance toward God and faith in our Lord Jesus Christ. This is the way Paul operated in the Roman Empire and the way any Christian must operate in a missionary situation.

How then can the state avoid the idolatry of making itself God? Twentieth-century secularism shows that it is very difficult for a state to resist this tendency. It can, however, be checked whenever there is at least the recognition that in addition to 'the things of Caesar' there are also 'the things of God' and that, although these two areas can ordinarily function compatibly, there may be instances when for some citizens they will conflict and call for the primary allegiance to 'the things of God' to take precedence. The ancient Roman state thus made some allowances for Jewish monotheism. In the American context we have been blessed, largely because of Christian influences through Western civilization, with a sense of a 'higher law' above and beyond even the U.S. Constitution. Whether this higher law be derived from custom, natural law, the will of the people, or the Scriptures, it has at least meant that those who govern are subject to the law, and the law itself is subject to the Constitution, which is interpreted to embody certain underlying, lasting principles. Obviously, much depends on who has the power to interpret the Constitution. Certainly we should seek to have officials who will bring a Christian understanding to such tasks. We can be thankful that the United States, in contrast to the former Soviet Union, still recognizes

---

20. Bahnsen, *Theonomy*, 399-400.

theistic possibilities for an understanding of the higher law, and we should learn from the Soviet example the necessity to contend earnestly for the protection of that theistic expression.

Some Reformed friends ask me, in light of my view, how we are to understand such passages as Psalm 2:10-12, which calls upon the kings of the earth to 'serve the Lord with fear' and to 'kiss the Son, lest he be angry and [they] be destroyed in the way.' The answer is that this is in the context of the nations raging and the rulers gathering together against the Lord and against his Anointed One. What we ask of the civil government is that it not oppose Christ but serve the Lord by following his law in the area of human relations and allowing his people the freedom to preach the gospel. It is the missionary mandate and the freedom to pursue it that is the intention of our King.

Matthew weaves the discourses of Jesus together to form the tapestry of his Gospel. The statement concerning the tribute money is integral to what is said in the beginning, in the Sermon on the Mount, and at the conclusion, in the Great Commission. Our righteousness surpasses that of the Pharisees and of the teachers of the law when we have entered the kingdom through repentance and faith, being baptized into the name of the Father and of the Son and of the Holy Spirit, being disciples who recognize that all authority is given to Jesus Christ in heaven and on earth, and making disciples, teaching them to obey everything he has commanded. Among these things is to give to Caesar the things that are Caesar's and to God the things that are God's. It is not Caesar's prerogative to enforce the true religion. The kingdom of King Jesus comes through the faith that comes by the hearing of the word.

This was the testimony of Justin Martyr in his *First Apology* after referring Emperor Antoninus Pius and his sons to Jesus' statement about the tribute money: 'So we worship God only, but in other matters we gladly serve you, recognizing you as emperors and rulers of men, and praying that along with your imperial power you may also be found to have a sound mind.'[21]

This was the testimony of Tertullian in his *De Idolatria*: 'The Lord ... said, "Render to Caesar what are Caesar's, and what are God's to God"; that is, the image of Caesar, which is on the coin, to Caesar, and the image of God, which is on man, to God; so as to render to Caesar money, to God yourself.'[22]

This was also the testimony of Daniel in his interpretation of Nebuchadnezzar's dream of the kingdoms and empires that would succeed his own:

> In the time of those kings, the God of heaven will set up a kingdom that will never be destroyed, nor will it be left to another people. It will crush all those kingdoms and bring them to an end, but it will itself endure forever. This is the meaning of the vision of the rock cut out of a mountain, but not by human hands – a rock that broke the iron, the bronze, the clay, the silver and the gold to pieces (2:44-45).

This is the history of the church. The victory of our King comes not through civil government, but through his witnesses – people like Daniel, Justin and Tertullian, and like you and me – those who testify that all authority is the Lord's.

---

21. Justin Martyr, *First Apology*, ch. 17; English translation in Cyril C Richardson, ed., *Early Christian Fathers*, Library of Christian Classics, vol. 1 (New York: Macmillan, 1970), 253.
22. Tertullian, *De Idolatria*, ch. 15; English translation in *Ante-Nicene Fathers*, 3:70.

Part 2

The Westminster Confession of Faith

Doctrinally conservative Presbyterians have rightly stressed commitment to the Westminster Confession of Faith and Catechisms, Shorter and Larger. But how strict should this commitment be? Does subscription to the Westminster Standards mean belief in every proposition of the Confession and Catechisms? The ordination vows for American Presbyterians call for adopting the Westminster Standards as embodying the system of doctrine contained in the Scriptures. In my view, honest or 'good faith' subscription allows for exceptions to certain statements in the Standards as long as this does not compromise the Reformed system of doctrine. This method of subscribing is revealed in the first heresy case in American Presbyterianism in 1735. Appreciation of the Confession and Catechisms is enhanced by acquaintance with the remarkable preachers, scholars, and London clergyman who composed the Westminster Assembly in the 1640s. The 350th anniversary of the Assembly, celebrated in London in 1993, led to my exploration of the Westminster Divines. The importance of the Westminster Confession and Catechisms was acknowledged by the next generation of Puritan leaders, such as Richard Baxter, John Owen, and Thomas Watson.

9

Profiles in Puritanism

Question: What is the chief end of man?
Answer: Man's chief end is to glorify God, and to enjoy Him forever.

Question: What rule hath God given to direct us how we may glorify and enjoy Him?
Answer: The word of God, which is contained in the scriptures of the Old and New Testaments, is the only rule to direct us how we may glorify and enjoy Him.

Question: What do the scriptures principally teach?
Answer: The scriptures principally teach what man is to believe concerning God, and what duty God requires of man.

Question: What is God?
Answer: God is a Spirit, infinite, eternal, and unchangeable, in His being, wisdom, power, holiness, justice, goodness and truth.

So begins the *Westminster Shorter Catechism*. For those of us who memorized it in childhood, along with scores of Bible verses, it proved to be a precious introduction to Christian theology. In more mature years we typically moved to the *Westminster Confession of Faith*, some devouring its systematic setting forth of Christian teaching in a single sitting upon their first enthusiastic encounter with its thirty-three concise chapters. Usually, only later, in our development did we come to appreciate the *Larger Catechism*, some four or five times longer than the *Shorter Catechism*, and with its detailed exposition of the Ten Commandments and the Lord's Prayer, valuable helps to one's devotional meditation and Bible study.

Where did these documents come from, and how were they produced?

The Westminster Assembly of Divines (or clergymen) was a group of 121 English Puritan ministers, assisted by six Scottish commissioners and thirty laymen, ten from the House of Lords and twenty from the House of Commons, who met from July 1, 1643, to February 22, 1649, with an average of sixty to eighty in attendance, as an advisory body to Parliament for the further reformation of religion and the church in England, Ireland, and Scotland. The political context was one of Civil War, as the Parliamentary forces, eventually led by Oliver Cromwell, were already engaged militarily with the Cavalier Army of King Charles I by October 23, 1642. The immediate roots of this conflict lay in the uprising of the Scots, rallying behind their National Covenant of 1638, against the imposition by Charles and Archbishop of Canterbury William Laud of episcopacy, Anglican liturgy, and Arminian doctrine. But the more remote roots go back to tensions between the Stuart monarchy, beginning with James I in 1603, and the English Puritans, leading up to the Short Parliament starting in November 1640, and even to the back-and-forth development of the English Reformation under the Tudor monarchs Henry VIII, Edward VI, Mary, and Elizabeth I in the sixteenth century. The Westminster Assembly comes at the culmination of the era of the Protestant Reformation and represents a consummation of that movement's effort to understand and apply the Bible's teaching.

Philip Schaff says of the Westminster Assembly:

> It forms the most important chapter in the ecclesiastical history of England during the seventeenth century. Whether we look at the extent or ability of its labors, or its influence upon future generations, it stands first among Protestant Councils.[1]

Almost a century later, John Leith claims even more:

> The place of the *Confession* in the history of Christian doctrine is such that a grasp of its significance is crucial for an understanding of the contemporary theological situation. The *Confession* was not only the conclusion of one hundred and twenty-five years of Protestant theology; it was also in a real sense, along with other seventeenth-century statements of the faith, the conclusion of sixteen centuries of theological work.[2]

But the work of the Westminster Assembly was influential not only among Presbyterians. Again, John Leith comments:

> The *Westminster Confession* was adopted with a few modifications as the *Savoy Declaration* of the English Congregational churches. It was adopted by the Congregational Synod of Cambridge, Massachusetts, in 1648, and with the Savoy modification, by the Synod of Boston in 1680, and by the Congregational churches of Connecticut at the Synod of Saybrook in 1708. It was adopted with modification by the London Baptists in

---

1. Philip Schaff, *The Creeds of Christendom,* 3 vols., 6th ed. (New York and London: Harper & Brothers, 1877, 1931), 1: 728.
2. John H. Leith, *Assembly at Westminster: Reformed Theology in the Making* (Richmond, Virginia: John Knox Press, 1973), 12.

1677 and in America as the Baptist Confession of 1742 (Philadelphia)....

Certainly the number of children who received their religious instruction from the *Shorter Catechism* must be estimated in the millions.[3]

Philip Schaff says further:

> The *Westminster Confession*, together with the Catechisms, is the fullest and ripest symbolical statement of the Calvinistic system of doctrine. In theological ability and merit it is equal to the best works of the kind, and is not surpassed by the *Lutheran Formula of Concord* or the *Roman Decrees* of the Councils of Trent and the Vatican (I). Its intrinsic worth alone can explain the fact that it has supplanted the older Scottish standards of John Knox and John Craig in the land of their birth, and that it was adopted by three distinct denominations: by Presbyterians in full, and by the Congregationalists and the Regular Baptists with some slight modifications.... Altogether it represents the most vigorous and yet moderate form of Calvinism....[4]

If all of this is even nearly the case, then we naturally want to know what sort of people were involved in this Assembly. The main focus of this article will be a consideration of three important Puritan leaders.

There were 121 members of the Assembly originally nominated by Parliament (two for each English county, one for each Welsh county, two each for the Universities of Oxford and Cambridge, four for London, and one for each of the Channel Islands), plus almost twenty more who replaced those who died or did not participate, and also the thirty Members of Parliament and the six Scottish commissioners. To profile even a few of these men is daunting – a task that demands selections be

---

3. Ibid., 11-12.
4. Schaff, *Creeds of Christendom,* 1: 788.

made to the exclusion of others. In writing a book on this subject I chose forty-six members. In this briefer article I will choose only three as representative.[5]

1. Stephen Marshall (c. 1594–November 19, 1655) – 'A Noted Puritan Preacher'

Stephen Marshall was the favorite preacher of the Long Parliament. According to Thomas Fuller:

> He was their Trumpet, by whom they sounded their solemn Fasts, preaching more publick Sermons on that occasion, than any foure of his Function. In their Sickness he was their Confessor, in their Assembly their Councellour, in their Treaties their Chaplain, in their Disputations their Champion.[6]

---

5. It should be acknowledged that I have not had the opportunity to read many of the primary sources, but my work is largely derivative from many excellent secondary sources. At the same time, where possible, I have quoted from the Westminster Divines themselves so that one may hear the voice of the Assembly. Copious endnotes are intended to guide those who are interested to test my conclusions or to pursue further research. Certainly such figures as Stephen Marshall, Cornelius Burgess, Edmund Calamy, William Gouge, Thomas Gataker, Herbert Palmer, Thomas Goodwin, and Alexander Henderson deserve modern full-length studies. As will be apparent to anyone who peruses the endnotes, I am especially indebted to the works on the Assembly by Robert S. Paul, John Richard De Witt, S. W. Carruthers, and Alexander F. Mitchell. For biographical information I owe much to the standard reference works, such as A. G. Matthews' *Calamy Revised* and the *Dictionary of National Biography,* in which the entries on Assembly members that I have used are almost half by Alexander Gordon, no other contributor doing more than two. The 1979 Yale Ph.D. dissertation by Larry Jackson Holley contains much helpful biographical information for the period up to 1643, but also several errors. James Reid's *Memoirs of the Westminster Divines* (1811, 1815) is an invaluable source of information not to be found elsewhere, but it also tends to be fulsome and excessively devotional. I have relied on him to be the channel, nevertheless, for accounts from earlier biographers such as Samuel Clarke, Thomas Fuller, Daniel Neal, and Benjamin Brook. A more concise source for much of the same information is the anonymous *History of the Westminster Assembly ... and Biographical Sketches of Its Most Conspicuous Members* published in 1841, which the minutes of the Presbyterian Board of Publication at the Presbyterian Historical Society in Philadelphia show most likely to be by Archibald Alexander of Princeton Theological Seminary.
6. Quoted in William Haller, *Liberty and Reformation in the Puritan Revolution* (New York and London: Columbia University Press, 1955), 36. Cf. James Reid, *Memoirs of the Westminster Divines,* 2 vols. in 1 (Edinburgh and Carlisle, Pennsylvania: Banner of Truth, 1982 reprint of 1811 and 1815 edition), 2: 73.

During the course of the Westminster Assembly he preached eight times before the Houses of Parliament on the regular monthly Fast Days, plus three times before the monthly system was established, and he was enlisted to preach on ten other special occasions, as well as at the funeral of his patron John Pym. He also preached two more times to the Rump Parliament in 1649 and 1653. Of these twenty-four sermons, sixteen were printed. No one else matched this record.'[7]

Not only was Marshall the foremost preacher among the Westminster Divines, but he was also a leading activist among the English Presbyterians. Clarendon would later say, 'And without doubt, the Archbishop of Canterbury had never so great an influence upon the councils at court, as Mr. Marshall and Dr. Burgess had upon the Houses of Parliament.'[8] H. R. Trevor-Roper, with only one misleading statement, otherwise describes him accurately:

> In the Long Parliament he would emerge as the inseparable political and spiritual ally of Pym, the interpreter of Pym's policy after Pym's death. At every stage of the revolution we can see him. Now he is thumping his pulpit on great occasions; now he is meeting with Pym, Hampden and Harley to prepare parliamentary tactics; now he is bustling through Westminster Hall to push voters into the Parliament before the division; now he is retiring, exhausted, to recuperate in the well-appointed house of his good friend 'my noble Lord of Warwick.' Later he would be the Parliament's envoy to Scotland, its chaplain with the captive King; he would pass unscathed from Presbyterianism to Independency; and if he always appeared as the spokesman for the winning side, his

---

7. John F. Wilson, *Pulpit in Parliament* (Princeton, New Jersey: Princeton University Press, 1969), 87, 109-10.
8. Quoted in Reid, *Memoirs*, 2: 73.

changes can be explained by one consistent aim, which was also the aim of Pym: to preserve the unity of opposition against royal and clerical reaction.⁹

Marshall did not move from Presbyterianism to Independency, as we shall see, but his political realism did lead him to cooperate with Oliver Cromwell, the Army, and the Independents when he perceived this as the necessary way to maintain the Puritan-Parliamentary cause. He was a Presbyterian of the English sort who sometimes puzzled his Scottish allies.

Stephen Marshall was born about 1594 at Godmanchester, Huntingdonshire, son of a poor glover. As a boy he had to glean in the fields. He entered Cambridge April 1, 1615, and enrolled in Emmanuel College, received the B.A. in 1618, the M.A. in 1622, and later the B.D. in 1629. In 1618 he became lecturer at Wethersfield, Essex, after the death, on April 21, of the famous Puritan preacher there, Richard Rogers. In 1625 he became Vicar of Finchingfield, Essex, just a couple of miles from Wethersfield. In 1636 he was reported to the ecclesiastical authorities for 'irregularities and want of conformity', and in March 1637, Sir Nathaniel Brent described him to Archbishop Laud as

> a dangerous person, but exceeding cunning. No man doubteth but that he hath an inconformable heart, but externally he observeth all.... He governeth the consciences of all the rich puritans in those parts and in many places far remote, and is grown very rich.¹⁰

---

9. H. R. Trevor-Roper, *The Crisis of the Seventeenth Century: Religion, the Reformation and Social Change* (New York and Evanston, Illinois: Harper & Row, 1968), 297-98. Trevor-Roper says, 'There is no adequate biography of Marshall, whose importance, at least as the spokesman for policy, seems to me greater than has been allowed' (298 n. 1).
10. *Dictionary of National Biography*, eds. Leslie Stephen and Sidney Lee, 22 vols. (London: Oxford University Press, 1921–22), 12: 1128; Larry Jackson Holley, 'The Divines of the Westminster Assembly' (New Haven: Yale University Ph.D. diss., 1979), 325.

He had become a client of Robert Rich, second Earl of Warwick and Lord-Lieutenant of Essex, and in the first quarter of 1640 he spoke on behalf of Warwick's candidates for Parliament throughout Essex.

Marshall was scheduled to preach on the first Fast Day of the Short Parliament, but it was dissolved on May 5, 1640, before this could take place. When the Long Parliament opened in November 1640, Marshall and Cornelius Burgess were the preachers on that momentous first Fast Day on November 17.[11] He would preach again on September 7, 1641 (with Jeremiah Burroughes), and then again on December 22, 1641 (with Edmund Calamy). What further brought him to national attention, however, was the response to Bishop Joseph Hall's claims for the divine right of episcopacy produced by Marshall with Edmund Calamy, Thomas Young, Matthew Newcomen, and William Spurstowe under the name 'Smectymnuus', taken from their initials. In a literary exchange running through 1641, with three pieces written on each side, the third in support of the Smectymnuans from John Milton in 1642, Marshall and his colleagues set the stage for the abolition of episcopacy. The five Smectymnuans would all support Presbyterianism in the Westminster Assembly.[12]

It was for his preaching, though, that Marshall was primarily known. James Reid says: 'His sermons which have been printed abound with striking comparisons, and pointed appeals to the hearers....'[13] Much of his effectiveness apparently resided in his personal delivery. Alexander Gordon comments:

> His sermons, denuded of the preacher's living passion, often have the effect of uncouth rhapsodies. His

---

11. Wilson, *Pulpit in Parliament*, 36-37.
12. Robert S. Paul, *Assembly of the Lord* (Edinburgh: T. & T. Clark, 1985), 119; Haller, *Liberty and Reformation*, 34-35.
13. Reid, *Memoirs*, 2: 79.

funeral sermon for Pym (December 1643) made an indelible impression, and is the finest extant specimen of his pulpit eloquence as well as of his 'feeling and discernment'.... His ordinary preaching is described as plain and homely, seasoned with 'odd country phrases' and 'very taking with a country auditory.' ... He was listened to because no man could rival his power of translating the dominant sentiment of his party into the language of irresistible appeal.[14]

His most famous sermon was *Meroz Cursed,* based on Judges 5:23 where Deborah in her victory song pronounces a curse on the Israelite city in Naphtali that would not come to the aid of the Lord's people. It was preached before Parliament at the first of the regular monthly Fast Days, on February 23, 1642, and was a stirring call to arms that left royalists like Clarendon outraged. Trevor-Roper calls it 'the first of a long series of incendiary sermons which, from now on, scandalized royalists and moderate men alike'.[15] It found favor with the majority of his hearers as a call to commitment to the Parliamentary cause, for, by his own account, 'he afterwards preached it, up and down the country, sixty times, and it was several times printed.'[16]

The freedom to preach was revolutionary, and the preaching itself had revolutionary consequences. After the first Fast Day sermons of Marshall and Cornelius Burgess, Thomas Knyvett wrote home to a friend in Norfolk on November 24, 1640, 'Now reformation goes on again as hot as a toast. If thou didst but hear what sermons are preached to Parliament men, thou wouldst

---

14. *D. N. B.,* 12: 1131.
15. Trevor-Roper, *Crisis,* 307-08; cf. Wilson, *Pulpit in Parliament,* 63-64, and Haller, *Liberty and Reformation,* 69.
16. Trevor-Roper, *Crisis,* 307; cf. *D. N. B.,* 12: 1131. Extracts from the sermon are to be found in George Yule, *Puritans in Politics* (Appleford, Oxfordshire: Sutton Courtenay Press, 1981), 297-304.

bless thyself.' Paul Seaver comments: 'In effect, from the opening of the Long Parliament those Puritans who commanded London pulpits were for the first time free to preach without fear of episcopal censure.'[17] William Haller adds: 'The fixing of the custom of regular fast days, with special services at St. Margaret's for the house of commons, gave the preachers recognition and responsibility such as they had never known.'[18]

When apocalyptic themes were combined with this new freedom of preaching, the effect could indeed be revolutionary. On June 15, 1643, Marshall preached from Revelation 15:2-4:

> He used the imagery of the Apocalypse in order once more to bring the struggle of parliament against the king and the prelates into line with the legend of the true church beset by Antichrist and of Christ's expected advent and triumph. He would have his hearers see themselves again in the most valid and compelling of perspectives. The great stream of history, directed by God from eternity to eternity, having reached its present point, would inevitably go on, and they were called to be the agents and actors of its next advance.[19]

While not as extreme as some others, Marshall had commended the millenarian writings of Joseph Mede[20] and the Scot Robert Baillie was to comment on the English clergy, '... the most of the chief divines here, not only Independents, but others, such as Twiss, Marshall, Palmer, and many more, are express Chiliasts.'[21]

John F. Wilson draws out the possible implication of such preaching:

---

17. Paul S. Seaver, *Puritan Lectureships* (Stanford, California: Stanford University Press, 1970), 268.
18. Haller, *Liberty and Reformation*, 68.
19. Ibid., 101.
20. Wilson, *Pulpit in Parliament*, 221.
21. Quoted in Paul, *Assembly of the Lord*, 394 n. 24.

... even such relatively moderate sentiments as those articulated by the equivocal Marshall testify that the apocalypticism and millenarianism which were clearly present in some of the preaching to the Long Parliament worked toward revolutionary ends, whether or not they were directly intended to do so. Stated very simply, whereas prophetic and reformist puritans sought merely to make the times intelligible, another strain within Puritanism labored to interpret the times according to a calculus which required their basic transformation. That latter rhetoric, in effect if not intent, was basically disruptive of all acknowledged authority.[22]

It is clear that neither Parliament nor Marshall himself perceived the imminent kingdom of Christ as undermining all other legitimate authority. Early in 1642, Parliament, overriding a petition from the church in Finchingfield to retain his services, recommended that the people of the parish of St. Margaret's, Westminster, appoint Marshall as a regular lecturer.[23] On February 28, 1644, he was appointed one of the seven daily lecturers at Westminster Abbey.[24] It is true that Marshall preached to the House of Lords on January 31, 1649, the day after the execution of Charles I, thus condoning that act,[25] but his associate Giles Firmin tells us that he was 'so troubled about the king's death' that on Sunday, January 28, he interceded with the heads of the Army, 'and had it not been for one whom I will not name, who was very opposite and unmovable, he would have persuaded Cromwell to save the king. This is truth.'[26] Preaching

---

22. Wilson, *Pulpit in Parliament*, 233-34.
23. *D. N. B.*, 12: 1129; Haller, *Liberty and Reformation*, 67.
24. Wilson, *Pulpit in Parliament*, 16.
25. Trevor-Roper, *Crisis*, 337; Wilson, *Pulpit in Parliament*, 95. This sermon was not published, so we do not know what he preached.
26. Quoted in *D. N. B.*, 12: 1130.

before the Barebones Parliament in November 1653, he spoke in favor of tithes to support a national ministry.[27] Marshall was not one for overthrowing all authority.

In the Assembly's debates over church polity Marshall moved gradually to a *jure divino* Presbyterian position,[28] but as Robert Baillie observed, he was seeking a 'middle way of his own'. At the beginning of the Assembly he was commissioned, with Philip Nye, to accompany Sir Henry Vane, Jr., to Scotland, where they negotiated the Solemn League and Covenant on August 17, 1643, for uniformity with the Scottish church. He was concerned, however, to find a way that would avoid a breach with the Independents, granting local congregations some powers of discipline and ordination, though not without involvement with presbytery.[29] In December 1643, he had drafted a pamphlet, *Certane Considerations to Desswade Men From Further Gathering of Churches in This Present Juncture of Time,* and had gotten several leading men of the Assembly and also of the Independents to endorse it, in order to wait to see what polity the Assembly would decide on. But this counsel of patience was not followed by the 'Five Dissenting Brethren', who produced their *Apologeticall Narration* in January 1644, appealing the Congregational cause directly to Parliament and the public.[30] In the summer of 1647, when the Army, having seized the King, threatened the City of London, it 'was Stephen Marshall, who once again, in a moment of crisis, emerged as the politician of the hour'.

Like other men who were neither Cromwellians nor radicals, Marshall believed that, at that moment, the unity of Parliament and Army was all-important

---

27. Tai Liu, *Discord in Zion* (The Hague: Martinus Nijhoff, 1973), 128-29.
28. *D. N. B.*, 12: 1130; George Yule, *Puritans in Politics,* 150; John Richard De Will, *Jus Divinum* (Kampen: J. H. Kok, 1969), 149 and n. 32, 223-24.
29. Yule, *Puritans in Politics,* 139-40.
30. Haller, *Liberty and Reformation,* 116; De Witt, *Jus Divinum,* 87.

and that the alternative would be confusion leading to unconditional royal reaction. So, in these last days of July, he flung himself into action. He made a party in the Westminster Assembly, worked on the aldermen of the City, darted to and fro between Lords, Commons, and Army headquarters, and finally, with seventeen supporters in the Assembly, presented a petition to Parliament and City offering to make their peace with the Army. His efforts were successful. The City militia offered no resistance, and the Army entered London without a struggle. When all was over, the defeated party recognized Marshall as the chief architect of their ruin. 'In that nick of time,' wrote Baillie, when 'one stout look more' would have established Presbyterianism forever, it was Mr. Marshall, 'the main instrument' of the Solemn League and Covenant, who, with 'his seventeen servants of the Synod ... put presently in the Army's power both Parliament, City and nation.'[31]

Marshall maintained his Presbyterian convictions to his deathbed, but he was able to cooperate with Cromwell and the increasingly prevalent Independents. He was among a group of Presbyterians, Independents, and Baptists with whom Cromwell consulted for the sake of reconciliation and peace in October and November 1653, with some of whom he was appointed 'Triers' by Cromwell on March 20, 1654.[32] Perhaps it helped that one of his daughters had married John Nye, a son of Independent leader Philip Nye.[33]

Marshall's broad and accommodating spirit is shown also in the manner in which the Assembly's Directory for Worship was drawn up. As chairman of the committee responsible for doing the preliminary work, he presented

---

31. Trevor-Roper, *Crisis*, 327-28.
32. Liu, *Discord*, 133; *D. N. B.*, 12: 1131.
33. Liu, *Discord*, 128. Marshall was not Philip Nye's father-in-law, as many modern sources have it.

the general reasons for a Directory and the criteria adopted by his committee – to find a mean between a completely fixed liturgy and a form of worship in which everyone would be 'left to his own will'.[34]

As Alexander Mitchell described it:

> In other words those who conducted the ordinary services were not directly prohibited from turning the materials furnished to them into an unvarying form of prayer, keeping as near to the words of the Directory as they could; but at the same time they were not only not restricted or counseled to do so, but they were counseled and encouraged to do something more, according to their ability and opportunities.[35]

This spirit has continued in Presbyterian worship to the present day.

Marshall himself felt great freedom in prayer and sometimes prayed at great length in public. When he and Joseph Caryl were chaplains to the commissioners treating with the King at Newcastle in 1646, they were at the dinner table with Charles, and Marshall

> put himself more forward than was meet to say grace; and, while he was long in forming his chaps, as the manner was among the saints, and making ugly faces, his Majesty said grace himself, and was fallen to his meat, and had eaten up some part of his dinner, before Marshall had ended the blessing.... [36]

In 1651, Marshall had left Finchingfield to become town preacher at Ipswich at St. Mary's at the Quay. He died of consumption on November 19, 1655, and was buried in Westminster Abbey. On September 14, 1661,

---

34. Paul, *Assembly of the Lord*, 364.
35. Alexander F. Mitchell, *The Westminster Assembly: Its History and Standards*, 2nd ed. (Philadelphia: Presbyterian Board of Publication, 1897), 240-41.
36. Reid, *Memoirs*, 2: 78.

however, by royal warrant of Charles II, his remains were taken up and cast into a grave in St. Margaret's churchyard. He had married, about 1629, a rich widow, Elizabeth, daughter of Robert Castell of East Hatley, Cambridgeshire, and they had a son and six daughters. He was described as 'of middle height, swarthy, and broad shouldered, rolling his eyes in conversation; not fixing them on those he addressed; his gait was "shackling", and he had no polish.' It is said that he was an indulgent father, allowing his daughters to dress in unpuritanical fashion. He could jest, and 'he frequently read himself asleep with a playbook or romance'.[37]

Richard Baxter regarded him 'a sober and worthy man' and said that if all the Bishops had been of the same spirit as Archbishop Ussher, the Independents like Jeremiah Burroughes, and the Presbyterians like Stephen Marshall, the divisions of the church would soon have been healed.[38]

Not long before his death Marshall said, 'I cannot say, as one did, I have not so lived that I should now be afraid to die; but this I can say, I have so *learned Christ*, that I am not afraid to die.'[39]

2. Robert Harris (1581–December 1 or 11, 1658) – 'A Noted Puritan Scholar'

When Sir Anthony Cope, Member of Parliament, sought to fill the vacancy in the church of Hanwell, Oxfordshire, with Robert Harris in 1607, Archbishop Richard Bancroft was not going to make it easy for another Puritan to succeed the ejected John Dod. He first said that Harris must be examined by his most

---

37. *D. N. B.*, 12: 1131. Eliza Vaughan, *Stephen Marshall, A Forgotten Essex Puritan* (London: Arnold Fairbairns & Co., 1907), 15-16, 121, refers to Marshall's wife as Susanna Castell.
38. Reid, *Memoirs*, 2: 81.
39. Ibid., 2: 80.

learned chaplain, who upon sufficient examination reported him to be 'moderately learned'. Unsatisfied, the Archbishop committed Harris to William Barlow, Bishop of Rochester (and later to be a translator of the Authorized Version), a man of great wit and learning, who was glad for the opportunity to conduct the further examination. He covered divinity, then other branches of learning, and finally the Greek language: 'They Greeked it till they were both run aground for want of words, upon which they burst into a fit of laughter, and so gave it over.'[40] Harris served as pastor at Hanwell for the next thirty-five years.

Harris served faithfully in the Westminster Assembly and then was appointed president of Trinity College, Oxford, on April 12, 1648, at which time he received the degree of D.D. It is said that in the Assembly he heard all and said little.[41] He was, however, one of the seven English divines most influential in preparing the *Confession of Faith* along with Edward Reynolds, Cornelius Burgess, Thomas Temple, Charles Herle, Joshua Hoyle, and Thomas Gataker.[42] This important role makes his life and theological development of special interest.

Born in 1581 to a large family of modest means in Broad Campden, Gloucestershire, Harris did not receive the best schooling before entering Magdalen Hall, Oxford, on June 10, 1597, but his tutor there, a Mr. Goffe or Gough, encouraged him spiritually while instructing him in philosophy. Eventually Harris instructed Goffe in Greek and Hebrew, and they read together Calvin's

---

40. *D. N. B.*, 9: 23; Reid, *Memoirs*, 2: 12.
41. Reid, *Memoirs*, 2: 15.
42. Jack Bartlett Rogers, *Scripture in the Westminster Confession* (Kampen: J. H. Kok, 1966), 174-76. Rogers' careful analysis concludes that the main supporters in this work were Matthew Newcomen, Anthony Tuckney, Jeremiah Whitaker, and John Arrowsmith, along with the Scottish divines Alexander Henderson, Robert Baillie, George Gillespie, and Samuel Rutherford. Cf. Mitchell, *Westminster Assembly*, 367–68.

Institutes. Harris received the B.A. on June 5, 1600, and decided to pursue the ministry rather than the law, which was his original intention.[43]

He preached his first sermon in 1604 at Chipping Camden, where he had attended school. Upon his arrival at the church, there was no Bible to be found from which he could read his text. Even in the greater town there was not one to be obtained. Finally, in the house of the vicar of the parish one was located although it had not been seen for some months. Harris preached from Romans 10:1, 'Brethren, my heart's desire and prayer to God for Israel is, that they might be saved.' His sermon was so well received that his friends sought to persuade him that he needed no further education. He returned to Oxford, however, only to be thwarted by the plague, which had closed down the University. A Mr. Doyly invited Harris to stay in his home near Oxford, and there he met the rector of Chiselhampton, Mr. Pries, who was in a weak condition and needed assistance in his church. Harris's effective preaching there brought him to the attention of Mr. Doyly's brother-in-law, Sir Anthony Cope, who secured his appointment to the church in Hanwell in 1607.[44]

Although the congregation at Hanwell was still loyal to John Dod, who had been their pastor for twenty years, Dod helped to get the younger Harris established there.[45] It also helped that at about the same time two contemporaries of Harris were appointed to churches within a couple of miles of Hanwell, William Whately at Banbury and Henry Scudder (who would also become a member of the Westminster Assembly) at Drayton. The three young ministers met together weekly to translate and analyze a chapter of the Bible, and eventually Harris

---

43. *D. N. B.*, 9: 23; Holley, 'Divines,' 314; Reid, *Memoirs*, 2: 8-9.
44. *D. N. B.*, 9: 23; Holley, 'Divines,' 314; Reid, *Memoirs*, 2: 10-11.
45. Haller, *Rise of Puritanism*, 57.

married Whately's sister and Scudder married Whately's wife's sister, Elizabeth Hunt.[46] Harris's wife suffered a long and difficult illness upon the birth of their first child, and late in life experienced mental disorder and spiritual torment, although she had lived a devout life and managed a large household well with Harris for about fifty years.[47]

Harris continued his studies, receiving the B.D. from Oxford on May 5, 1614. His reputation as a preacher apparently spread, for he preached at St. Lawrence Jewry in London in the summer of 1619,[48] gave a sermon at Paul's Cross in 1622,[49] served as lecturer at St. Saviour's in Southwark from September 1623 to January 1625, and was invited to be lecturer at St. Mary Aldermanbury when the Archbishop put a stop to it.[50] On February 18, 1629, he preached for a Fast Day to the House of Commons.[51] From 1629 to 1631 he preached every other week at Stratford-upon-Avon, and crowds came to hear him.[52] The Long Parliament invited him to preach on the monthly Fast Day, May 25, 1642.[53]

When the Battle of Edgehill, the first battle of the Civil War, took place on Sunday, October 23, 1642, just a few miles from Hanwell, Harris held his customary services without being aware of it: ' ... the wind being contrary, he did not hear the least noise of it until the public exercises of the day were over; nor could he believe the report of the battle till soldiers, besmeared with blood, come to make it known.'[54]

---

46. Reid, *Memoirs*, 2: 12-13; Holley, 'Divines,' 340.
47. Reid, *Memoirs*, 2: 3, 19.
48. Holley, 'Divines,' 314; Paul S. Seaver, *Puritan Lectureships* (Stanford, California: Stanford University Press, 1970), 234.
49. Seaver, *Puritan Lectureships*, 57.
50. Ibid., 135, 137-38, 272.
51. John F. Wilson, *Pulpit in Parliament* (Princeton, New Jersey: Princeton University Press, 1969), 35. Holley, 'Divines,' 314-15.
52. Emerson, *English Puritanism*, 260; Holley, 'Divines,' 314.
53. Wilson, *Pulpit in Parliament*, 65, 204.
54. Reid, *Memoirs*, 2: 14.

Royalist troops were quartered in his home, and some of those abused him with derogatory names and swearing. The latter he could not tolerate, and so he preached on James 5:12, 'But above all things, my brethren, swear not.' This was so offensive that they threatened to shoot him if he should preach upon that text again. When he preached on the same verse again the next Sunday, 'he observed a soldier preparing his firelock, as if he designed to shoot; but Mr. Harris went on without fear, apprehending that the soldier intended only to disturb him, and he finished his discourse without interruption.'[55] Eventually his property was burned and his and his family's safety was sufficiently endangered that they fled to London.

While serving in the Assembly, he ministered at St. Botolph's, Bishopsgate, and continued to preach to other audiences, such as the London City Council on April 7, 1645, where he encouraged order and mercy to the poor.[56] Of Harris's preaching, Samuel Clarke the biographer said that he

> could so cook his meat that he could make it relish to every pallate: He could dress a plain discourse, so as that all sorts should be delighted with it. He could preach with learned plainness, and had learned to conceal his Art. He had clear Notions of high Mysteries, and proper language to make them stoop to the meanest capacity.[57]

Sermons, he said, should not be divinity lectures.[58] He complained that some preachers spent too much time insisting upon doctrinal points and too little upon applications, 'wherein ... a Sermons excellency doth

---

55. Ibid., 2: 4-15.
56. George Yule, *Puritans in Politics* (Appleford, Oxfordshire: Sutton Courtenay Press, 1981), 167, 199 n. 108, 109.
57. Quoted in Haller, *Rise of Puritanism*, 132.
58. Ibid., 129.

consist.' He for his part 'contrived the Uses first', and 'did often handle the same Texts, and the same Points, and yet still would pen new Applications'.[59]

He said of the Bible that 'We must be careful to read it, hear it, lodge it in our hearts, apply it close to our consciences, and then it will heal our hearts'.[60]

With regard to the *Westminster Confession's* doctrine of Predestination, Harris was an infralapsarian, emphasizing that unbelievers were responsible for their own condemnation.[61] Committed to the doctrine of Election, he also declared that God's Fatherhood was universal in some sense:

> God's adversaries are in some way his own. He is a piece of a Father to them also. For he is a *common Father by office* to all, a *special Father by adoption* to saints, *a singular Father by nature* to Christ. A Prince, besides his particular relation to his children, is *pater patriae*,... and is good to all, though with a difference. So here, though Christ hath purchased a peculiar people to himself, to the purpose of salvation, yet others taste of this his goodness.[62]

Harris had a very practical approach to the covenant of grace, emphasizing the personal application of the doctrine. When Noah looked outward into the flood he saw 'nothing but feare and death'. And when he looked inward 'there were no neighbours but Bears and Lyons, and other beasts'. But Noah and his Ark are 'a pledge of God's care'. And so too 'stands our case', for 'looke wee inward into our selves, there's nothing but guilt, sin, death,

---

59. Ibid., 135.
60. Quoted in Ryken, *Worldly Saints*, 153.
61. John von Rohr, *The Covenant of Grace in Puritan Thought* (Atlanta, Georgia: Scholars Press, 1986), 41.
62. Quoted in Alexander F. Mitchell, 'Introduction,' lxiii, n. 1, in *Minutes of the Westminster Assembly*, ed. Mitchell and Struthers. Cf. Mitchell, *Westminster Assembly*, 396 n. 1.

rottennesse, corruptions crawling in every roome in the soule; looke we outward ... there's nothing before our eyes but confusion and destruction, every place is a sea.' But we too have a pledge and, Harris added, 'for such as are already enrolled within the covenant ... there is not onely a possibility, but a certainty too of their blessedness.'[63]

He stressed that a troubled soul should make use of the means of grace available in the church:

> Especially apply your selves to the communion of the Saints: A dead coale, put to live coales, will take fire from them, which it would never do lying in the dead heape: so here ... sort your selves with such as are godly, and frequent the ordinances ... that you may have part in the new covenant.[64]

> He saw assurance of salvation as a matter of degree, something to be desired, but not necessarily complete in every believer: 'There be Christians of all ages and of all sizes in Gods family,' meaning that 'all Gods children have some assurance, though all have not alike'.[65]

In characteristic Puritan fashion Harris kept a spiritual diary for the sake of self-examination. He would write down 'the evidences which he found in himself, on account of which he hoped to reach heaven.' Usually these were propositions from Scripture or syllogisms that contributed to his own assurance.[66] The way such a spiritual diary functioned in place of the confessional for Puritans is illustrated by Harris's pastoral care of Elizabeth Wilkinson. This young woman had become

---

63. Von Rohr, *Covenant of Grace*, 12, quoting from Harris's *The Way to True Happinesse* (1632), twenty-four sermons on the Beatitudes.
64. Von Rohr, *Covenant of Grace*, 57, quoting from Harris's *A Treatise of the New Covenant* (1632).
65. Von Rohr, *Covenant of Grace*, 156-57.
66. [Alexander], *History*, 307; Reid, *Memoirs*, 2: 18-19.

concerned about her soul at age twelve, being assailed by atheistic doubts. These were relieved by reading Calvin's *Institutes*, but then she despaired that she had committed the sin against the Holy Ghost. She was helped by reading Henry Scudder's *Christians Daily Walk* and by Christian fellowship.

The upshot of her struggle was that she wrote out a 'particular account of Gods gracious dealing' toward her and sent it to Robert Harris, then Master of Trinity, Oxford, begging him to admit her to communion. He granted her request; she entered upon the life of a saint, kept a diary, and when she died (in 1654), the story of her spiritual progress was published by Edmund Staunton, the preacher chosen to pronounce the sermon at her funeral.[67]

Harris spent the last ten years of his life as president of Trinity College, Oxford, and as rector of Garsington, near Oxford. He preached regularly on Sundays at Garsington and once a week at All Soul's College, also preaching in turn at the University in English and in Latin.[68] He died on December 1 or 11, 1658, at the age of 77.[69] One of his sayings was 'That a preacher has three books to study: the *Bible, himself*, and the *people* – That preaching to the people was but one part of the pastor's duty: he was to live and die in them, as well as for, and with them.'[70] Robert Harris exemplified the Puritan preacher/pastor/theologian.

3. *Edmund Calamy (February 1600–October 29, 1666) –'A Noted London Clergyman'*

From the events leading up to the Westminster Assembly on through the outworking of the Assembly's actions

---

67. Haller, *Rise of Puritanism*, 99.
68. Reid, *Memoirs*, 2: 16; *D. N. B.*, 9: 23.
69. *D. N. B.*, 9: 23 has December 1; Reid, *Memoirs*, 2: 22 has December 11.
70. Reid, *Memoirs*, 2: 23.

in Revolutionary England, no single figure provided greater leadership for the Presbyterians than Edmund Calamy. As Archibald Alexander says:

> No minister of his time was more popular; and none had more energy and public spirit, together with a fearless boldness in declaring his sentiments, and going forward in the path which conscience directed. He may well be considered the leader of the Presbyterian party; their confidence in his courage, prudence, and integrity, was unbounded; and they manifested their estimation of his talents and address, by generally making him their chairman, at all their meetings.[71]

James Reid says: 'Mr. Calamy was well acquainted with the subjects appropriate to his profession: as a preacher, he was plain and practical; and he boldly avowed his sentiments on all necessary occasions.'[72] William Haller, comparing him to Stephen Marshall, the greatest preacher of the Assembly, says: 'Calamy, his colleague in the pulpit on several occasions, was, perhaps, among all the preachers, the next greatest favorite with parliament.'[73] Tai Liu says that

> ... Calamy commanded unparalleled prestige and exercised an irrefutable influence in the City of London during the revolutionary era. As his grandson would later say: 'No Minister in the City was more follow'd; nor hath there ever been a Week-day lecture so frequented as his; which was attended not only by his own Parish, but by Eminent Citizens, and many Persons of the Greatest Quality, and constantly for 20 years together;

---

71. [Archibald Alexander], *A History of the Westminster Assembly of Divines* (Philadelphia: Presbyterian Board of Publication, 1841), 222-23.
72. James Reid, *Memoirs of the Westminster Divines*, 2 vols. in 1 (Edinburgh and Carlisle, Pennsylvania: Banner of Truth, 1982 reprint of edition of 1811 and 1815), 1: 185.
73. William Haller, *Liberty and Reformation in the Puritan Revolution* (New York and London: Columbia University Press, 1955), 37.

for there seldom were so few as 60 coaches.' Indeed it was often in Calamy's house in Aldermanbury that strategy and actions of the London Puritan brethren were planned...[74]

Edmund Calamy was born in February 1600, the only son of a tradesman in Walbrook, London, who came from the island of Guernsey where, according to family tradition, he was a Huguenot refugee from the coast of Normandy.[75] Young Edmund entered Pembroke Hall, Cambridge, on July 4, 1616, and received the B.A. in 1620 and the M.A. in 1623.[76]

His aversion to Arminianism prevented him from becoming a Fellow, in the English reaction to the Synod of Dort, but he was elected *Tanquam Socius*, an arrangement peculiar to Pembroke Hall that allowed him most of the privileges of Fellow without any share in the government of the College.[77]

Nicholas Felton, Bishop of Ely, made him a chaplain of his household, permitting him to spend much time in study. During this stage of his life Calamy not only acquainted himself with the writings of Robert Bellarmine and Thomas Aquinas, but read over Augustine's works five times.[78] Bishop Felton presented him to the vicarage of St. Mary, Swaffham Prior, Cambridgeshire, on March 6, 1626, but in the next year he resigned this position to become a lecturer at Bury St. Edmunds, Suffolk. He would remain there for ten years, with Jeremiah Burroughes, his colleague, from around 1627 to 1631. The enforcement of Bishop Matthew Wren's articles of 1636 drove him from Bury, but Robert Rich, second Earl

---

74. Tai Liu, *Puritan London* (Newark, Delaware: University of Delaware Press, 1966), 74.
75. *D. N. B.*, 3: 679. Holley, 'Divines,' 288, says he was born in Walbrook, Suffolk.
76. Holley, 'Divines,' 288; *D. N. B.*, 3: 679.
77. Reid, *Memoirs*, 1: 166.
78. Ibid., 167.

of Warwick, secured him a position at Rochford, Essex, where he served as rector or lecturer from November 9, 1637, until May 1639.[79] The marshes of Essex did not agree with him, however, and an illness left him with a chronic dizziness that prevented him from mounting a pulpit, so that he always afterward preached from the reading-desk.[80]

Calamy was elected on May 27, 1639, to the perpetual curacy of St. Mary Aldermanbury, London, a parish with a strongly Puritan tradition and with many prominent citizens in its membership.[81] It also paid its minister handsomely. From the beginning Calamy was given what was 'probably the highest annual stipend a London minister received so early in this period'. [82] It was from this base that Calamy became involved in the attack upon episcopacy. From early in 1641 he joined with Cornelius Burgess, John White, Stephen Marshall, and various noblemen and lay leaders to plot their strategy.[83] When Bishop Joseph Hall published his defense of episcopacy by divine right, Calamy joined with Stephen Marshall, Thomas Young, his brother-in-law, Matthew Newcomen, and William Spurstowe to produce responses over the name 'Smectymnuus', an anagram of their initials. The full title of their first treatise reveals their subject matter: *An Answer to a Book entitled, An Humble Remonstrance; in which the Original of Liturgy and Episcopacy is discussed: and Queries propounded concerning both. The Parity of Bishops and Presbyters in Scripture demonstrated. The occasion of*

---

79. *D. N. B.*, 3: 679; Holley, 'Divines,' 288; *Calamy Revised*, ed. A. G. Matthews (Oxford: Clarendon Press, 1934), 97; Reid, *Memoirs*, 1: 169.
80. Reid, *Memoirs*, 1: 171; *D. N. B.*, 3: 679.
81. Liu, *Puritan London*, 29, 75-76, 173.
82. Ibid., 151-52.
83. Jacqueline Eales, *Puritans and Roundheads*, (Cambridge, New York, etc.: Cambridge University Press, 1990), 112-13; Paul S. Seaver, *The Puritan Lectureships* (Stanford, California: Stanford University Press, 1970), 264; Richard L. Greaves, *Saints and Rebels: Seven Nonconformists in Stuart England* (Macon, Georgia: Mercer University Press, 1985), 15.

their Imparity in Antiquity discovered. The Disparity of the Ancient and our Modern Bishops manifested. The Antiquity of Ruling Elders in the Church vindicated. The Prelatical Church bounded.[84] Five years later Calamy wrote:

> After my coming to London at the beginning of this Parliament I was one of those that did joyn in making Smectymnuus, which was the first deadly blow to Episcopacy in England of late years... I was the first that openly before a Committee of Parliament did defend that our Bishops were not only not an Order distinct from Presbyters, but that in Scripture a Bishop and Presbyter were all one.[85]

It was toward the beginning of the Long Parliament that Calamy for the Presbyterians and Phillip Nye for the Independents made an agreement at Calamy's house in Aldermanbury,

> That (for advancing of the publicke cause of a happy Reformation) neither side should Preach, Print, or dispute, or otherwise act against the other's way; And this to continue 'til both sides, in a full meeting, did declare the contrary.[86]

Presbyterians and Independents thus were aware of their differences before the Westminster Assembly, but were united in opposing episcopacy.

On December 22, 1641, Calamy and Stephen Marshall preached before the House of Commons for a special Fast Day for the Irish crisis. Calamy's sermon, *Englands Looking-Glasse,* based on Jeremiah 18:7-10 , developed four points that made Parliament's responsibility clear:

---

84. Reid, *Memoirs,* 1: 172. Cf. Haller, *Liberty and Reformation,* 34-35.
85. Tai Liu, *Discord in Zion* (The Hague: Martinus Nijhoff, 1973), 36 n. 24.
86. Ibid., 9. George Yule, *Puritans in Politics* (Appleford, Oxfordshire: Sutton Courtenay Press, 1981), 122-23.

(1) 'That God hath an independent and illumi-nated Prerogative over all Kingdoms and Nations to build them, or destroy them as he pleaseth'; (2) 'Though God hath this absolute power over Kingdoms and Nations, yet he seldome useth this power, but first he gives warning'; (3) 'That Nationall turning from evill, will divert Nationall judgments, and procure Nationall blessings' [repentance he construed as 'Humiliation for sins past, Reformation for the time to come']; (4) 'That when God begins to build and plant a Nation; if that Nation do evill in Gods sight, God will unbuild, pluck up, and repent of the good he intended to do unto it.'

Along with other preachers Calamy urged Parliament to call a 'free Nationall Synod' for the sake of reform.[87]

When the system of regular monthly Fast Days was established, Calamy and Marshall were selected by the House of Commons to begin the series on February 23, 1642. Calamy's sermon, based on Ezekiel 36:32, was titled *Gods free Mercy to England. Presented as a Pretious, and Powerful motive to Humiliation.* John F. Wilson refers to it as 'something of classic exposition of puritan doctrine for the times'. Steering between Arminian moralism and Antinomian irresponsibility, it argues 'That Nationall mercies come from free grace, not from free will; Not from mans goodnes, but Gods goodnes.'

'The contemplation of Gods free mercy to Nations and persons ought to be a mighty incentive, and a most effectuall argument to make them ashamed to sin for the time to come.' Repentance for the past and reform for the future, or change in attitude and change in action, were the available means of salvation. Sundered from each other, both were ineffectual and potentially heretical. Conjoined, they defined the religious practices

---

87. John F. Wilson, *Pulpit in Parliament* (Princeton, New Jersey: Princeton University Press, 1969), 55-56. Cf. Liu, *Discord in Zion*, 20, 31, 35.

appropriate to a people or a nation in explicit covenant with God.[88]

In another move to pave the way for cooperation between the London clergy and the Westminster Assembly, the Puritans gained control of Sion College in London. In April 1643, Andrew Janaway of All Hallows was elected president, and Calamy and Henry Roborough, who would be one of the two scribes for the Assembly, were elected assistants. Calamy would serve as president in 1650.[89] On June 15, 1643, as the Assembly was about to get under way, Calamy preached to the House of Lords a sermon, *The Nobleman's Pattern of true and real thankfulness*, from Joshua 24:15; he said, 'It is the duty of all men, but especially of such as are Joshuah's, such as are Rulers and Nobles, to ingage themselves and their Families to serve God resolutely, speedily, and publickely... .'[90]

In the Assembly itself Calamy was the fourteenth most active speaker in the debates on church government, just behind William Bridge in number of speeches recorded in Minutes down to November 15, 1644, and ahead of Joshua Hoyle.[91] His role in the debates shows him arguing for distinctively Presbyterian positions from the beginning of the Assembly.[92] He served on the Grand Committee for the treaty obligations to the Scots.[93] He

---

88. Wilson, *Pulpit in Parliament*, 183-84; cf. 63, 158-159. For other references to this sermon, cf. Haller, *Liberty and Reformation*, 68-69; Liu, *Discord in Zion*, 19; H. R. Trevor-Roper, *The Crisis of the Seventeenth Century* (New York and Evanston: Harper & Row, 1968), 306-07.
89. Robert S. Paul, *The Assembly of the Lord* (Edinburgh: T. & T. Clark, 1985), 118-19; *Calamy Revised*, 97. E. H. Pearce, *Sion College and Library* (Cambridge: Cambridge University Press, 1913), 344, shows the following Assembly members to have been president: John Ley (1644), George Walker (1645), Cornelius Burgess (1647–48), William Gouge (1649), Lazarus Seaman (1651–52), and Edward Reynolds (1659).
90. Wilson, *Pulpit in Parliament*, 70. Cf. Haller, *Liberty and Reformation*, 100-10; Liu, *Discord in Zion*, 23.
91. Wayne R. Spear, 'Covenanted Uniformity in Religion' (Pittsburgh, Pennsylvania: University of Pittsburgh Ph.D. diss., 1976), 362.
92. John Richard De Witt, *Jus Divinum* (Kampen: J. K. Kok, 1969), 72, 84.
93. Paul, *Assembly of the Lord*, 243 and n. 87.

also served on the committee to consider the 'Reasons' offered by the Independents.[94] He and Stephen Marshall were entrusted with distribution of money paid by Parliament to the Assembly on January 3, 1644, and he, Marshall, Cornelius Burgess, and William Spurstowe said that they did not wish to share in the distribution of April 7, 1645, evidently because of being better off than most of the divines.[95]

Repeatedly in the discussions Calamy showed an awareness of actual situations in English parishes and a concern for the practical consequences of decisions made at the Assembly.[96]

From 1643 to 1648 he had as his assistant at St. Mary Aldermanbury his brother-in-law and fellow Smectymnuan, Matthew Newcomen, who was also a member of the Assembly.[97] Meanwhile, when the idea of toleration had been broached in Parliament, Calamy preached to the House of Commons on the special Fast Day of October 22, 1644, *England's Antidote against the Plague of Civil War*, based on Acts 17:30 . In this sermon he said:

> If you do not labour according to your duty and according to your power, to suppress the errors and heresies that are spread in the Kingdom, all these errors are your errors.... You are Anabaptists and you are the Antinomians, and it is you that hold all religions are to be tolerated, even Judaism and Turkism.[98]

---

94. Ibid., 427 and n. 190.
95. S. W. Carruthers, *The Everyday Work of the Westminster Assembly* (Philadelphia: The Presbyterian Historical Societies of America and of England, 1943), 62, 64.
96. Cf. Paul, *Assembly of the Lord*, 371, 373-74, 439 n. 10, 435 and n. 228, 450–51 n. 62; Greaves, *Saints and Rebels*, 25-28.
97. Seaver, *Puritan Lectureships*, 273. Newcomen's wife was sister of Calamy's first wife, Mary Snelling, who died between 1638 and 1641. They were probably of the same family in Ipswich from which William Ames's mother, Joane Snelling, came (*D.N.B.*, 3: 681) which was also connected by marriage to the family of John Winthrop (Keith L. Sprunger, *The Learned Doctor William Ames* [Urbana, Chicago, London: University of Illinois Press, 1972], 3, 9).
98. Yule, *Puritans in Politics*, 139.

Just two months later, on December 25, 1644, the regular Fast Day, Calamy preached to the House of Lords on *An Indictment against England because of her self-murdering Divisions; with an Exhortation to Concord,* based on Matthew 12:25. With the differences between Independents and Presbyterians in mind he said: 'Divisions, whether they be Eclesiasticall, or Politicall, in Kingdomes, Cities, and Families, are infallible causes of ruine...' He concluded that if England should perish in the Civil War, her epitaph could be written: 'Here lyeth a Nation that hath broken Covenant with God...'[99] Incidentally, since the regular Fast Day fell on Christmas Day, Calamy expressed some Puritan sentiments on the superstition and profaneness connected with that day and opined that since Christmas could not be reformed, it should be dealt with as Hezekiah dealt with the bronze serpent.[100]

On January 14, 1646, Calamy preached to the Lord Mayor with the sheriffs, aldermen, and Common Council of London on the occasion of their renewing the Solemn League and Covenant. His text was 2 Timothy 3:3, and his title was *The Great Danger of Covenant-refusing, and Covenant-breaking*. He said that 'the famous City of London is become an Amsterdam, separation from our churches is countenanced, toleration is cried up, authority lieth asleep'.[101]

This and other sermons, according to George Yule, stressed that settling the Presbyterian system, having no toleration and maintaining the Covenant were all of a piece, and thus helped the Council see the issue as a whole, which was a powerful weapon against the Erastians.[102] After this date Calamy seems not to have preached on

---

99. Wilson, *Pulpit in Parliament*, 177; Liu, *Discord in Zion*, 52. Cf. Yule, *Puritans in Politics*, 142.
100. Reid, *Memoirs*, 1: 186-87. Cf. Carruthers, *Everyday Work*, 44.
101. Quoted in C. Gordon Bolam, Jeremy Goring, et al., *The English Presbyterians* (Boston: Beacon Press, 1968), 50.
102. Yule, *Puritans in Politics*, p. 169.

the Parliamentary Fast Days. He was invited for June 24, July 29, and August 26, 1646, but asked to be excused on account of illness on the first date and declined the other invitations. Since he was previously enthusiastic about the monthly Fast Days, either his illness continued or he had become disenchanted with the practice.[103]

Part of his disillusionment may have stemmed from an incident in his own parish. Henry Burton was permitted to hold a 'catechisticall lecture' on alternate Tuesdays at St. Mary Aldermanbury, and on September 23, 1645, he spoke out in favor of 'his congregationall way'. At the instigation of Calamy the churchwardens locked Burton out, and an exchange of pamphlets ensued: *The Door of Truth Opened*, by Calamy, and *Truth still Truth, though Shut Out of Doors*, by Burton, both in 1645, and *A Just and Necessary Apology* (i.e., defense), by Calamy in 1646.[104] The kind of atmosphere that was increasingly developing in London in the late 1640s is described by Christopher Hill:

> In 1648 the General Baptist, Edward Barber, was invited by parishioners of St. Benet Fink, London, to come to the parish church and add to what the minister (Edmund Calamy) should say, or contradict him if erroneous. Hanserd Knollys created several 'riots and tumults' by going around churches and speaking after the sermon. One can imagine the irritation this practice might cause when, as time went on, the parson himself became the

---

103. Wilson, *Pulpit in Parliament*, 88-89. In 1641 Calamy had written: 'Blessed be God, we have now our Christian new moons and evangelical feast of trumpets. We have not only our monthly sacrament feast to refresh our souls withal in most of our congregations ... but our monthly fasts in which the word is preached, trading ceaseth, and sacrifices of prayer, praises, and alms are tendered up to God,' thus indicating that the Lord's Supper was observed monthly at that time (Alexander F. Mitchell, *The Westminster Assembly*, 2nd ed. [Philadelphia: Presbyterian Board of Publication, 1897], 243 n. 1).
104. *D. N. B.*, 3: 680; Haller, *Liberty and Reformation*, 145; Seaver, *Puritan Lectureships*, 281; Geoffrey F. Nuttall, *Visible Saints* (Oxford: Basil Blackwell, 1957), 134; Greaves, *Saints and Rebels*, 23-24.

main target of itinerant interrupters, professionally skilled hecklers, denouncing his self-righteousness and his greed in taking tithes.[105]

After the triumphant Army occupied London in the summer of 1647, Calamy 'openly denounced the latter in a sermon for the morning exercise at St. Michael Cornhill', with the result that a pamphlet responded:

> When we come to hear you, we expected to be instructed in Divinity, and not to be corrupted in Civility; if we had a desire to learn the language of *Billingsgate*, we should not have gone to Michael Cornhill in London, especially when Mr. Calamy was the Teacher.[106]

Under these circumstances it is understandable that the English Puritan majority sided with the Scottish Presbyterians for reasons such as Robert S. Paul enumerates: 'fear of the growing sectarianism, determination to maintain an established state church, and a strong desire to maintain the status and authority of the clergy.'[107]

Calamy was a member of the Presbyterian Sixth London Classis.[108] He was one of the signatories of Cornelius Burgess's *A Vindication of the Ministers of the Gospel in, and about London* that opposed the Army's actions leading to the trial and eventual execution of the King.[109] Under the Protectorate he 'kept himself as private as he could', but he was the main author in 1650 of *Vindication of the Presbyteriall-government*, reaching out to Independents, and in 1654 of *Jus divinum ministerii evangelici*, or *The divine right of the Gospel-ministry*, appealing to the Episcopalians

---

105. Christopher Hill, *The World Turned Upside Down: Radical Ideas During the English Revolution* (New York: Viking Press, 1972), 85, Cf. also Greaves, *Saints and Rebels*, 29.
106. Liu, *Puritan London*, 74.
107. Paul, *Assembly of the Lord*, 322 n. 44.
108. Liu, *Puritan London*, 73.
109. Liu, *Discord in Zion*, 163.

as well as to Independents.[110] Oliver Cromwell did consult with some of the London clergy, including Edmund Calamy, when he was contemplating expulsion of the Rump Parliament, probably in early April 1653. Calamy advised that it was both unlawful and impracticable that one man should assume the government of the country. Concerning its being unlawful Cromwell appealed to the safety of the nation as the supreme law. When asked why he thought it impracticable, Calamy said, 'Oh, it is against the voice of the nation; there will be nine in ten against you.' But Cromwell responded, 'Very well; but what if I should disarm the nine, and put the sword in the tenth man's hand, would not that do the business?'[111]

In the period following Oliver Cromwell's death on September 3, 1658, Calamy was involved with other Presbyterian ministers in support of Richard Cromwell and the restored Long Parliament, but when the government began to disintegrate, he worked for the restoration of monarchy.[112] He went to Holland with Edward Reynolds, William Spurstowe, Thomas Case, and Thomas Manton to consult with Charles II, and their delegation was well received.[113] Along with all of the delegation plus John Wallis, Simeon Ashe, Richard Baxter, and one or two others, he was appointed a Royal Chaplain.[114] On the one occasion when he preached before the King, August 12, 1660, Samuel Pepys commented in

---

110. Bolam, Goring, et al., *English Presbyterians*, 50-51, and n. 1, 59; A. H. Drysdale, *History of the Presbyterians in England* (London: Publication Committee of the Presbyterian Church of England, 1889), 312 and n. 1.
111. Reid, *Memoirs*, 1: 175. Both Robert S. Paul, *The Lord Protector* (Grand Rapids, Michigan: William B. Eerdmans, 1964), 264-65 and n. 4, and Antonia Fraser, *Cromwell, Our Chief of Men* (London: Mandarin, 1993 reprint of 1973 ed.), 416, believe Cromwell's statement to be not so much political cynicism as a sense of providential use of force to support what is right.
112. Cf. Bolam, Goring, et al., *English Presbyterians*, 74-79.
113. George R. Abernathy, Jr., 'The English Presbyterians and the Stuart Restoration, 1648–1663,' *Transactions of the American Philosophical Society*, New Series, 55, Part 2 (1965), 65-66.
114. Abernathy, 'The English Presbyterians,' 68; Drysdale, *History*, 375 and n. 1.

his *Diary* that he 'made a good sermon upon these words, "To whom much is given of him much is required." He was very officious with his three reverences to the King, as others do.'[115]

At the crucial point of negotiations with the King's representatives and the Bishops, Calamy joined with Edward Reynolds in seeking to tone down some of Richard Baxter's response, but even so the Presbyterian exceptions were more than the Bishops would accept.[116] Offered the Bishoprics of Hereford, Norwich, and Lichfield and Coventry respectively, Baxter declined, Reynolds accepted, and Calamy hesitated and then declined.[117] J. I. Packer explains what was operative for Calamy at this juncture:

> ... these Puritan clergy were prevented from trying to stretch their consciences by the sense that the eyes of their own flocks –indeed, of all Englishmen – were upon them, and that they could not even appear to compromise principles for which they had stood in the past without discrediting both themselves, their calling, and their previous teaching. Calamy records a contemporary comment which focuses their fear: 'had the ministers conformed, people would have thought there was nothing in religion.' It had become a question of credibility. The Puritan clergy held that they should be ready to confirm what they had publicly maintained as truth by suffering, if need be, rather than risk undermining their whole previous ministry by what would look like time-serving abandonment of principle.[118]

---

115. *Calamy Revised*, 97-98.
116. Abernathy, 'The English Presbyterians,' 74-75; Greaves, *Saints and Rebels*, 50–51.
117. Bolam, Goring, et al., *English Presbyterians*, 76; Abernathy, 'The English Presbyterians,' 77, says Calamy was dissuaded by his wife and Matthew Newcomen, his brother-in-law.
118. J. I. Packer, *A Quest for Godliness: The Puritan Vision of the Christian Life* (Wheaton, Illinois: Crossway Books, 1990), 121.

When it became clear that the King and his advisers were not going to accommodate those who could not conform, Calamy did not hide his feelings. On one occasion when General George Monck, who had persuaded him and Simeon Ashe that the Long Parliament must be dissolved, was present in his church, he had occasion in his sermon to refer to filthy lucre:

> 'and why,' said he, 'is it called filthy, but because it makes men do base and filthy things? Some men,' said he, 'will betray three kingdoms for filthy lucre's sake.' Saying this, he threw his handkerchief, which he generally waved up and down while he was preaching, toward the General's pew.[119]

With the passage of the Act of Uniformity, knowing he would be ejected, he preached his Farewell Sermon on August 17, 1662, a week before the Act would take effect, on the text of 2 Samuel 24:14 . James Reid summarizes it:

> The chief design of it is to illustrate and improve this point, 'that sin brings persons and nations into great perplexities.' He observes, That beside many outward troubles, this brings a spiritual famine upon a land: a famine of the word.... Have not some of you *itching ears* who would fain have a preacher who would feed you with dainty phrases; and who begin not to care for a Minister that unrips your consciences, and speaks to your hearts: some who by often hearing sermons are become sermon proof? There is hardly any way to raise the price of the gospel-ministry, but the want of it.... Give glory to God by confessing and repenting of your sins, before darkness comes; and who knoweth but that may prevent that darkness.[120]

---

119. Reid, *Memoirs*, 1: 176; Greaves, *Saints and Rebels*, 42-43 n. 49, regards this story as 'probably apocryphal.'
120. Ibid., 1: 177-78.

On August 20, just days before St. Bartholomew's Day (August 24), Simeon Ashe, who had been Sunday-afternoon lecturer at St. Mary Aldermanbury since 1651 and Calamy's assistant there until January 1655, 'went seasonably to Heaven at the very Time when he was cast out of the Church.'[121] Calamy preached his funeral sermon on August 23, at St. Austin's Church on the text Isaiah 57:1, 'The righteous perisheth, and no man layeth it to heart: and merciful men are taken away, none considering that the righteous is taken away from the evil to come.'

After St. Bartholomew's Day, Calamy continued to attend St. Mary Aldermanbury from which he had been ejected. On December 28, he was present as usual when the assigned preacher did not appear. Urged by the people, he entered the desk 'and preached with some warmth'.[122] His sermon was based on 1 Samuel 4:13: 'And when he came, lo, Eli sat upon a seat by the wayside watching; for his heart trembled for the ark of God.' It was later written out and published in the collections of farewell sermons as *Trembling for the Ark of God* . His fifth and final application was:

> The ark was called the ark of the covenant. Keep covenant with God, and God will preserve the ark. But if you break the covenant of the ark, the covenant made in baptism, and that covenant often renewed in the sacrament, if you break covenant, God will take away the ark.[123]

On January 6, 1663, Calamy was arrested and committed to Newgate Prison, the first of the Nonconformists to be penalized for disobeying the Act of Conformity for preaching without permission. Many of Calamy's friends came to visit him in prison, their coaches jamming

---

121. *Calamy Revised*, 16; Seaver, *Puritan Lectureships*, 271-72.
122. *D. N. B.*, 3: 681.
123. *Sermons of the Great Ejection*, ed. Iain Murray (London: Banner of Truth, 1962), 34.

the traffic in Newgate Street. 'A certain Popish lady,' apparently the King's mistress, was detained by the jam and, inquiring as to its cause, learned from disturbed people standing by that 'a person much beloved and respected, was imprisoned there for a single sermon.' She immediately reported this to the King, whose express order set Calamy free, although the House of Commons said that the Act had not provided for longer restraint and took steps to tighten the regulations against toleration.[124]

Edmund Calamy lived to see the Great Fire of London of September 3, 1666. It is said to have overrun 373 acres within the city's walls, burning down 13,200 houses, 89 parish churches, besides chapels, and leaving only eleven parish churches within the walls still standing. Driven in a coach through the ashes and ruins as far as Enfield, Calamy was devastated by the sight. Heartbroken, he never again emerged from his room and died on October 29, 1666. He was buried on November 6 in the ruins of the church he had served for twenty-three years, 'as near to the place where his pulpit had stood as they could guess.'[125]

Calamy was the first of six Edmund Calamys, and to avoid confusion is known as Edmund Calamy the Elder. His son Edmund Calamy the Younger (1635?–1685) was one of three children of his first wife, Mary Snelling. He was educated at Sidney Sussex College, and Pembroke Hall, Cambridge, and was ordained as a Presbyterian in 1653, was ejected from the rectory of Moreton, Essex, in 1662, and attended his father in London until his death. Edmund Calamy the Elder's second wife was Anne Leaver, of the Lancashire Leavers, who bore him three sons, Benjamin, James, and John. The older two became

---

124. Reid, *Memoirs*, 1:180-81; *D. N. B.*, 3: 185.
125. *D. N. B.*, 3: 681; Reid, *Memoirs*, 1: 185.

ministers who conformed to the Church of England after the Restoration, but enjoyed cordial relations with their Nonconformist half-brother, Edmund. Benjamin Calamy (1642–86) gained the D.D. in 1680 and, as vicar of St. Lawrence Jewry (with St. Mary Magdalene Milk Street annexed) and a prebendary of St. Paul's, was a prominent churchman.

Edmund Calamy the Younger had one son, Edmund Calamy (1671–1732), the great biographical historian of Nonconformity, often referred to as 'Dr. Calamy' since he received the D.D. from the University of Edinburgh upon a journey to Scotland in 1709. His eldest son, Edmund Calamy (1697?–1755), was a Dissenting minister who served on the Presbyterian Board, as did his son, Edmund Calamy (1743–1816), who became a barrister of Lincoln's Inn. His son, Edmund Calamy, the great-great-great-grandson of Edmund Calamy the Elder, died August 27, 1850, at age 70. His younger brother, Michael Calamy, who occasionally preached for the Unitarians at Exeter and Topsham, died unmarried on January 3, 1876, aged 85, the last of a notable line.[126]

Conclusion

An American Presbyterian friend, when taking the guided tour of Westminster Abbey, asked the tour guide if he could see the Jerusalem Chamber. The guide responded by inquiring why he would want to see the Jerusalem Chamber. When my friend replied, 'Because that is where the Westminster Assembly met,' the guide had to be informed as to what the Westminster Assembly was.

There is a certain irony about the influence of the Westminster Assembly. A half-dozen Scottish delegates came south to London for more than four years to get

---

126. *D. N. B.*, 3: 678-87.

a group averaging from sixty to eighty Englishmen to produce a *Confession of Faith*, two catechisms, a *Directory for Worship*, and a *Form of Government* which became standards for the Kirk of Scotland, and for Presbyterianism wherever English-speaking Christians take them around the world, but which have had only a very momentary influence on England itself. It is perhaps not so unusual that our God would work in such a way 'that no flesh should glory'.

The lives of the members of the Westminster Assembly help to fill a gap in the story of the English Puritan movement. Because the products of the Assembly were not lastingly adopted in England, they are sometimes overlooked in the study of English Puritanism. Learned articles on English Puritan ethics have been produced, for example, that skip from William Perkins and William Ames to the period of Richard Baxter without commenting on the important statements in the *Westminster Larger Catechism* on the proper understanding and application of the Ten Commandments. The work of the Westminster Assembly should be seen as reflecting the core of English Puritan theology and spirituality.

For those churches that profess to adhere to the Westminster Standards, the lives of the members of the Assembly shed much light on the foundations of continuing truths. The extended discussions on church government, including such matters as the office and role of the ruling elder, can be studied profitably still today. The same can be said about the Lord's Supper, the reading of Scripture in worship, the conscience, and many other topics. The writings of Joseph Caryl on 'what is good' are still relevant to the study of biblical ethics. The fact that Independents, Erastians, Scots, and English Presbyterians – good Puritans all! – did not always agree was a healthy stimulus to study of the Bible in depth and thorough debate as to its meaning and application in the immediate context of the mid-seventeenth century.

The historical context of the Westminster Assembly must not be forgotten. There were differences of theological emphasis and nuance among the members, all of whom were Calvinists. The supralapsarian/infralapsarian issue was not pressed, nor was the matter of the millennium, on which there were differences. It is also interesting to see that there were differences among the members on the specific role of the active obedience of Christ in the justification of the believer.

Most instructive is to realize the strong interest in evangelism and missions on the part of many members of the Assembly. Thomas Hill sought to see missionaries sent not only into the dark corners of the realm, but also abroad. John White, Anthony Tuckney, William Gouge, Edmund Calamy, and others maintained an active interest in the American missions to the Indians. Herbert Palmer's dying prayers were for the spread of the gospel around the world.

It was a rare collection of God's servants with a rich variety of gifts that gathered in the Westminster Assembly to produce the documents that continue to bear fruit in the understanding and living out of God's Word. The members of the Westminster Assembly, imperfect as they were, were nevertheless gifts to the church from the ascended Christ, to whom be thanks and all glory given.

10

A BODY OF DIVINITY BY THOMAS WATSON

The author of *A Body of Divinity*, Thomas Watson, was a Puritan pastor in London from 1646 until near the time of his death in July of 1686. Active in the tumultuous times of the Civil War and the Westminster Assembly of 1640s, the Commonwealth of Oliver Cromwell in the 1650s, the Restoration of the Monarchy in 1660 and the Great Ejection of many non-conforming ministers in 1662, and the subsequent persecutions of Puritan Nonconformists into the 1680s, he was recognized as a popular preacher who was called upon to speak on some significant public occasions.

The exact date and place of his birth are unknown, but he was educated at Emmanuel College, Cambridge, receiving his B.A. in 1639 and his M.A. in 1642.[1] After preaching at Hereford in 1641, he resided for some time with the family of Mary, the widow of Sir Horace Vere, Baron Tilbury, who had been military leader of the English Protestant forces in the Netherlands. Lady Vere,

---

This chapter appeared in *The Devoted Life* (2004), eds., Kelly M. Kapic and Randall C. Gleason, IVP.
1. Iain Murray, ed., *Sermons of the Great Ejections* (London: Banner of Truth, 1962), 113.

whose religious views were 'of Dutch complexion', thus favoring Parliament in the Civil War, nevertheless had the care of King Charles I's children, Elizabeth and Henry, Duke of Gloucester, for a short time in the spring of 1645.[2]

In 1646 Watson married Abigail, daughter of John Beadle, rector of Barnston, Essex.[3] In the same year he was appointed Rector of the parish of St. Stephen's Walbrook, in the heart of London. For nearly sixteen years he served there as a faithful pastor, known for his effective preaching and also for his public prayer. Dr. Edmund Calamy tells of the time when

> the learned Bishop Richardson came to hear him at St. Stephen's, who was much pleased with his sermon, but especially with his prayer after it, so that he followed him home to give him thanks, and earnestly desired a copy of his prayer. 'Alas!' (said Mr. Watson) 'that is what I cannot give, for I do not use to pen my prayers; it was no studied thing, but uttered, *pro re nata*, as God enabled me, from the abundance of my heart and affections.' Upon which the good Bishop went away wondering that any man could pray in that manner extempore.[4]

Watson was of Presbyterian convictions. After Cromwell's Colonel Pride had purged Parliament of its Presbyterian members, because of their willingness to negotiate with the king, on December 6, 1648, Watson was nevertheless selected, along with the Independent Thomas Brooks, to preach before the 'Rump Parliament'

---

2. *Dictionary of National Biography*, eds. Leslie Stephen and Sidney Lee, 22 volumes (London: Oxford University Press, 1908-09) 20:238, under 'Vere, Sir Horace.'
3. Hamilton Smith, ed., 'Biographical Introduction,' in *Gleanings from the Past: Extracts from the Writings of Thomas Watson* (London, 1915), reprinted as *Gleanings from Thomas Watson* (Morgan, Pa.: Soli Deo Gloria, 1995), xi.
4. Quoted in C. H. Spurgeon, 'Brief Memoir of Thomas Watson,' in Thomas Watson, *A Body of Divinity* (London: Banner of Truth, rev. ed. 1965, reprinted from the 1890 edition), viii.

on December 27. Whereas Brooks urged that justice be done to malefactors (meaning the King), Watson warned Parliament that all things were naked to the eye of God. Significantly, Parliament authorized the printing of Brooks's sermon, but not that of Watson.[5] He joined some sixty Presbyterian ministers in a remonstrance to Cromwell and the council of war against the death of Charles I, who was, however, executed on January 30, 1649. In 1651 Watson was implicated in the plot of fellow Presbyterian minister Christopher Love to negotiate with Charles II, then in Holland, against the Commonwealth. Love was executed by Cromwell, but Watson and some other ministers were released after several months' imprisonment in the Tower, and on June 30, 1652 he was formally reinstated as Vicar of St. Stephen's, Walbrook.[6]

Upon the Restoration of the monarchy in the person of Charles II in 1660, Watson continued at St. Stephen's until the Great Ejection of some 2000 Puritan ministers on St. Bartholomew's Day, August 24, 1662, when he was among those who could not agree to the Act of Uniformity. He delivered two farewell sermons to his congregation, on John 13:34 and 2 Corinthians 7:1, on Sunday, August 17, and a third on Isaiah 3:10,11, on Tuesday, August 19. In the second of these he said:

> I have now exercised my ministry among you for almost sixteen years; ... I have received many signal demonstrations of love from you. Though other parishes have exceeded you in number of houses, yet I think,

---

5. William Haller, *Liberty and Reformation in the Puritan Revolution* (New York and London: Columbia University Press, 1955), 336, 383 n.23. Hugh Trevor-Roper calls this 'one of the boldest sermons that was ever uttered to the Long Parliament' (*The Crisis of the Seventeenth Century* [New York and Evanston: Harper & Row, 1968], 334-35); cf. John F. Wilson, *Pulpit in Parliament* (Princeton, N.J.: Princeton University Press, 1969), 95, 155-57.
6. *Dictionary of National Biography*, 20:949, under 'Watson, Thomas.'

none for the strength of affection. I have with much comfort observed your reverent attention to the word preached; you rejoice in this light, not for a season, but to this day. I have observed your zeal against error in a critical time, your unity and amity. This is your honour. If there should be any interruption in my ministry among you, though I should not be permitted to preach to you again, yet I shall not cease to love you, and to pray for you. But why should there be any interruption made? Where is the crime? Some, indeed, say that we are disloyal and seditious. Beloved, what my actions and sufferings for his Majesty has been is known to not a few of you. However, we must go to heaven through good report and bad report; and it is well if we can get to glory though we press through the pikes.[7]

In spite of legal penalties Watson and other nonconformists managed to preach from time to time in a variety of secret places. As the English Presbyterians divided between the 'Dons' and the 'Ducklings' after the 'Five Mile Act' of October 1665, Watson belonged to the latter group, those who 'did not fear the water', or who were willing to take the plunge in breaking the law and setting up conventicles.[8] After the great fire of London in 1666, when many of the churches were burned, he fitted up a large room for public worship for any who wished to attend. Upon the Declaration of Indulgence in 1672, he obtained license for use of the great hall in Crosby House, on the east side of Bishopsgate Street in London. He preached here for several years, Stephen Charnock becoming co-pastor with him of the Presbyterian church at Crosby Hall from 1675 until Charnock's death in 1680.[9] Watson

---

7. *Sermons of the Great Ejection*, 136-37; also quoted by Spurgeon, 'Brief Memoir,' pp. ix-x, in Watson, *Bod y of Divinity*.
8. C. G. Bolam and Jeremy Goring, 'The Cataclysm,' in C. Gordon Bolam, *et. al.*, *The English Presbyterians: From Elizabethan Puritanism to Modern Unitarianism* (Boston: Beacon Press, 1968), 87.

published several works in the 1650s and '60s, but his *Body of Divinity*, published posthumously in 1692, probably represents some three-and-a-half years of his preaching on Sunday afternoons at the Crosby Hall church before his own death.[10] His health failed in the mid-1680s, and he retired to Barnston in Essex, where he died suddenly while at prayer and was buried in the grave of his father-in-law, John Beadle, on July 28, 1686.

1. *A Body of Practical Divinity*

Thomas Watson's best-known work was originally published in 1692 as *A Body of Practical Divinity*. It consists of 176 sermons based on the Shorter Catechism produced by the Westminster Assembly of Divines in 1647. The modern edition available today was published in three separate volumes by the Banner of Truth Trust in Edinburgh, Scotland, and Carlisle, Pennsylvania, as *A Body of Divinity* (1958), *The Ten Commandments* (1959), and *The Lord's Prayer* (1960), all reprinted from the 1890 edition, superintended by Rev. George Rogers, Principal of Charles Haddon Spurgeon's Pastors' College, who reported:

> The style has been modernized, so far as could be done without detracting from its own peculiar characteristics. Long sentences have been divided into two or three, when it could be done without injury to the clearness or force of the signification. Modern words have been substituted for such as had become obsolete; Latin quotations restored to their correct form, as far as their sources could be ascertained; and divisions of subjects more perspicuously arranged.[11]

---

9. *Dictionary of National Biography*, 2:134, under 'Charnock, Stephen'; William Symington, 'Life and Character of Charnock,' in Stephen Charnock, *Discourses Upon the Existance and Attributes of God*, 2 vols. (Grand Rapids, Mich.: Baker Book House, 1979, reprint of 1853 edition), 1:7-8.
10. Watson, *Body of Divinity*, 5.
11. Quoted in Spurgeon, 'Brief Memoir,' pp. xi-xii.

Spurgeon stated in this 1890 edition concerning the original one-volume folio of 1692: 'For many a year this volume continued to train the common people in theology, and it may still be found very commonly in the cottages of the Scottish peasantry.'[12] There were numerous subsequent editions, including one in London (1838) and one in New York (1855).

The Westminster Shorter Catechism is the most concise statement of the theology of the Assembly which met from 1643 to 1648 to provide a clarified declaration of the Reformation doctrines of the English church, producing also the fuller Westminster Confession of Faith and Larger Catechism. These documents were adopted by the Parliament in England, where they had temporary official standing, and also by the Church and Parliament of Scotland, where they had more lasting influence among Presbyterians, but also Congregationalists and Baptists in America and all the English-speaking world. Generations in such circles have been brought up on the Shorter Catechism and thus have had their piety shaped by the doctrine that Thomas Watson is expounding in the three volumes of *A Body of Divinity.*

Watson follows the general outline of the Shorter Catechism as indicated in its third question and answer: 'The Scriptures principally teach what man is to believe concerning God, and what duty God requires of man.' Volume 1 goes up through Q. & A. 38, covering 'what man is to believe concerning God'. Watson treats the classic definition of the chief end of man ('to glorify God and to enjoy him forever') and then the doctrine of Scripture as the foundation. Then almost one third of the volume is on 'God and His Creation', with a detailed treatment of the attributes of God, then God's unity, the Trinity, and creation and providence. Under

---

12. Spurgeon, 'Brief Memoir,' p. xi.

'The Fall' Watson deals with the Covenant of Works, sin, Adam's sin, and original sin, and man's misery by the fall. Under 'The Covenant of Grace and the Mediator', Watson describes Christ's prophetic, priestly, and kingly offices, giving twice the space to the priestly office as to each of the others, before covering Christ's humiliation and exaltation. Under 'The Application of Redemption' Watson deals with faith, effectual calling, justification, adoption, sanctification, and assurance, then breaks out from 'the benefits of redemption' separate sections on peace, joy, growth in grace, and perseverance, thus showing his special concern for the practical application of doctrine. Finally, he deals with the death of the righteous and the resurrection.

In Volume 2, 'The Ten Commandments,' covering Catechism questions 39-98, Watson moves into the latter half of what 'the Scriptures principally teach' with the 'duty that God requires of man'. After introductory sections on obedience and love, he describes at length the preface to the Ten Commandments, and then deals with each one of the Commandments in turn. The Second Commandment, on worship, and the Fourth Commandment, on the Sabbath, receive the longest treatment, in characteristic Puritan fashion. Then, under 'The Law and Sin', he deals with man's inability to keep the moral law, degrees of sin, and the wrath of God. Finally, under 'The Way of Salvation', he treats faith, repentance, and then in separate sections the means of grace: the word, baptism, the Lord's Supper, and prayer.

In Volume 3, 'The Lord's Prayer,' covering Catechism questions 99-107, Watson takes up the preface to the Lord's Prayer and then each of the six petitions in turn. The fact that this third volume has more pages (332) than either Volume 1 (316 pages) or Volume 2 (245 pages), even though it covers far fewer Catechism questions than the others, shows Watson's emphasis on the Christian's piety in terms of worship and private devotion.

Although Watson follows closely the outline and content of the Shorter Catechism, he typically begins a section with an exposition of Scripture. Then the Scripture quotations and allusions tend to tumble over each other in his development of a doctrinal topic. Other sources that frequently come into play are Church Fathers – including Irenaeus, Tertullian, Cyprian, Athanasius, Ambrose, Basil, Jerome, Chrysostom, Gregory the Great, but especially Augustine; also Reformers such as Luther, Oecolampadius, Melanchthon, Calvin, Bullinger, and Beza; even Medieval figures such as Anselm, Bernard, Aquinas, and other Scholastics; plus more recent theologians such as William Perkins, Joseph Scaliger, and Hugo Grotius. Mingled with these are numerous references to classical sources, including Socrates, Plato, Aristotle, Plutarch, and Caesar. The fruit of Watson's diligent study at Emmanuel College, Cambridge is clearly displayed.

As learned as Watson was, his style was that of a popular preacher. He is eminently readable, racy, and rich with abundant illustrations from common life of the time or from biblical or classical literature. He is also repetitious in a way that can be as tedious as ringing the changes on church-tower bells or as beautiful and interesting as Brahms's *Variations on a Theme by Haydn*.

A taste of some of his aphorisms may whet the appetite of the potential reader. 'In the Word we hear God's voice, in the sacrament we have his kiss' (*Body of Divinity*, p. 21). 'Let us pray that God will preserve pure ordinances and powerful preaching among us. Idolatry came in at first by the want of good preaching. The people began to have golden images when they had wooden priests' (*Ten Commandments*, p. 64). Commenting on distractions during Sabbath worship, he says: 'Does it not please Satan to see men come to the word, and as good stay away? They are haunted with vain thoughts; they are taken off from the duty while they are in it; their body is in the assembly, their heart in their shop' (*Ten Commandments*, p. 111). 'Prayer is the gun we shoot with, fervency is the fire that discharges it, and faith is the bullet which pierces the throne of grace. Prayer is the key of heaven, faith is the hand that turns it' (*Lord's Prayer*, p. 32). Speaking of a person's particular besetting sin, he says: 'Men can be content to have other sins declaimed against; but if a minister put his finger upon the sore, and touches upon one special sin, then *igne micant oculi* [their eyes flash with fire], they are enraged, and spit the venom of malice' (*Lord's Prayer*, p. 117). Comparing the glory of creation and the glory of redemption, he says:

> Great wisdom was seen in making us, but more miraculous wisdom in saving us. Great power was seen in bringing us out of nothing, but greater power in helping us when we were worse than nothing. It cost more to redeem than to create us. In creation it was but speaking a word (Psa. cxlviii. 5); in redeeming there was shedding of blood, I Pet. I.19. Creation was the work of God's fingers, Psa. viii. 3, redemption was the work of his arm, Luke i.51. In creation, God gave us ourselves; in the redemption, he gave us himself. By creation, we have life in Adam; by redemption, we have life in Christ, Col iii 3. By creation, we had a right to an earthly paradise: by redemption, we have a title to a heavenly kingdom (*Ten Commandments*, p. 96).

These are but a few samples of his eloquence and of the vivid analogies that tend to come in almost every paragraph.

Always concerned with the practical application of doctrine, Watson is not without a polemical side. Frequently he contrasts the biblical teaching with that of Roman Catholicism or Islam ('the Pope' or 'Papist', 'the Turk'), that of the Arminians or the Antinomians, or that of the Anabaptists or the Socinians. There is an awareness of false teaching in the knowledge that right behavior or practice finds its foundation only in Scriptural truth.

2. Theological Analysis

The theology of Watson and *A Body of Practical Divinity* is standard seventeenth-century Calvinism. This is naturally to be expected since his work is an exposition of the Westminster Shorter Catechism. As such it furnishes a helpful elaboration on the Westminster Standards for those desiring deeper interpretation of the Catechisms and Confession of Faith. For example, on the question of preparation for salvation, he says concerning effectual calling: 'Before this effectual call, a humbling work passes upon the soul .... Conviction is the first step in conversion.'[13] In regard to assurance, he says: '... the heart must be ploughed up by humiliation and repentance, before God sows the seed of assurance.'[14] On the other hand, in answer to the question 'How may deserted souls be comforted who are cast down for want of assurance?' he answers '(1.) Want of assurance shall not hinder the success of the saint's prayers,' and '(2.) Faith may be strongest when assurance is weakest', and '(3.) When God is out of sight, he is not out of covenant.'[15] Here is his definition of assurance:

> It is not any vocal or audible voice, or brought to us by the help of an angel or revelation. Assurance consists of a practical syllogism, in which the word of God makes the major, conscience the minor, and the Spirit of God,

---

13. Watson, *Body of Divinity*, 224.
14. *Body of Divinity*, 252.
15. *Body of Divinity*, 256-57.

the conclusion. The Word says, "He that fears and loves God is loved of God;" there is the major proposition; then conscience makes the minor, "But I fear and love God;" then the Spirit makes the conclusion, "Therefore thou art loved of God;" and this is what the apostle calls "The witnessing of the Spirit with our spirits, that we are his children," Rom viii. 16.[16]

Like the Westminster Confession and Catechisms, *A Body of Divinity* reflects the structure of covenant theology, with sections on the Covenant of Works and the Covenant of Grace. Its section on the doctrine of adoption reflects Westminster's unique inclusion of this element in a confessional statement along with justification and sanctification. In his exposition of the Second Commandment, Watson expresses what would later become 'the regulative principle of worship':

> Avoid superstition, which is a bridge that leads over to Rome. Superstition is bringing any ceremony, fancy, or innovation into God's worship which he never appointed. It is provoking God, because it reflects much upon his honour, as if he were not wise enough to appoint the manner of his own worship. He hates all strange fire to be offered in his temple, Lev x 1.[17]

In the Lord's Supper, there is a real spiritual presence of the Lord, in contrast to the Roman Catholic view of transubstantiation: 'We say, we receive Christ's body spiritually.'[18] Faith is the instrument for the believer's reception of Christ: 'Faith makes Christ present to the soul. The believer has a real presence in the sacrament.'[19] On the role of the Law in the believer's life, Watson

---

16. *Body of Divinity*, 251.
17. *Ten Commandments*, 63.
18. *Ten Commandments*, 225-26.
19. *Ten Commandments*, 237.

provides eight rules for rightly interpreting the Ten Commandments that correspond fairly closely to the eight rules of interpretation that are given in the Larger Catechism question 99. In almost all respects Watson's work is perfectly consistent with the Westminster Assembly's position.

In some places he so expands on the Shorter Catechism's teaching that he signals some personal distinctive tendencies. His exposition of the second petition of the Lord's Prayer, 'Thy kingdom come,' constitutes almost one-third of the volume on the Lord's Prayer and practically amounts to a theological treatise on its own. Here he rings the changes on the kingdom of grace and the kingdom of glory: 'The kingdom of grace is glory in the seed, and the kingdom of glory is grace in the flower. The kingdom of grace is glory in the daybreak, and the kingdom of glory is grace in the full meridian. The kingdom of grace is glory militant, and the kingdom of glory is grace triumphant.'[20] Towards the conclusion of this section he provides 'twenty-three persuasives or arguments to exert and put forth your utmost diligence for obtaining the kingdom of heaven'.[21] These are similar in spirit to the 'twenty directions' he gave to his parishioners 'as advice and counsel with you about your souls' in his second farewell sermon to the St. Stephen's, Walbrook congregation in the Great Ejection of 1662, and which can be given here more concisely:

1. I beseech you, keep your constant hours every day with God.
2. Get good books in your houses.
3. Have a care of your company.
4. Have a care whom you hear.

---

20. *Lord's Prayer*, 59.
21. *Lord's Prayer*, 145; cf. 136.

5. Follow after sincerity.
6. As you love your souls, be not strangers to yourselves.
7. Keep your spiritual watch.
8. You that are the people of God, often associate together.
9. Get your hearts screwed up above the world.
10. Trade much in the promises.
11. To all you that hear me, live in a calling.
12. Let me entreat you to join the first and second tables of the law together, piety to God, and equity to your neighbor.
13. Join the serpent and the dove together, innocence and prudence.
14. Be more afraid of sin than of suffering.
15. Take heed of idolatry.
16. Think not the worse of godliness because it is reproached and persecuted.
17. Think not the better of sin because it is in fashion.
18. In the business of religion serve God with all your might.
19. Do all the good you can to others as long as you live.
20. Every day think upon eternity.[22]

These counsels were given in a time of crisis, but they represent the advice of Watson for every day of a believer's life and also of *A Body of Divinity* for every generation in which it is read.

Three traits of *A Body of Divinity* stand out for application to the church of this generation of the twenty-first century. One is the importance of doctrinal truth. Watson's primary concern is for application to the Christian's life, yet he constantly recognizes that truth is the foundation for behavior, doctrine must come before life. Hence *A Body of Divinity* is a compact and readable version of systematic theology and Christian ethics.

---

22. *Sermons of the Great Ejection*, 137-45.

A second distinctive trait of great usefulness to Christians today is Watson's recurring emphasis on meditation. This is a key to private devotion. It is not enough to hear sermons, engage in small-group Bible studies, read the Word for oneself. One must also develop the ability to meditate on God's truth, to reflect on all that God has done, is doing, and will do, on those things that transcend the natural and material, on eternity.

A third characteristic distinctive of Watson's *A Body of Divinity* is his emphasis on what he terms 'the ordinances'. These are the means of grace – the Word, the sacraments, and prayer. And these are to be found preeminently in the fellowship of the church, in the regular services of worship on the Sabbath. In all these respects, *A Body of Divinity* is indeed a Puritan classic that has ministered God's truth to generations and can continue to do so for those still to come.

11

SYSTEM SUBSCRIPTION

1. *Introduction*

Events in recent decades have reminded us of the value of confessional statements for safeguarding the teaching of the truth of Scripture. Whether we think of the very recent struggles within the Christian Reformed Church, those somewhat earlier in the Southern Baptist Convention, or still others, we see the importance not only of affirming the inerrancy of Scripture, but also of declaring corporately what we believe Scripture teaches.

Throughout church history, creeds, confessions, and catechisms have served this purpose. When officially adopted by the church, such documents become dogma, constituting the tradition of that church.[1] Such creeds, confessions, and catechisms are clearly secondary to Scripture, which is the only infallible rule of faith and practice, a point underscored in the *Westminster Confession* in its first chapter on Scripture, in its declaration that

---

1. We should not be afraid of this term. As Jaroslav Pelikan has said, 'Tradition is the living faith of the dead,' as contrasted with traditionalism, which is the 'dead faith of the living' (*The Emergence of the Catholic Tradition* (100–500) [The Christian Tradition 1; Chicago: University of Chicago Press, 1971], 9).

synods and councils of the church can err and many have erred, and in several other places.

While different denominations handle their confessional statements differently, the method of subscription of American Presbyterianism, if properly understood and practiced, is the best method of safeguarding and promoting the teaching of the church's doctrine. In this essay, I will defend the view that we should require that those who are ordained subscribe to the system of doctrine taught in confessional standards (system subscription) by taking a primarily historical approach. First, I will use as my point of departure the second ordination vow as it appears in the Presbyterian Church in America's (PCA's) *Book of Church Order* (roughly equivalent to the second vow in the Orthodox Presbyterian Church [OPC]). Second, I will clarify the methodology of system subscription by construing the Adopting Act of 1729 and referring to the first heresy trial in American Presbyterianism. Third, I will attempt to articulate a philosophical principle for following such a practice, which is essentially that of Charles Hodge and of the Old Princeton Seminary. Fourth, I will discuss certain contemporary exceptions that have been or are taken to the doctrinal standards. Finally, I will discuss the reunion of the Old Side and New Side (1758–1788), which provides us with a positive model for today.

2. The Ordination Vow

The second ordination vow in the PCA's *Book of Church Order* reads as follows:

> Do you sincerely receive and adopt the *Confession of Faith* and *Catechisms* of this Church, as containing the system of doctrine taught in the Holy Scriptures; and do you further promise that if at any time you find yourself out of accord with any of the fundamentals of

this system of doctrine, you will on your own initiative, make known to your Presbytery [Session, in the case of ruling elders and deacons] the change which has taken place in your views since the assumption of this ordination vow? (BCO, 21-5, 24-5.)

This vow raises several points. First, the candidate for ordination adopts the *Westminster Confession* and *Catechisms* as his statement of faith as part of the corporate body of the denomination. That does not mean that he would necessarily say everything the same way as it is said in the Standards, but he stands with the church in testifying with this statement of faith.

Second, he adopts them as containing the system of doctrine taught in Scripture. That means that he affirms that the Bible teaches not merely various propositions and precepts, but a coherent system of doctrine, which the *Westminster Standards* embody.

Third, this system of doctrine has certain fundamentals, or essential doctrines, exceptions to which must be reported to the appropriate church judicatory. By implication, there might be exceptions to parts of the Standards which might not be deemed as fundamentals of the system of doctrine.

The language of the second ordination vow was adopted by the first General Assembly in 1788: 'Do you sincerely receive and adopt the confession of faith of this church, as containing the system of doctrine taught in the holy Scriptures?' At the same time, the Assembly approved amendments to Chapter XXXI as well as Chapters XX and XXIII, as well as one to the *Larger Catechism*, regarding the civil magistrate. The language 'system of doctrine', however, goes back at least to 1758, when the Old Side and New Side reunited as the Synod of New York and Philadelphia. The relevant parts of their joint declaratory statement were as follows:

Both Synods having always approved and received the Westminster Confession of Faith, and Larger and Shorter Catechisms, as an orthodox and excellent *system of Christian doctrine,* founded on the word of God, we do still receive the same as the confession of our faith, and also adhere to the plan of worship, government, and discipline, contained in the Westminster Directory, strictly enjoining it on all our members and probationers for the ministry, that they preach and teach according to the form of sound words in said Confession and Catechisms, and avoid and oppose all errors contrary thereto... .

The Synod of 1758 clearly viewed itself as in continuity with the Synods of the past in adopting the *Westminster Standards* as a whole, even though they were aware of the scruples previously allowed with regard to the civil magistrate. This leads us back to consideration of the Synod of 1729, when the American Presbyterian Church originally adopted the *Westminster Standards.*

3. The Adopting Act of 1729

Much controversy has swirled around the interpretation of the Adopting Act of 1729 whereby the General Synod of the Presbyterian Church in colonial America adopted the *Westminster Confession* and *Catechisms* as its doctrinal standards. In both the Old Side/New Side division of the eighteenth century and the Old School/New School division of the nineteenth century, the stricter subscriptionists have emphasized the actual adopting action on the afternoon of September 19, and the fact that the only exceptions taken were to portions of Chapters XX and XXIII of the *Confession* having to do with the civil magistrate. The other side has emphasized the 'Preliminary Act', adopted on the morning of the same day, which makes reference to 'all the essential and necessary articles'.

1. The Language of the Adopting Act

A balanced position must take the two together as the action of the Synod on a single day, the afternoon's adopting action as the concluding act and the morning's preliminary action as part of the immediate historical context. The reference to 'essential and necessary articles' occurs five times in the 'Preliminary Act', in which a method is proposed for dealing with any scruple a minister or candidate may have:

> [W]e ... agree that all the ministers of this Synod ... shall declare their agreement in, and approbation of, the Confession of Faith, with the Larger and Shorter Catechisms of the Assembly of Divines at Westminster, as being in all the essential and necessary articles, good forms of sound words and systems of Christian doctrine, and do also adopt the said Confession and Catechisms as the confession of our faith.
>
> [A]ll the Presbyteries ... shall always take care not to admit any candidate of the ministry ... but what declares his agreement in opinion with all the essential and necessary articles of said Confession... .
>
> [I]n case any minister ... or any candidate for the ministry, shall have any scruple with respect to any article or articles of said Confession or Catechisms, he shall at the time of his making said declaration declare his sentiments to the Presbytery or Synod, who shall, notwithstanding, admit him to the exercise of the ministry ..., if the Synod or Presbytery shall judge his scruple or mistake to be only about articles not essential and necessary in doctrine, worship, or government.
>
> But if the Synod or Presbytery shall judge such ministers or candidates erroneous in essential and necessary articles of faith, the Synod or Presbytery shall declare them uncapable of communion with them.
>
> And the Synod do solemnly agree, that none of us will traduce or use any opprobrious terms of those that

differ from us in these extra-essential and not necessary points of doctrine... .

The adopting action that afternoon was as follows:

> All the ministers of this Synod now present, except one that declared himself not prepared, viz., [eighteen names follow], after proposing all of the scruples that any of them had to make against any articles and expressions in the Confession of Faith, and Larger and Shorter Catechisms of the Assembly of Divines at Westminster, have unanimously agreed in the solution of those scruples, and in declaring the said Confession and Catechisms to be the confession of their faith, excepting only some clauses in the twentieth and twenty-third chapters, concerning which clauses the Synod do unanimously declare, that they do not receive those articles in any such sense as to suppose the civil magistrate hath a controlling power over Synods with respect to the exercise of their ministerial authority; or power to persecute any for their religion, or in any sense contrary to the Protestant succession to the throne of Great Britain.[2]

2. The Interpretation of the Adopting Act
Eighteen of the nineteen ministers present adopted the *Confession* and *Catechisms* as their confession. They provided a way for men to express their exceptions concerning articles of faith or doctrine including worship or government and concerning articles of the *Catechisms* as well as of the *Confession,* although the only unresolved exceptions involved portions of the *Confession* concerning the civil magistrate. The Westminster doctrinal standards were adopted with only one qualification concerning the civil magistrate, and a method was established for deciding

---

2. Quoted from the Synod minutes in Maurice W. Armstrong, Lefferts A. Loetscher, and Charles A. Anderson, eds., *The Presbyterian Enterprise* (Philadelphia: Westminster Press, 1956), 30-32.

whether exceptions violated essential and necessary articles – namely, to have the candidate or minister express his exception and let the Presbytery or Synod decide.

This construction is correct, as evidenced by the very 1727 overture proposing adoption of the *Westminster Standards* – from John Thompson, the leader on behalf of strict subscription – which overture included the possibility of teaching something contrary to the Standards if first discussed by Presbytery or Synod:

> [I]f any minister within our bounds shall take upon him to teach or preach anything contrary to any of the said articles, unless, first, he propose the said point to the Presbytery or Synod to be by them discussed, he shall be censured so and so.[3]

The Adopting Act thus was a compromise, satisfying both strict subscriptionists like John Thompson and also broader evangelicals like Jonathan Dickinson, because it provided a doctrinal standard with which all were in general accord, and it also provided a method of dealing with possible exceptions.[4] That it was a compromise also appears from the departure at this point of a few dissatisfied strict subscriptionists who joined some of the Scottish secessionist groups in America.[5]

3. The First American Heresy Trial

The Synod of 1730 sought to clear up some contemporary misunderstanding of the Adopting Act by passing unanimously the following:

---

3. Quoted in Charles Hodge, *Constitutional History of the Presbyterian Church of the United States of America* (Philadelphia: Presbyterian Board of Publication, 1851), 1:141.
4. This is the view of Charles Hodge (*Constitutional History,* 1:152) and also of John Murray ('Creed Subscription in The Presbyterian Church in the U.S.A.' [Unpublished article, Westminster Theological Seminary Library, 1979], 4).
5. Leonard J. Trinterud, *The Forming of an American Tradition: A Re-examination of Colonial Presbyterianism* (Philadelphia: Westminster Press, 1949), 49.

> Whereas some Persons have been dissatisfied at the Manner of wording our last years [sic] Agreement about the Confession &c: supposing some Expressions not sufficiently obligatory upon Intrants; overtured yt [sic] the Synod do now declare, that they understand those Clauses that respect the Admission of Intrants or Candidates in such a sense as to oblige them to receive and adopt the Confession and Catechisms at their Admission in the same Manner and as fully as the Members of the Synod did that were then present.[6]

This action makes it clear that a minister seeking to join the Presbyterian Church in America must adopt the *Westminster Confession* and *Catechisms*. What remained unclear is whether he may express scruples only with regard to the civil magistrate or any difference, letting the Synod or presbytery determine if such a difference is acceptable, being not essential or necessary.

These issues were resolved in the first American heresy trial involving Samuel Hemphill, an eloquent young preacher, who came to America from Northern Ireland and eventually garnered the support of Benjamin Franklin for his deistic and moralistic sentiments. He turned out, however, to have plagiarized his sermons from some leading Unitarians in England. In determining that he should be removed from the Presbyterian ministry, the Commission of Synod issued *A Vindication of the Reverend Commission*, in which crucial light is shed on the method of confessional subscription following the Adopting Act.

In particular, the Commission took umbrage with Hemphill's defense that, at the time of his ordination, '*all he declared to at his Admission into the Synod, were the*

---

6. Guy S. Klett, ed., *Minutes of the Presbyterian Church in America, 1706–1788* (Philadelphia: Presbyterian Historical Society, 1976), 108.
7. *A Vindication of the Reverend Commission of the Synod: in answer to some observations on their proceedings against the Reverend Mr. Hemphill* (Philadelphia: Andrew Bradford, 1735), 22.

fundamental Articles of the Confession of Faith.'[7] In fact, Hemphill had '(d)eclared his Assent to every Article in the *Westminster Confession of Faith,* and in the Larger and Shorter *Catechisms,* without one Exception' and had made assurances that 'he had before Subscribed the same in *Ireland*'.[8] In this context, the Synod summarizes the Adopting Act of 1729:

> [T]he Synod came to an unanimous Agreement about a Test of Orthodoxy, and of our Union in the essential Articles of Christianity, in the following method. It was agreed that all of the Ministers in this Synod, do Declare their Agreement in and Approbation of the *Confession of Faith,* with the Larger and Shorter *Catechisms* of the Assembly of Divines at *Westminster,* as being in all the essential and necessary Articles, good Forms of sound Words, and Systems of Christian Doctrine; and do adopt them as the Confession of their Faith, *&c.* And in Case any Minister of this Synod, or any Candidate of the Ministry, shall have any Scruple with respect to any Article or Articles of the said *Confession* or *Catechisms,* he shall at the Time of his making said Declaration, declare his Scruples to the Presbytery or Synod, who shall notwithstanding admit him to the Exercise of the Ministry within their Bounds, and to ministerial Communion; if the Synod or Presbytery shall judge his Scruple or Mistake to be only about Articles not essential or necessary, in Doctrine, Worship or Government.[9]

The Synod then goes on to explain that 'if Mr. *H-ll* had any Objection to make, against any Thing in the *Confession* or *Catechisms,* he should have particularly offered his Objections, and submitted it to the Judgment of the Synod, whether the Articles objected against, were essential and necessary, or not.' Hemphill's sincerity was then called into question because he took no exceptions

---
8. Ibid.
9. Ibid., 23.

to the Standards when given a chance to do so during his ordination examination. The Synod also refuted one of the arguments upon which Hemphill apparently relied:

> Nor is it any Excuse, that the Synod have not defined how many fundamental Articles there are in the *Confession*; since they have reserved to themselves the Liberty to judge upon each Occasion, what are, and what are not Fundamental.[10]

Here we have again the preliminary part of the Adopting Act from the morning of September 19, 1729, with two very significant aspects that shed light on how to construe the Adopting Act. First, five years after the Confession was adopted, with exceptions acknowledged only with regard to clauses in the Chapters XX and XXIII concerning the civil magistrate, Hemphill was asked not just whether he only took exception to Chapters XX and XXIII, but whether he took *any* exceptions to the *Westminster Standards.* Second, the Synod declined to define which articles are fundamental, but reserved the right to make that judgment on a case by case basis.

4. *Methodology for Subscription*
The methodology made clear in the Synod's response to the Hemphill case is the historic method of subscription in American Presbyterianism. It is also the method that we should employ today. The candidate professing to adopt the *Westminster Standards* should declare any exceptions that he may have, and then the Presbytery should decide whether his exceptions are such that he cannot be deemed as sincerely taking his ordination vow (e.g., the second ordination vow). If that is the case, then

---
10. Ibid., 24.

the Presbytery should not approve him for ordination. On the other hand, if the Presbytery determines that his exceptions do not represent a violation of his ordination vow, he should be ordained and should also be able to teach such exceptions, since he is conscience-bound to teach the whole counsel of God, as revealed in Scripture, whose authority he also has affirmed elsewhere in his ordination vows. But he should teach such exceptions with utmost sensitivity to the peace and purity of the church.

1. Four Practical Results
Four practical results follow from this view of subscription. First, it safeguards orthodoxy. By allowing – indeed requiring – that officer candidates declare exceptions to the *Westminster Standards*, we avoid a glib kind of total subscription and thus safeguard purity of doctrine by forcing all differences out into the open. Second, it promotes knowledge of the *Westminster Standards* since it compels candidates to study them seriously, carefully comparing their teachings with Scripture. Third, it promotes honesty by avoiding mental reservations as the presbytery – the court of the church most intimately acquainted with the candidate and most readily able to deal with stated exceptions – has the original responsibility to examine, always with the prospect of review by the higher court. Fourth, it promotes rule by Scripture. We value the *Westminster Standards* and sincerely receive and adopt them as the corporate confession to which we are personally committed; nevertheless, we must maintain a distinction between them (which are subject to correction and revision) and Scripture (the very Word of God, the only infallible rule of faith and practice).

2. Charles Hodge's Understanding

Any substantial discussion of confessional subscription in Presbyterianism necessarily entails the views of Charles Hodge (1797–1878).[11] This major Princeton theologian wrote significantly on the subject on at least four occasions, primarily in *The Constitutional History of the Presbyterian Church*, first published in 1839 (vol. I, 127ff.) and then subsequently in articles from the 1858 and 1867 *Princeton Review* reprinted in *The Church and Its Polity* (1879), as well as an earlier article in the *Princeton Review* of 1831.[12]

Some claim that Hodge changed his view from an earlier (*Constitutional History*) to a later (*Church Polity*) position on subscription;[13] however, he himself claimed in 1858 that his views were the same then as those he expressed in October 1831. At that earlier date, in an article entitled 'Remarks on Dr. Cox's Communication' in the old *Princeton Review,* Hodge opposed, on the one hand, the 'substance of doctrine' view and, on the other hand, the 'every proposition' view. What a Presbyterian minister subscribed to in the second ordination vow, he said, was the 'system of doctrine' of the *Westminster Standards*. According to Hodge:

> In professing to adopt the Confession of Faith as containing the system of doctrines taught in the sacred Scriptures, a man professes to believe the whole series of doctrines constituting that system, in opposition to every other. That is, he professes to believe the whole

---

11. Cf. Murray, 'Creed Subscription,' 8-10, 19-24. ('The position argued by Dr. Hodge is a thoroughly reasonable interpretation of the Question concerned. There can be, furthermore, little doubt but it is the understanding upon which generations of those subscribing have proceeded in adopting the formula of subscription' [19-20].)
12. See Hodge, *Constitutional History*, 1:127ff.; *The Church and Its Polity* (London: T. Nelson, 1879), 317-42; and 'Remarks on Dr. Cox's Communication,' *Biblical Repertory and Princeton Review* 3 (1831), 514-43.
13. Murray, loc. cit., 22; cf. also a paper, 'Confessional Subscription,' commended for study by the Tenth General Assembly of the Presbyterian Church in America (*Minutes of the Tenth General Assembly of the Presbyterian Church in America* [Atlanta: The Committee for Christian Education and Publications, 1982], 221).

series of doctrines which go to make up the Calvinistic system, in opposition to the Socinian, Pelagian, Semi-Pelagian, Arminian, or any opposite and inconsistent view of Christianity.[14]

When asked what latitude of explanation should be allowed, he answered: 'any which does not really affect the essentials of a doctrine.' And when further asked who is to judge, he answered that it is first a matter for every man to judge in the sight of God, but secondly, 'the Presbytery has a right of judgment in all such cases.'[15] He concludes this section by saying that the great mass of Presbyterians

> are ready to say that no man can consistently be a minister in our Church who rejects any one of the constituent doctrines of the Calvinistic system contained in the Confession of Faith; while from necessity and from principle, they are willing to allow any diversity of view and explanation not destructive of their nature, that is, not amounting to their rejection.[16]

The mature views of Hodge in 1858 were essentially the same as the views he set forth in 1831. In 1858 he opposed a 'substance of doctrine' view and also an 'every proposition' view. In his discussion of the Adopting Act of 1729, he equated the 'necessary and essential articles' with 'the system of doctrine'.[17] By equating these concepts, he did not mean the necessary and essential articles of the gospel, or of the Christian faith broadly understood, but rather, the necessary and essential articles of the Reformed, Calvinistic, or Augustinian faith – that is, the

---

14. Charles Hodge, 'Remarks on Dr. Cox's Communication,' *Biblical Repertory and Theological Review* 3:4 (October 1831), 522.
15. Ibid., 523.
16. Ibid., 524-25.
17. C. Hodge, *The Church and Its Polity* (London, England: 1879), 329.

system of doctrine of the *Westminster Standards*.[18] Hodge claimed that this was a matter of history, which his contemporaries could readily recognize.[19]

The *Westminster Confession,* he said, contains three classes of doctrines: (1) those common to all Christians as summed up in the ancient creeds, (2) those common to all Protestants and by which they are distinguished from Romanists, and (3) those peculiar to the Reformed Churches and by which they are distinguished from the Lutherans, from the Arminians, and from other sects of later origin. To all of these doctrines a Presbyterian minister subscribes when he adopts the system of doctrine of the *Westminster Standards.*

Did Hodge, then, hold a different view in 1839 when he wrote *The Constitutional History of the Presbyterian Church* as a justification of the Old School position? In this historical context, he stressed that 'the adopting act, as understood and intended by its authors, bound every new member to receive the *Confession of Faith* and *Catechisms,* in all their parts, except certain specified clauses in chapters twentieth and twenty-third'.[20] But in 1858 he wrote: 'It is a perfectly notorious fact, that there are hundreds of ministers in our Church, and that there always have been such ministers, who do not receive all the propositions contained in the *Confession of Faith* and *Catechisms.*'[21] When we examine *Constitutional History* further, however, we find that Hodge was perfectly consistent. He clearly regarded the 'Preliminary Act' as

---

18. Ibid., 323.
19. 'If the question, "What is the system of doctrine taught by the Reformed Churches?" be submitted to a hundred Romanists, to a hundred Lutherans, to a hundred members of the Church of England, or to a hundred sceptics, if intelligent and candid, they would all give precisely the same answer. There is not the slightest doubt or dispute among disinterested scholars as to what doctrines do, and what do not belong to the faith of the Reformed' (Ibid., 333).
20. C. Hodge, *The Constitutional History of the Presbyterian Church* (Philadelphia, Pa.: 1851), 1:155-56.
21. C. Hodge, *Church and Its Polity,* 330.

part of the Adopting Act of 1729, which he viewed as a compromise. His emphasis in interpreting the meaning of 'the essential and necessary articles' was that it meant, not the essential and necessary articles of the *gospel* (which was his understanding of the New School approach[22]), but the essential and necessary articles of the *Confession:*

> Ever since the solemn enactment under consideration, every new member or candidate for the ministry has been required to give his assent to this confession, as containing the system of doctrines taught in the word of God. He assents not merely to absolutely essential and necessary articles of the gospel, but to the whole concatenated statement of doctrines contained in the Confession.[23]

Hodge describes the system as 'concatenated', by which he means those doctrines connected as with a chain to form the Reformed or Calvinistic or Augustinian tradition. As shown above, Hodge's view did not move from an early, stricter position to a later, more lax one; rather, he maintained a position throughout his career which he believed was consistent with the language and intent of the Adopting Act of 1729 – that is, a subscription that required adoption of the *Westminster Standards* with its Calvinistic system of doctrine, although not necessarily with agreement to every proposition. The Presbytery would have to decide if a candidate's exception to the *Westminster Standards* was contrary to the system of doctrine. Hodge did not regard such matters

---

22. A. A. Hodge in Appendix I to his *A Commentary on the Confession of Faith* (Philadelphia, Pa.: 1869), 539-43, describes his father's discovery by 1870 that the New School, as represented by Dr. Henry B. Smith, had not held officially to such a 'substance of doctrine' view. Cf. George M. Marsden, *The Evangelical Mind and the New School Presbyterian Experience: A Case Study of Thought and Theology in Nineteenth-century America* (New Haven: Yale University Press, 1970), 215-27.
23. C. Hodge, *Constitutional History*, 1:183; cf. 149, 150, 151, 158, 159, 185 and 215 for further discussion of the 'essential and necessary articles'.

as 'vows and oaths, of the civil magistrate, of marriage' as essential to the system,[24] but he did so regard the distinctive doctrines of the Augustinian system.[25] In this context, he comments about the Augustinian system:

> That such is the system of doctrine of the Reformed church is a matter of history. It is the system which, as the granite formation of the earth, underlies and sustains the whole scheme of truth as revealed in the Scriptures, and without which all the rest is as drifting sand. It has been from the beginning the life and soul of the church, taught explicitly by our Lord himself, and more fully by his inspired servants, and always professed by a cloud of witnesses in the church. It has moreover ever been the esoteric faith of true believers, adopted in their prayers and hymns, even when rejected from their creeds. It is this system which the Presbyterian Church is pledged to profess, to defend, and to teach; and it is a breach of faith to God and man if she fails to require a profession of this system by all whom she receives or ordains as teachers and guides of her people. It is for the adoption of the Confession of Faith in this sense that the Old-school have always contended as a matter of conscience.[26]

Hodge's view, then, is consistently contrasted with a 'substance of doctrine' view, or what is essential to Christianity or the gospel (which is what he understood the New School view to be in the nineteenth century), and with an 'every proposition' view. What one is subscribing to in adopting the *Westminster Standards* is the Reformed system of doctrine, with every doctrine essential to that system.

---

24. C. Hodge, *Church and Its Polity*, 31.
25. Ibid., 338-40. Hodge made further comments on subscription in his articles, 'Presbyterian Reunion,' *Princeton Review* 40 (Jan. 1868), 57ff.; 'The New Basis of Reunion,' *Princeton Review* 41; (July 1869), 462-66; 'Retrospect on the History of the Princeton Review,' *Biblical Repertory and Princeton Review: Index Volume, 1825-1868* (Philadelphia, Charles Scribner and Co., 1871), 1-39, esp. 22-26.
26. *Biblical Repertory and Princeton Review* 39 (1867), 511-12.

Hodge's view was the Old School position of Old Princeton, as represented also by B. B. Warfield, who held that the ordination vow is 'a vow demanding of all who accept our *Confession of Faith* that they accept it as a system of doctrine; and that they affirm by their acceptance of it that this system of doctrine is the system of doctrine that is taught in Holy Scripture.'[27] The language 'only as containing the system of doctrine taught in the Holy Scriptures,' according to Warfield, means:

> 'only in this sense, namely, as containing the *system* of doctrine' – that is to say, not in its every proposition or mode of statement, but only in the system of doctrine it contains, to wit, the Calvinistic system. There is, so far as we know, no difference of opinion as to the import of the ordination vow in our Churches: it is everywhere understood and administered as binding those taking it merely to the system and not to the detailed manner of stating that system; but as binding them strictly to the system in its integrity and in its entirety. As such it has been justly lauded as combining in itself all reasonable liberty with all reasonable strictness – binding as it does to the great system of doctrine expressed in the Confession with absolute strictness, and yet leaving room for all possible individual preferences in modes of conceiving and stating this system. Under this combined strictness and liberty every genuine form of Calvinism has an equal right of existence under the Confession.... But beyond the limits of generic Calvinism the right of adoption ceases. Our vow of ordination is not a solemn farce: and the terms of our adoption of the Confession are not so phrased as to enable us to seem to adopt it while not adopting it at all.[28]

---

27. Benjamin B. Warfield, 'The Proposed Union with the Cumberland Presbyterians,' *Princeton Theological Review* 2 (1904): 295-316, quotation on pages 314-15.
28. Ibid.

In an earlier article, Warfield warned of an overly strict subscription as being then practiced in Scotland and concluded:

> We observe, then, ... [t]hat so long as we remain a Calvinistic Church, the American Church, with its free and yet safe formula of acceptance of the Confession, is without the impulse which drives on some other churches to seek to better their relation to the Standards. We have always accepted the Confession only for 'the system of doctrine' contained in it, and hence since 1729 have possessed what the great Scotch churches are now seeking after.[29]

For Warfield, then, American Presbyterianism excelled Scottish Presbyterianism by requiring that those ordained to office subscribe to the system of doctrine contained in the *Westminster Standards*.

5. Examples Facing the Twentieth-Century Church

Having demonstrated that system subscription has been the consistent view of American Presbyterianism, we can learn from a few examples the twentieth century church has faced.

1. J. Gresham Machen on Premillennialism

In *The Presbyterian Guardian*, J. Gresham Machen wrote that though the *Westminster Standards* oppose Premillennialism, a Premillennialist in the Presbyterian Church of America (now the OPC) can still hold to the system of doctrine taught in those standards:

> It is true, the Westminster Confession of Faith and Catechisms teach not the Premillennial view but a view that is opposed to the Premillennial view. That

---

29. *Presbyterian Review* 10, no. 40 (Oct. 1889), 656-57.

is particularly plain in the Larger Catechism (Q. 87 and 88).

But subscription to the Westminster Standards in The Presbyterian Church of America is not to every word in those Standards, but only to the *system* of doctrine which the Standards contain.

The real question, then, is whether a person who holds the Premillennial view can hold that system. Can a person who holds the Premillennial view be a true Calvinist; can he, in other words, hold truly to the Calvinistic or Reformed system of doctrine which is set forth in the Westminster Standards? We think that he can; and for that reason we think that Premillennialists as well as those who hold the opposing view may become ministers or elders or deacons in The Presbyterian Church of America....

It is no new thing to take this position regarding creed-subscription. It is the position which has long been taken by orthodox Calvinistic theologians.[30]

2. Amendments Concerning the Civil Magistrate

The American Presbyterian Church amended parts of Chapters XX, XXIII, and XXXI of the *Westminster Confession* in the late eighteenth century, but somehow neglected to amend the Larger Catechism Q. 191 on the second petition of the Lord's Prayer: '... we pray that...the Church [may be]...countenanced and maintained by the civil magistrate....' This is one statement to which I have taken exception. (Other amendments have pertained to the Pope as the Antichrist and to degrees of affinity and consanguinity in marriage in Chapter XXIV.4.)

3. Pictures of Jesus

Although I do not advocate pictures or portrayals of Jesus, I find it difficult to be in accord with *Larger Catechism*

---

30. 'Premillennialism,' *The Presbyterian Guardian* (October 24, 1936), 21.

Q. 109 on sins forbidden in the second commandment: ('...the making any representation of God, ...of any of the three Persons, either *inwardly in our mind,* or outwardly in any kind of image ...'), when reading such a passage as John's vision of our Lord in Revelation 1:10-16. I believe the *Larger Catechism* statement represents a Puritan over-reaction to Roman Catholic abuses, and therefore, I have declared an exception to this particular part of the Standards.

4. Sabbath Practice
A more common example of a modern-day exception concerns Sabbath observance. I believe it is incumbent upon candidates, elders, and ministers in Presbyterian churches to be sabbatarian – that is, to hold to the continuing relevance of the fourth commandment. The *Larger Catechism* QQ. 117 and 119, however, appear to me to go beyond the teaching of Scripture with regard to some 'recreations as are on other days lawful'. We should seek to maintain the spirit of the Sabbath as our Lord Jesus taught and exemplified it in Mark 2:23–3:6.

6. The Model of the 1758 Reunion of Old Side and New Side
Not quite a century after the reunion of Old Side and New Side in 1758, Hodge could write of the united Synod's five-page, eight-point statement:

> This noble declaration is for our church what the declaration of independence is for our country. It is a promulgation of first principles; a setting forth of our faith, order, and religion, as an answer to those who question us. It is the foundation of our ecclesiastical compact, the bond of our union. Those who adhere to the principles here laid down, are entitled to a standing in our church; those who desert them, desert not merely

the faith but the religion of our fathers, and have no right to their name or their heritage.[31]

What this declaration represented was a reaffirmation of both emphases that the two sides had stressed – the Old Side doctrinal orthodoxy of adherence to the *Westminster Standards* and the New Side commitment to revivalistic preaching for the sake of evangelism. The number of ministers in the New Side had almost quadrupled during the seventeen-year division, but such leaders as Gilbert Tennent had come to recognize the evils of extreme enthusiasm in religion and of the censorious spirit of itinerant preachers who would denounce the character of the local minister. Thus, the reunion represented a renewed commitment to both orthodox doctrine and spiritual experience with consequent obedient life and witness. The declaration stated:

> Accordingly we unanimously declare our serious and fixed resolution, by divine aid, to take heed to ourselves that our hearts be upright, our discourse edifying, and our lives exemplary for purity and godliness; to take heed to our doctrine that it be not only orthodox, but evangelical and spiritual, tending to awaken the secure to a suitable concern for their salvation, and to instruct and encourage sincere Christians.[32]

The statement concluded on this note:

> Finally, we earnestly recommend it to all under our care, that instead of indulging a contentious disposition, they would love each other with a pure heart fervently, as brethren who profess subjection to the same Lord, adhere to the same faith, worship, and government, and entertain the same hope of glory. And we desire

---
31. *The Constitutional History of the Presbyterian Church in the United States of America* (Philadelphia: Presbyterian Board of Publications, 1851), 281.
32. Ibid., 280-81.

that they would improve the present union for their mutual edification, combine to strengthen the common interests of religion, and go hand in hand in the path of life; which we pray the God of all grace would please to effect, for Christ's sake. AMEN.[33]

This prayer appears to have been answered, as during the next thirty years, the Presbyterian Church experienced rapid growth and an influence surpassed perhaps only by the Congregationalists. Concerning the unity of the Synod of New York and Philadelphia in this period, Hodge comments: 'It is probable there never was a period of equal length in the history of our church in which there was such a general and cordial agreement among our ministers on all doctrinal subjects.' As he concludes his survey of the Synod minutes of this period, he states:

> The members of this Synod were, to a remarkable degree, harmonious in their doctrinal views. There is no indication of diversity of opinion on any important subject; there were no doctrinal controversies, and but one instance of the infliction of censure for erroneous opinions. Besides this negative evidence, we have the positive proof to be found in the frequent declarations of the adherence of the Synod to the Westminster Confession, and the unanimous adoption of that formula as a part of the new constitution.[34]

This period would seem to provide us with an exemplary model, to unify Presbyterians who are agreed on the truth of Scripture and committed to spread the gospel.

---

33. Ibid.
34. Ibid., 281.

12

THE SAMUEL HEMPHILL HERESY CASE (1735) AND THE HISTORIC METHOD OF SUBSCRIBING TO THE WESTMINSTER STANDARDS

On Monday morning, September 22, 1735, the Synod of the Presbyterian Church, meeting in Philadelphia, received the following letter:

> To the Revd. Members of ye Synod,
> By way of Answer to ye Notification which I received Saturday last, I have only to observe, yt ye Dispute between the Synod and me being made publick in the World, which was first begun by the Commission, what I have at present to offer to the Synod, is contained in an Answr. to the Vindication of the Revd. Commision now in the Press and will be speedily published, and yt I despise the Synod's claim of Authority.
>
> > Your humble Servt.
> > Sam: Hemphill
> > Monday morning
> > P.S. I shall think you'll do me a deal of Honour if you entirely excommunicate me.[1]

When the promised publication appeared on October 30, it included this 'Postscript':

---

1. Guy S. Klett, ed., *Minutes of the Presbyterian Church In America, 1706-1788* (Philadelphia: Presbyterian Historical Society, 1976), 130.

Since the writing of this, Mr. *Hemphil* has been inform'd that the Rev. Synod has with great Formality, Gravity and Solemnity, excommunicated him entirely out of their Society. As Gratitude is a Debt always due for a Favour bestow'd, and as expelling the said *Hemphil* out of so bad Company, was the greatest Favour and Honour these Rev. Gentlemen were capable of doing him, he takes publick Opportunity of thanking them very heartily for it.[2]

Such was the ultimately bitter tenor of the controversy surrounding the first heresy trial in American Presbyterian history. Samuel Hemphill himself appears on the scene for only about a year, but because his trial and the ensuing literary debate involved such significant figures as the young Benjamin Franklin and Jonathan Dickinson, the Hemphill case has attracted some attention from scholars.[3] What has been only casually noticed, however, is the light this controversy sheds on the understanding of subscription to the Westminster Confession and Catechisms only six years after the Adopting Act of 1729.[4]

---

2. [Benjamin Franklin], *A Defence of the Rev. Mr. Hemphill's Observations: or, An Answer to the Vindication of the Reverend Commission* (Philadelphia: B. Franklin, 1735), 48. Franklin's four published writings on behalf of Hemphill can also be found in *The Papers of Benjamin Franklin*, ed. Leonard W. Labaree et al., 24 vols. (New Haven: Yale University Press, 1959-), II, 28-33, 37-65, 66-88, and 90-126.
3. The following all deal with the Hemphill case primarily out of interest in Franklin: Merton A. Christensen 'Franklin on the Hemphill Trial: Deism Versus Presbyterian Orthodoxy,' *William and Mary Quarterly*, Third Series, X (July 1953), 422-40; Alfred Owen Aldridge, *Benjamin Franklin and Nature's God* (Durham, N.C.: Duke University Press, 1967), 86-98; Melvin H. Buxbaum, *Benjamin Franklin and the Zealous Presbyterians* (University Park and London: Pennsylvania State University Press, 1975), 76-115; and Elizabeth E. Dunn, 'From a Bold Youth to a Reflective Sage: A Revelation of Benjamin Franklin's Religion,' *Pennsylvania Magazine of History and Biography*, CXI (1987), 501-24.
4. Charles Augustus Briggs gave it some attention in connection with subscription in *American Presbyterianism: Its Origin and Early History* (New York: Charles Scribner's Sons, 1885), 230-35. Leonard J. Trinterud, *The Forming of an American Tradition: A Re-examination of Colonial Presbyterianism* (Philadelphia: Westminster Press, 1949), 62-63, discusses it only briefly. Details on Hemphill and the case can be found in Richard Webster, *A History of the Presbyterian Church in America, From*

The Samuel Hemphill Heresy Case (1735)

From nearly the very beginning the significance of the Adopting Act has been variously understood. On the one hand strict subscriptionists have emphasized the Synod's action of the afternoon of September 19, 1729 in which the ministers declared the Westminster Confession and Catechisms to be the confession of their faith, excepting only some clauses in the twentieth and twenty-third chapters pertaining to the civil magistrate.[5] On the other hand there are those who have emphasized the action of the morning of that same day in which there was repeated reference to 'essential and necessary' articles of faith and the possibility of expressing scruples with regard to 'extra-essential and not-necessary points' of doctrine.[6] The Synod of 1730 sought to clear up some

---

Its Origin Until the Year 1760, with Biographical Sketches of Its Early Ministers (Philadelphia: Joseph M. Wilson, 1857), 416-20 and 110-15. Most recently the trial has been discussed by Marilyn J. Westerkamp, *Triumph of the Laity: Scots-Irish Piety and the Great Awakening, 1625-1760* (New York and Oxford: Oxford University Press, 1988), 158-61.

5. Klett, *Minutes*, 104. Old School Presbyterian theologians have generally taken this view. The views of Charles Hodge are discussed in William S. Barker, 'Subscription to the Westminster Confession and Catechisms,' *Presbuterion: The Covenant Seminary Review*, X (1984), 11-14. For James Henley Thornwell, see his *Collected Writings* (Edinburgh: Banner of Truth, 1974) IV, 313, 366-67, 442-43, and 493-94. More recent examples would be Morton H. Smith, *How the Gold is Become Dim: The Decline of the Presbyterian Church U.S., as reflected in Its Assembly Actions*, 2nd ed. (Jackson, Miss.: Steering Committee for a Continuing Presbyterian Church, 1973), 38-39; and George W. Knight, III, 'Subscription to the Westminster Confession of Faith and Catechisms,' *Presbuterion: The Covenant Seminary Review*, X (1984), 21-23.

6. Klett, *Minutes*, 103-04. Those who understand the Adopting Act in this way would include Frederick W. Loetscher, 'The Adopting Act,' *Journal of the Presbyterian Historical Society*, XIII (Dec. 1929), 337-55; Trinterud, *Forming*, 48-49, 66-67; James Hastings Nichols, 'Colonial Presbyterianism Adopts Its Standards,' *JPHS*, 34 (March 1956), 53-66, and Thomas A. Schafer, 'The Beginnings of Confessional Subscription in the Presbyterian Church,' *McCormick Quarterly*, 19 (Jan. 1966), 102-19. James R. Payton, Jr. 'Background and Significance of the Adopting Act of 1729,' 131-45 in *Pressing Toward the Mark: Essays Commemorating Fifty Years of the Orthodox Presbyterian Church*, ed. Charles G. Dennison and Richard C. Gamble (Philadelphia: Committee for the Historian of the Orthodox Presbyterian Church, 1986) agrees with this interpretation in his extended review of Samuel Miller's *Letters to Presbyterians on the Present Crisis in the Presbyterian Church in the United States* (Philadelphia: A. Finley, 1833) that ran in the Christian Advocate from July 1833 to April, 1834; cf. XI, 364-66, 411-13 (Aug., Sept., 1833).

contemporary misunderstanding of the Adopting Act by passing unanimously the following:

> Whereas some Persons have been dissatisfied at the manner of wording our last years Agreement about the Confession & c: supposing some Expressions not sufficiently obligatory upon Intrants; overtured yt the Synod do now declare, that they understand those Clauses that respect the Admission of Intrants or Candidates in such a sense as to oblige them to receive and adopt the Confession and Catechisms at their Admission in the same Manner and as fully as the members of the Synod did that were then present.[7]

This action makes it clear that a minister seeking to join the Presbyterian Church in America must adopt the Westminster Confession and Catechisms. What remains unclear is whether he may express scruples only with regard to the passages concerning the civil magistrate or that he may express whatever differences he may have and let the Synod or a presbytery determine if such a difference is acceptable, being not essential or necessary.

Such was the situation when Samuel Hemphill was received by the Synod in 1734. In the year following his trial the Synod of 1736 sought to tighten up the matter of confessional subscription by adopting without dissent the following overture:

> That the Synod do declare, yt inasmuch as we understand yt many Persons of our Perswasion both more lately and formerly have been offended with some Expressions or Distinctions in the first or preliminary act of our Synod, contained in the printed Paper, relating to our receiving or adopting the westminster Confession and

---

7. Klett, *Minutes*, 108.

Catechisms & c: That in order to remove said offence and all Jealousies yt have arisen or may arise in any of our People's minds on occasion of sd. Distinction and Expressions, the Synod doth declare, yt the Synod have adopted and still do adhere to the westminster Confession Catechisms and Directory without the least variation or alteration, and without any Regard to sd. Distinctions. And we do further declare yt this was our meaning and true Intent in out first adopting of sd. Confession, as may particularly appear by our adopting act which is as followeth.[8]

And then the afternoon action of September 19, 1729 is quoted without the morning's preliminary action referring to essential and necessary articles. Charles Augustus Briggs comments, 'This act does not antagonize the Adopting Act, but it points in the direction of strict subscription,' and he shows in a lengthy footnote how those in attendance at the 1736 Synod were predominately of the stricter subscription viewpoint.[9] James Hastings Nichols, however, says that this 1736 action 'in effect constituted a substitute constitution',[10] and Thomas Schafer concludes that in '1736 the subscriptionists had scuttled the 1729 agreement....'[11]

Is there a way to harmonize the actions of 1736 and of 1730 with the whole Adopting Act of 1729, indeed of harmonizing the morning and the afternoon actions of 1729? Exponents of a broad or looser style of subscription have tended to champion the preliminary action of the 1729 Synod as representing the church's spirit of genuine compromise and to see the 1736 action as a one-sided decision engineered by a momentarily dominant minority faction. On the other side, exponents of a very

---

8. Klett, *Minutes*, 141.
9. Briggs, *American Presbyterianism*, 235-38.
10. Nichols, 'Colonial Presbyterianisms,' 61-62.
11. 'The Beginnings,' 118.

strict style of subscription have tended to emphasize the 1736 action as consistent with the afternoon adopting action of 1729, thus neglecting the morning's preliminary action as representing the sentiments of those like Jonathan Dickinson, architect of compromise, who had earlier opposed subscription.

It seems strange, however, that the unanimous actions of church courts within a short span of time, or indeed on the morning and afternoon of the same day, should be contradictory of each other. There were differing convictions about confessional subscription within the Synod, but there was a larger measure of unity than has usually been recognized. This unity revolved around the method of subscription. The controversy over Hemphill shows the particular procedure of subscription that evidently satisfied both sides at the time.

Because it is critical to a proper understanding of early American Presbyterian confessional subscription to see that the view ascribed to Dickinson was not merely his own but became the expression of the entire Synod, and because some of the authorities on Franklin have not fully understood the Presbyterian Church's procedure in the controversy, the sequence of events and the authorship of the documents relevant to the Hemphill case are here laid out in great detail in the first section. Then in the second section, the specific role of the Westminster Confession in the controversy is described.

1. *The Sequence of Events*

It is important, first of all, to identify the main figures in the controversy and to place the documents properly in the sequence of events. Who was Samuel Hemphill? Precious little is known about him, and no one seems to know what became of him after 1735. Franklin says simply, in his *Autobiography*, 'On our Defeat he left us, in search elsewhere of better Fortune....'[12] Franklin does furnish some further information about his age, style, and origins:

> About the Year 1734, there arrived among us from Ireland, a young Presbyterian Preacher named Hemphill, who delivered with a good Voice, & apparently extempore, most excellent Discourses, which drew together considerable Numbers of different Persuasions, who join'd in admiring them. Among the rest I became one of his constant Hearers, his Sermons pleasing me, as they had little of the dogmaticall kind, but inculcated strongly the Practice of Virtue, or what in the religious Stile are called good works.[13]

A similar version of the facts, from quite a different angle, is provided by the senior pastor of the (First) Presbyterian Church of Philadelphia, Jedidiah Andrews:

> There came from Ireland one Mr Hemphill at yt Time to sojourn in Town for the winter, as was pretended, till he could fall into Business among some People in the Country (tho' some think he had other views at first, considering the Infidel disposition of too many here). Some desiring I shd have assistance and some leading Men not disaffected to the way of Deism so much as they shd be, yt Man was imposed upon me and the Congregatn. Most of the best of the People were soon so dissatisfied yt they would not come to meeting. Free-thinkers, Deists and Nothings getting a scout of him flocked to hear. I attended all winter, but making Complaint brought the Ministrs together, who acted as is shown in the books I send you. Never was there such a Tryal known in the American world.[14]

---

12. *The Autobiography of Benjamin Franklin: A Genetic Test*, ed. J. A. Leo Lemay and P. M. Zall (Knoxville: University of Tenn. Press, 1981), 97.
13. Ibid., 96.
14. Letter of June 14, 1735 from Jedidiah Andrews to 'Reverend and Dear Sir' (a clergyman in the Boston area, but not Benjamin Colman or Thomas Prince since they are both referred to in the final sentence); photocopy in the Presbyterian Historical Society, Philadelphia.

Records of the Irish Presbyterian Church show that Hemphill, having studied at Glasgow, was received by the Presbytery of Strabane 'on first tryals' by June of 1729, was licensed and had 'subscribed according to order' by June of 1730. On June 18, 1734 Strabane Presbytery reported to the General Synod at Londonderry that 'they have in tryals for ordination Mr Saml Hemphill; who designs to pass into the Plantations in America.'[15]

The minutes of the Synod of Philadelphia show that he was present in September of 1734 and 'being recommended by the Presbry of Straban in Ireland, to all their Revnd. Brethren where the Providence of God shall call him; and he also bringing ample and satisfactory Certificates from the same Presbry of his Qualifications for and Ordination to the sacred Ministry, he is, upon his Desire, admitted a member of this Synod, and recommended to the Regards and Assistance of which so ever of our Presbry's his Abode shall be fixed among.' At that same meeting Hemphill and three others 'declared for and adopted the Westminster Confession Catechisms and Directory commonly annexed, the former as the Confession of their faith and the latter as the Guide of their Practice in Matters of Discipline as far as may be agreeable to the Rules and Prudence & c: as in the adopting Acts of this Synod is directed.'[16] But Hemphill was accompanied not only by satisfactory certification. An Irish minister named Patrick Vance had also sent word to his brother-in-law in America, a Mr. J. Kilpatrick, that Hemphill's doctrine was not sound.[17]

---

15. *Records of the General Synod of Ulster, From 1691 to 1820*, 3 vols. (Belfast, 1890–98), II, 140, 149, 189. Cf. Briggs, *American Presbyterianism*, 230 footnote: He subscribed ... according to the Synodical formula: 'I believe the Westminster Confession of Faith to be agreeable to the Scriptures of the Old and New Testaments and founded thereupon and as such I own it to be the confession of my faith. Subscribed Sam. Hemphill.' (See MS. Minutes Presbytery of Strabane, McGee College Library, Londonderry.)'
16. Klett, *Minutes*, 121.

When Hemphill preached two sermons to the people of New London in Chester County, he was summoned before the Presbytery of New Castle but was cleared.[18] By November of 1734 he was serving as Jedidiah Andrews' assistant in the (First) Presbyterian Church of Philadelphia and attracting people such as Franklin. Other than his role in the trial itself and the following literary debate little else is known about him.[19]

Benjamin Franklin was twenty-nine years old at the time of the Hemphill trial, but was already well established in Philadelphia with a successful printing business. He was a leading member of the Junto club, founder of the Philadelphia Library Company, owner of the *Pennsylvania Gazette* and of his *Poor Richard's Almanac*, and a grand master of the Masons.[20] He had previously attended the Presbyterian Church, once for five Sundays in a row, but found the preaching of Andrews doctrinal and unedifying. The arrival of Hemphill in the pulpit kindled his interest, and it is in accord with the evidence to see him as the ringleader of those in support of Hemphill. He reports on events at the trial as though present,[21] and it is easy to imagine him as

---

17. [Benjamin Franklin], *Some Observations on the Proceedings Against the Rev. Mr. Hemphill; With a Vindication of His Sermons*, 2nd ed. (Philadelphia: B. Franklin, 1735), 3-4. The Irish church subsequently heard charges against Vance for having 'written to the prejudice of Mr. Hemphill's character' (*Records of the General Synod of Ulster*, II, 208-9, 215, 223). Vance defended himself as having evidence, and eventually he was vindicated by the Sub-Synod of Derry and the General Synod (Westerkamp, *Triumph*, 158).
18. [Franklin], *Some Observations*, 5. Cf. Webster, *A History of the Presbyterian Church*, 11.
19. There is a Samuel Hemphill in the *Dictionary of National Biography*, who is a contemporary but somewhat older. He received an M.A. from Glasgow College on April 30, 1716, just eight weeks after the date that Briggs reports our Samuel Hemphill entered there. He was ordained on December 24, 1718 by Augher Presbytery, served congregations in Castleblayney and Antrim, and died on March 28, 1741. Ironically, he engaged in the controversy over subscription in the Irish church, opposing the anti-subscriptionists.
20. Buxbaum, *Benjamin Franklin*, 76-77.
21. [Franklin], *Some Observations*, 10.

practically the counsel for the defense. Many years later he would write in his *Autobiography*: 'I became his zealous Partisan, and contributed all I could to raise a Party in his Favour; and we combated for him a while with some Hopes of Success. There was much Scribbling pro & con upon the Occasion; and finding that tho' an elegant Preacher he was but a poor Writer, I lent him my Pen and wrote for him two or three Pamphlets....'[22] Experts on Franklin are agreed that the writing on Hemphill's side are properly to be ascribed to Franklin, in large part if not in toto.[23] The characteristic Franklin wit shines throughout the pamphlets, but there is a strident tone, particularly in his final piece, *A Defence of the Rev. Mr. Hemphill's Observations*, that is quite different from the persona portrayed in his *Autobiography*, written between 1771 and 1790, of a benevolent Deist who is above the hairsplitting of religious controversy.[24]

The other main actor in the Hemphill case is the Commission of Synod. Several misunderstandings about the Commission contribute to Melvin Buxbaum's regarding it as unfair in its treatment of Hemphill.[25] The Commission of Synod, from 1720 on, was a standing body designed to act with the authority of Synod between the annual meetings of the General Synod.[26] Each year a number of ministers would be chosen to

---

22. *Autobiography*, 96.
23. See the editorial comments in Volume II of *The Papers of Benjamin Franklin*; Buxbaum, *Benjamin Franklin*, 234 n. 140; Christensen, 'Franklin on the Hemphill Trial,' 434.
24. This is the contention throughout Buxbaum's *Benjamin Franklin*. Elizabeth Dunn comments: 'Ethics often occupied his thoughts, and he believed Hemphill's preaching to be more useful than the teaching of religious dogma for inculcating virtue in the populace. At the same time, he carefully avoided directly challenging the religious establishment of Philadelphia' ('From a Bold Youth,' 516), but that last sentence hardly accords with *A Defence of the Rev. Mr. Hemphill's Observations*.
25. Buxbaum, *Benjamin Franklin*, 95, 102, 111, 115, and 233 n. 81.
26. Charles Hodge, *The Constitutional History of the Presbyterian Church in the United States of America*, 2 vols. In 1 (Philadelphia: Presbyterian Board of Publication, 1851), I, 112. Klett, *Minutes*, 47.

serve in this capacity during the intervening months. On September 19, 1734 the following were appointed to the Commission for the year ensuing: Jedidiah Andrews, James Anderson, John Thomson, George Gillespie, Robert Cross, Jonathan Dickinson, John Pierson, Thomas Creaghead, and the moderator of Synod, who that year was Ebenezer Pemberton.[27] When Andrews brought charges against his younger associate Hemphill, he himself did not serve on the Commission – in fact, having presented the charge he 'left all to the Ministrs and meddled no more', describing himself as 'weary of these things'.[28]

Another significant thing to note about the Commission is that Jonathan Dickinson was not present to participate in the trial. The seven remaining regular members of the Commission were joined, however, by thirteen correspondents who participated in voting upon the verdict. These included William Tennent Sr., David Evans (who served as Clerk), Richard Treat, Adam Boyd, Joseph Houston, Andrew Archbold, Robert Jamison, Thomas Evans, Alexander Hutchison, Robert Cathcart, Nathaniel Hubbel, Gilbert Tennent, and William Tennent Jr.[29] These twenty ministers were more than half of the thirty-nine who were then members of the Synod, and they represent a fair balance of whatever factions may have existed at that time. In view of what the Commission would subsequently say about subscription, it is significant that John Thomson, the original proposer of subscription, was a member. When the Commission decided to suspend Hemphill, the minutes note: 'This is the unanimous Determination

---

27. Klett, *Minutes*, 119, 118.
28. Andrews, Letter of June 14, 1735.
29. *An Extract of the Minutes of the Commission of the Synod, Relating to the Affair of the Reverend Mr. Hemphil* (Philadelphia: Andrew Bradford, 1735), 3. (Webster, *A History of the Presbyterian Church*, 417, fails to include William Tennent, Jr.)

of the whole Commission and all the Correspondents,' and they gave thanks 'that in the whole Transaction we have not had one dissenting Vote'.[30]

It is important at this point to put the documents pertaining to the Hemphill affair in proper logical order. First is Franklin's *Dialogue between Two Presbyterians*, printed in *The Pennsylvania Gazette* on April 10, 1735, just one week before the Commission meeting concerning Hemphill was to begin. In it Mr. S. discusses with Mr. T. whether the Synod 'are going to persecute, silence and condemn a good Preacher [Mr. H], for exhorting them to be honest and charitable to one another and the rest of Mankind'.[31] The Commission began its sessions, on Thursday, April 17 and continued to Saturday, April 26 except for Sunday, April 20, when Robert Cross and Ebenezer Pemberton preached before the Commission 'and a very numerous audience, the Person accus'd being likewise present....'[32] *An Extract of the Minutes of the Commission of the Synod, Relating to the Affair of The Reverend Mr. Samuel Hemphill* was published in the first week of May, with the reason given as follows: 'The late Tryal of the Reverend Mr. Samuel Hemphill, before the Commission of the Synod, being the Subject of much Discourse; we thought it necessary to publish our Minutes upon that Affair, to prevent any Misrepresentations, and unjust Aspersions that might be cast upon us, and to give the World a View of the Grounds which we went upon in the Censure we have passed upon him.'[33] The verdict agreed upon was 'That Mr. Hemphill be suspended from all the parts of his ministerial Office until the next meeting of our Synod, and that it be referred

---

30. *An Extract*, 13.
31. *The Papers of Benjamin Franklin*, II, 31.
32. Robert Cross, *The Danger of perverting the Gospel of Christ, Represented in a Sermon preach'd before the Commission of Synod at Philadelphia. April 20th, 1735* (New York: John Peter Zenger, 1735), 30.
33. *An Extract*, 2.

to the Synod to judge, when met, whether the Suspension shall be continued or taken off, or whatever else shall be judged needful to be done, according as things shall then appear: And accordingly we do suspend the said Mr. Samuel Hemphill as above.'[34]

On June 14, as already mentioned, Jedidiah Andrews wrote a letter to a fellow clergyman in the Boston area, sending three copies of a book – evidently *An Extract of the Minutes of the Commission* – one each for his recipient, Benjamin Colman, and Thomas Prince, commenting that 'It has been, since last November, the most trying Time with me yt ever I met with in all my Life,' and indicating that: 'there is in the Press an Answr to the *Abstract* and a *Vindication of his sermons*. What it will be I know not; there are men appointed to defend what is done.'[35]

The work anticipated by Andrews, and no doubt expected by the Commission since a committee was set up to defend its actions, appeared on July 17 as *Some Observations on the Proceedings Against the Rev. Mr. Hemphill; With a Vindication of His Sermons*. This work, published anonymously but now ascribed to Franklin, was printed by Franklin after an illness of six or seven weeks and proved so popular that a second edition was required in August.[36]

Meanwhile the sermons of Robert Cross and of Ebenezer Pemberton, preached before the Commission on April 20, were published because they had been claimed by Hemphill to be prejudicial to his case, Franklin stating that he was willing to surrender his sermon notes to the Commission only after these sermons were preached.[37] These were

---

34. Ibid., 13.
35. Andrews, Letter of June 14, 1735 to 'Reverend and Dear Sir.'
36. [Benjamin Franklin], *Some Observations on the Proceedings Against the Rev. Mr. Hemphill; With a Vindication of His Sermons*, 2nd ed. (Philadelphia: B. Franklin, 1735), 2.
37. Cross, *The Danger of perverting the Gospel* (the text was Galatians 1:7-9);

published prior to September 4, when appeared the most important document for our understanding of confessional subscription, *A Vindication of the Reverend Commission of the Synod In Answer to Some Observations On their Proceedings against the Reverend Mr. Hemphill*. This work of sixty-three pages (the last fifteen of which are an 'Appendix' with fuller extracts from Hemphill's seven sermons that were considered) is often ascribed to Jonathan Dickinson, but is clearly not by Dickinson alone since at least parts of it bear the stamp of an eye-witness to the event of the trial, and Dickinson, though a member of the Commission for that year, was not listed as present for the Hemphill case.[38] The authorship of *A Vindication of the Reverend Commission* should rather be ascribed to the committee that was assigned (as shown by Andrews' letter) 'to defend what is done'. The Synod met in Philadelphia within two weeks of this work's publication, September 17-25, and after unanimously confirming the Commission's verdict by declaring Hemphill 'unqualified for any future Exercise of his Ministry within our Bounds', took this action: 'The Brethren appointed to justify the Commission against any Complaints from Mr Hemphill if he should publish any such, having complied with the Commissions order in yt Matter, are desired by the Synod to continue to answr. any further Publications of Mr. Hemphill's or his Friends in yt Cause if they shall think it necessary.'[39]

Ebenezer Pemberton, *Sermon Preach'ed before the Commission of the Synod, at Philadelphia, April 20th, 1735* (New York: John Peter Zenger, 1735) (the text was Luke 7:35); [Franklin], *Some Observations*, 13.
38. *A Vindication of the Reverend Commission of the Synod in Answer to Some Observations On their Proceedings against the Reverend Mr. Hemphill* (Philadelphia: Andrew Bradford, 1735). On page 12 concerning the sermons of Cross and Pemberton, by then published, it says: 'what Convictions these Sermons afforded Mr. *H-ll*, we cannot tell; but the next Morning he offered to read his Notes before *The Commission*, which proposal we readily accepted of, esteeming it the likeliest Way to prevent our being mistaken in the Principles he maintained; and the surest Method of obtaining a just and impartial View of the Doctrines he had Propagated.' On page 6 of this document is the first hint that Hemphill's sermons were plagiarized.

While the Synod was meeting, there appeared *A Letter to a Friend in the Country, Containing the Substance of a Sermon Preach'd at Philadelphia, in the Congregation of the Rev. Mr. Hemphill, Concerning the Terms of Christian and Ministerial Communion.* This forty-page work includes a three-page preface, 'The Publisher to His Lay-Reader,' signed by 'A LAYMAN,' who clearly is Franklin. The body of it purports to be a letter dated August 30, 1735, describing to an outsider the good qualities of a sermon preached on Hemphill's behalf. It is most likely that the entire work is Franklin's.[40]

By November 27 the answer appeared in *Remarks Upon a Pamphlet, Entitled, A LETTER to a Friend in the Country, containing the Substance of a SERMON preached at Phila-delphia, in the Congregation of the Rev. Mr. Hemphill.* This work is almost universally ascribed to Jonathan Dickinson although the title page does not include an author. It does contain the characteristically Dickinsonian position: 'We can't too often declare, that the Door of *Christian Communion*, should stand as wide open as the *Gates of Heaven*; and each Christian Society, have a right to judge for themselves how wide that is.'[41] It should rather be regarded, however, as by the committee established by the Commission and mentioned by the Synod's minutes.

Next in the sequence of responses, although it actually appeared on October 30, four weeks earlier than *Remarks upon a Pamphlet*, is Franklin's bitterest piece, *A Defence Of the Rev. Mr. Hemphill's Observations: or, An Answer to the Vindication*

---

39. Klett, *Minutes*, 130-31. The dates for the publication of these several documents are given in the editorial comments in *The Papers of Benjamin Franklin* as derived from contemporary announcements in Franklin's *Pennsylvania Gazette* or Andrew Bradford's *American Weekly Mercury*. Some of Christensen's dating, 432-33, is incorrect.
40. Buxbaum, *Benjamin Franklin*, 234 n. 140.
41. [Jonathan Dickinson?] *Remarks upon a Pamphlet, Entitled, A LETTER to a Friend in the Country, containing the Substance of a SERMON preached at Philadelphia, in the Congregation of the Rev. Mr. Hemphill* (Philadelphia: Andrew Bradford, 1735), 21.

of the Reverend Commission. Sometime during the summer it had become clear that Hemphill not only advocated a deistic theology, but he had plagiarized his sermons from Samuel Clarke, Benjamin Ibbot, and James Foster, British preachers known for their Arian views. Franklin describes this embarrassment in his *Autobiography*:

> During the Contest an unlucky Occurrence hurt his Cause exceedingly. One of our Adversaries having heard him preach a Sermon that was much admired, thought he had somewhere read that Sermon before, or at least a part of it. On Search he found that Part quoted at length in one of the British Reviews from a Discourse by Dr. Foster's. This Detection gave many of our Party Disgust, who accordingly abandoned his Cause, and occasion'd our more speedy Discomfort in the Synod. I stuck by him, however, as I rather approv'd his giving us good Sermons compos'd by others, than bad ones of his own Manufacture; tho' the latter was the Practice of our common Teachers. He afterwards acknowleg'd to me that none of those he preach'd were his own; adding that his Memory was such as enabled him to retain and repeat any Sermon after one reading only.[42]

In *A Defence* Franklin employed a Swiftean analogy: 'Thus the Difference between him and most of his Brethren, in this part of the World, is the same with that between the *Bee* and the *Fly* in a Garden. The one wanders from Flower to Flower, and for the use of others collects from the whole the most delightful Honey; while the other (of a quite different Taste) places her Happiness entirely in Filth, Corruption and Ordure.'[43]

A Defence clearly is the work that Hemphill had rudely informed the Synod, in his letter of September 22, was 'now in the Press and will be speedily published'.

---

42. Franklin, *Autobiography*, 96-97.
43. Franklin, *A Defence*, 10.

In it Franklin names Robert Cross, pastor of the church in Jamaica on Long Island, as the person previously described as 'one of the chief managers of the whole affair' on the Commission.[44] The final answer from the Synod's committee, appearing by January 6, 1736, was issued under the pseudonym of 'Obadiah Jenkins' and was entitled *Remarks upon the Defence of the Reverend Mr. Hemphill's Observations: In a Letter to a Friend*. It claims to be a letter dated November 24, 1735 from a gentleman in New York who has followed the controversy thus far and states to his correspondent: 'I am fully of your Mind, that the Commission will not undertake a Reply. I hope those Reverend Gentlemen will find better Employment than to rake the Kennels. They will doubtless esteem such a scurrilous Paper below their Notice.'[45] The editors of *The Papers of Benjamin Franklin* base their judgment that 'Obadiah Jenkins' is a pseudonym, and that Jonathan Dickinson was probably the author, on a contemporary note on the copy in the Historical Society of Pennsylvania.[46] This copy is bound together (in third place) with *A Vindication of the Reverend Commission* and *Remarks upon a Pamphlet*. A contemporary hand has written on top of page 1 of *A Vindication* 'By Mr. Dickinson' and on the title page of Obadiah Jenkins' *Remarks upon the Defence* the initials 'J.D.' above 'Obadiah' and 'Nomenfictum' after 'Jenkins'.[47]

A more specific handwritten note appears, however, on the microfilmed copy in the Speer Library of Princeton

---

44. Ibid., 18.
45. Obadiah Jenkins, *Remarks upon the Defence of the Reverend Mr. Hemphill's Observations: In a Letter to a Friend* (Philadelphia: Andrew Bradford, 1735), 2.
46. *The Papers of Benjamin Franklin*, II, 91 n.4.
47. This volume is actually stored for the Historical Society of Pennsylvania in the next-door Library Company of Philadelphia. There is no indication of authorship for *Remarks upon a Pamphlet*, but the reverse of the title page has written in a similar hand 'S. Horton's Book'. Perhaps all three works belonged to Simeon (or Simon) Horton, who joined the East Jersey Presbytery prior to the Synod of 1735, but was not present at the synod meeting.

Theological Seminary. Opposite the first page of Jenkins' *Remarks upon the Defence*, a contemporary hand has written 'Chiefly by Mr. D…… to p. 15' and 'Partly by Mr. P…… from p. 16…….' Most likely this refers to Jonathan Dickinson and Ebenezer Pemberton as main members of the committee assigned to respond to the publications of Hemphill or his supporters. Clearly the authors of Obadiah Jenkins' *Remarks* desired at this point to mask the fact that they were here responding officially for the Synod. For one thing, they descended to Franklin's level of argument, specifically indicating which sermons Hemphill had stolen from whom, and picking up the Swiftean analogy: '… Instead of imitating the *Bee*, in collecting Honey from every Flower, he has but acted the *Drone*, in stealing other Men's Labours.'[48] They also wanted it to appear that Hemphill's latest defense did not really merit a reply: '…I can't but think that the Commission have sufficiently vindicated themselves, from all his scurrilous Imputations of out-doing the Jesuits in *Subterfuge, Distinction* and *Evasion*….'[49] By this point neither side had more to say.

2. The Role of the Confession in the Controversy

Franklin had rejoiced in Hemphill's sermons because they expressed the sort of deistic religion that he had come to hold. The six articles that the Commission framed against the preacher included his teaching of a religion based on the Law of Nature, of no necessity of conversion for those born to Christian parents in a Christian society, of a Socinian Christ whose death was not a satisfaction of God's justice, of a faith involving persuasion of the mind upon rational grounds and producing suitable affects but not mentioning receiving

---

48. Jenkins, *Remarks upon the Defence*, 18.
49. Ibid., 19.

of Christ on the terms of the gospel, of salvation through the Light of Nature apart from divine revelation, and of justification by faith as not necessary for 'those who have been educated and instructed in the knowledge of the Christian Religion'.[50] But Franklin recognized that the obstacle standing in the way of acceptance of such views in the Presbyterian Church was the Westminster Confession of Faith. From the very beginning much of the literary debate revolved around the role of the Confession.

Franklin first argued against the finality of any creed or confession. In the *Dialogue between Two Presbyterians*, after Mr. T. says, 'We ought to abide by the Westminster Confession of Faith; and he that does not, ought not to preach in our Meetings,' Mr. S. responds, 'But has not a Synod that meets in King George the Second's Reign, as much Right to interpret Scripture, as one that met in Oliver's Time? ... why must we be forever confin'd to that, or to any, Confession?'[51] In his climactic speech Mr. S. concedes that Hemphill's doctrine may not be entirely in accord with all of the church's standard: '... he does not perhaps zealousy propagate all the Doctrines of an old Confession.'[52] Pursuing this line further in *Some Observations on the Proceedings*, Franklin makes a telling distinction: 'And if these Reverend Gentlemen were as acquainted with what they call their *well known* Confession of Faith as they pretend to be, they would not have found Hemphill's Sermons inconsistent with it; he will undertake to prove that all his Discourses are agreeable to the *fundamental* Articles of it, which was all he declared to at his Admittance into the Synod: And surely they would not offer to condemn him for

---

50. *An Extract of the Minutes*, 7-11.
51. *The Papers of Benjamin Franklin*, II, 31-32.
52. Ibid., II, 32.

differing with them about extra-essentials.'[53] At the conclusion he charges, '... it seems very hard that they should make this Book the Standard and Test, when at the same time they own'd to him, that *they knew not how many fundamental Articles were in it.*' Franklin was well aware of the discussions surrounding the Adopting Act of 1729:

> I shall only add, that many of these reverend Gentlemen, who are now so zealous for the Confession, that they seem to give it the Preference to the Holy Scriptures, were of late years more indifferent than Hemphill has yet appear'd to be; and altho' they then agreed, that there were some Articles in it of no great Moment whether Men believed 'em or not, nay some publickly declared they did not understand many of 'em, (which I sincerely believe was very true) yet they would now make 'em all Fundamentals, in order to serve a Turn.[54]

In *A Letter to a Friend*, he merely questions the necessity or usefulness of framing long confessions of faith if neither Christ nor his apostles did so.[55] By the time of *A Defence*, however, Franklin sees no point in hiding his true colors and, through Hemphill, renounces any allegiance to the Confession: 'Where Hemphill's Notions of Christianity be or be not inconsistent with the darling *Confession of Faith*, he is not at all concern'd to enquire; whatever Notions he might have formerly entertain'd of this idol Confession, he now declares it to be no more *his* Confession, &c.'[56] Franklin goes on to term the doctrines of the imputation of Adam's guilt and of the imputed righteousness of Christ as ridiculous and reveals that for him the final authority in religion is not even Scripture:

---

53. Franklin, *Some Observations*, 18.
54. Ibid., 30.
55. Franklin, *A Letter to a Friend*, 11.
56. Franklin, *A Defence*, 28.

'And if there was such a Text of Scripture, for my own Part, I should not in the least hesitate to say, that it could not be genuine, being so evidently contrary to Reason and the Nature of Things.'[57]

Over against this onslaught, the committee appointed by the Commission, and subsequently the Synod, to respond to Hemphill and his friends labored to show how the Westminster Confession functioned in the Presbyterian Church. In their final response, Obadiah Jenkins' *Remarks upon the Defense*, they testify to their respect for the authority of the Confession: '... if renouncing as an Idol, the Confession of Faith, received by the Presbyterian Churches in *England*, *Scotland*, and *Ireland*, as well as by our Synod, and subscribed by himself as the Confession of his Faith, are just reasons for refusing him Ministerial Communion, the Censure of the Synod is justified by his own Pen.'[58] In the second response, *Remarks Upon a Pamphlet*, it is made clear that Presbyterians are not imposing their beliefs on any but themselves: 'We allow of no *Confession of Faith*, as a *Test of Orthodoxy* for others, but only as a Declaration of our own Sentiments; nor may this be imposed upon the Members of our own Society, nor their Assent required to any Thing as the Condition of their Communion with us; but what we esteem essentially necessary. If others differ from us, they have *Liberty* to think for themselves, if they will but allow us the same *Liberty*.'[59] This work concludes with a quotation from 'the acute and ingenious Mr. Lock, in his *Letter concerning Toleration*':

> This is the fundamental and immutable Right of a spontaneous Society, that it has Power to remove any of its Members, who transgress the Rules of its Institution.

---

57. Ibid., 32.
58. Jenkins, *Remarks upon the Defense*, 22.
59. *Remarks Upon a Pamphlet*, 26.

> But it cannot by the Accession of any new Members, acquire any Jurisdiction over those, that are not joined with it. And therefore Peace, Equity, and Friendship, are always mutually to be observed, by particular Churches, in the same Manner, as by private Persons, without any Pretence of Superiority or Jurisdiction over one another.[60]

Then as an appendix to prove that the Presbyterian Church operates in such a fashion there is added verbatim the preliminary part of the Adopting Act from the morning of September 19, 1729.[61]

For clarification of the way confessional subscription was intended to work, however, a crucial passage from the first response by the committee, *A Vindication of the Reverend Commission*, deserves to be quoted fully:

> But we cannot overlook without some Remarks, this surprising Narrative here given, and elsewhere repeated, *that all he declared to at his Admission into the Synod, were the fundamental Articles of the Confession of Faith*. When it is certainly true, and can be attested by above Forty Members of the Synod then present, that he solemnly Declared his Assent to every Article in the *Westminster Confession of Faith*, and in the Larger and Shorter Catechisms, without one Exception; and assured us, he had before Subscribed the same in *Ireland*.
>
> That we may once for all give the Reader a just View of this Case, and obviate all further Complaints about this matter, it will be proper to observe, that in the Year 1729, the Synod came to an unanimous Agreement about a Test of Orthodoxy, and of our Union in the essential Articles of Christianity, in the following method. It was agreed that all of the Ministers in this Synod, do Declare their Agreement in and Approbation of the *Confession of Faith*, with the Larger and Shorter Catechisms of the

---

60. Ibid., 29-30.
61. Ibid., 31-32.

Assembly of Divines at Westminster, as being in all the essential and necessary Articles, good Forms of sound Words, and Systems of Christian Doctrine; and do adopt them as the Confession of their Faith, & c. And in Case any Minister of this Synod, or any Candidate of the Ministry, shall have any Scruple with respect to any Article or Articles of the said *Confession* or *Catechisms*, he shall at the Time of his making said Declaration, declare his Scruples to the Presbytery or Synod, who shall notwithstanding admit him to the Exercise of the Ministry within their Bounds, and to ministerial Communion; if the Synod or Presbytery shall judge his Scruple or Mistake to be only about Articles not essential or necessary, in Doctrine, Worship or Government. By which it appears, that if Mr. *H-ll* had any Objection to make, against any Thing in the *Confession* or *Catechisms*, he should have particularly offered his Objections, and submitted it to the Judgment of the Synod, whether the Articles objected against, were essential and necessary, or not: And accordingly at the Time of his adopting the *Confession* and *Catechisms*, he was called upon to propose his Objections, if he had any; but he replied, he had none to make, and that he had before subscribed the same in *Ireland*, as before hinted. And now the World must Judge, whether it would not have been more to Mr. *H-ll's* Reputation, to have past over this whole Affair in Silence, than to have thus expos'd himself to the just Censure of all those that see the Repugnancy of this Confession of Faith to his Sermons; and that know how to value Sincerity. Nor is it any Excuse, that the Synod have not defined how many fundamental Articles there are in the *Confession*; since they have reserved to themselves the Liberty to judge upon each Occasion, what are, and what are not Fundamental.[62]

---

62. *A Vindication of the Reverend Commission*, 22-24. Briggs, *American Presbyterianism*, 232-33, quotes a substantial portion of this, but it is important to have the full context.

Here we have again the preliminary part of the Adopting Act from the morning of September 19, 1729 with two very significant aspects included. First, five years after the Confession was adopted, with exceptions acknowledged only with regard to clauses in the twentieth and twenty-third chapters concerning the civil magistrate, the procedure was followed of asking Hemphill whether he had *any* exceptions to declare, not just to these portions of the Confession. Second, it is stated that the Synod has not defined which articles are fundamental but has reserved that judgment to itself.

It has been argued that this procedure, of operating according to the 'Preliminary Act' of the Synod of 1729, reflects simply the position of Jonathan Dickinson, who had after all opposed confessional subscription prior to 1729.[63] It must be remembered, however, that *A Vindication of the Reverend Commission* was published only two weeks before the Synod of 1735 met to approve the Commission's suspension of Hemphill and to exclude him from the ministry. There is no evidence that anyone in the Synod disapproved of the language of *A Vindication*, which surely would have been 'must' reading for every member. Second, *A Vindication* spoke for the whole Commission which included the original proposer of confessional subscription, John Thomson, and several others who were known to favor strict subscription. Third, as we have seen, the authorship of *A Vindication* could not have been Dickinson's alone since it bears the marks of an eye-

---

63. George W. Knight, III, 'A Response to Dr. William Barker's Article "Subscription to the Westminster Confession of Faith and Catechisms,"' *Presbuterion* X (1984), 58. On Jonathan Dickinson and subscription see Keith J. Hardman, *Jonathan Dickinson and the Course of American Presbyterianism* (Ph.D. diss., University of Pennsylvania, 1971), 48-65, and Bryan F. Le Beau, 'The Subscription Controversy and Jonathan Dickinson,' *Journal of Presbyterian History*, 54 (1976), 317-35. For a revision of Trinterud's analysis of factions in the church see Elizabeth I. Nybakken, 'New Light on the Old Side: Irish Influences in Colonial Presbyterianism,' *Journal of American History*, 68 (March, 1982), 813-32.

witness to the trial and Dickinson himself was not present. Once again a handwritten note on the microfilm copy in the Speer Library of Princeton Seminary may provide the answer concerning authorship. Opposite the first page there appears in a contemporary hand: 'Written from p. 1 to p. 14 by Mr. *Pemberton* of N.Y. The rest by Mr. *Dickinson* of Eliz. Town Except.g p. 37, & 38. which were inserted by Mr. Cross of Jamaica, in Vindica. of himself.'[64] Most probably Ebenezer Pemberton (who as Moderator of the Synod of 1734 served as Moderator of the Commission for Hemphill's trial[65]) and Jonathan Dickinson were the committee to which the task of responding to Hemphill and his friends was assigned, with the possible addition of Robert Cross, whom Franklin identified as 'one of the chief managers of the whole Affair'.[66] In any case, Cross, who was one of the strongest advocates for strict subscription, had a hand in the production of *A Vindication* and no doubt would have objected if this publication did not accurately describe the method of subscription from 1729 to 1735.

---

64. I am grateful to Herbert L. Samworth, author of *Those Astonishing Wonders of His Grace: Jonathan Dickinson and the Great Awakening* (Ph.D.diss., Westminster Theological Seminary, 1988), for calling my attention to this handwritten note. Ms. Jean Preston of the Special Collections, Firestone Library, Princeton University says it is an eighteenth-century hand, more likely the former half than the latter half. Ms. Christine Ruggere of the Special Collections, Van Pelt Library, University of Pennsylvania terms it mid-eighteenth century handwriting. This handwritten note is not in the copy in Yale's Beinecke Library nor is it in the copy at the Massachusetts Historical Society, the two copies listed in Charles Evans' American Bibliography.
65. *An Extract of the Minutes*, 3.
66. Franklin, *A Defence*, 18. On the same day as the Commission's committee was continued by the Synod, the following motion 'made by a Member' was adopted '... the Synod do agree yt if any of our members shall see Cause to prepare any Thing for the Press upon any Controversy in religious Matters, yt before such Member publish what he hath thus prepared, he shall submit the same to be perused by Persons to be appointed for yt Purpose, and yt Messrs. Andrews, Dickinson, Robt. Cross, Pemberton and Pierson northward of Philada. and Messrs. Anderson, Thomas Evans, Cathcart, Stevenson and Thomson in the Bounds of ye Synod southward of Philada. – Any three of each Committee to be a Quorum' (Klett, *Minutes*, 131). This may represent a response to George Gillespie's *A Treatise against the Deists or Free-Thinkers, proving the Necessity of Revealed Religion*, announced as 'Just Published' in the *American Weekly Mercury* for July 31–August 7, 1735.

The conclusion to be drawn from the evidence in the Hemphill case is that, whatever differences of emphasis may have existed among the members of the Synod concerning the 'Preliminary Act' of the morning or the 'Adopting Act' of the afternoon of September 19, 1729, both were regarded as of continuing validity. The Synod had in fact adopted all of the Westminster Confession and Catechisms as its doctrinal standard, and the method of subscribing was for a candidate to declare any exception that he might have, upon which the appropriate judicatory would decide if the exception was to an essential or necessary article, as it had decided concerning the parts about the civil magistrate in 1729. To be sure some, like Thomson, would tend to emphasize the adoption of the Confession and Catechisms as the church's doctrinal standards, and some, like Dickinson, would tend to emphasize the method of subscription; and these differences in emphasis would contribute to tensions leading to the division of 1741.

The immediate reaction of the Synod of 1735 to its experience with Hemphill was to adopt a lengthy overture from an unidentified source concerning future ministers from the north of Ireland, 'seeing it is too evident to be denied and called in Question, yt we are in great Danger of being imposed upon by Ministrs. and Preachers from thence, tho' sufficiently furnished with all Formalities of Presbyterial Credentials, as in the Case of Mr. H-ll....' The first of five points had to do with subscription:

> ... That no Ministr. or Probationer coming in among us from Europe be allowed to preach in vacant Congregations until first his Credentials and Recommendations be seen & approven by the Pry unto which such Congregatn. doth most properly belong, and until he preach with approbation before sd. Pry and

subscribe or adopt the westminster Confessn. of Faith & Catechisms before sd. Pry in Manner and Form as they have done; and yt no Ministr. employ such to preach in his Pulpit until he see his Credentials & be satisfied, as far as may be, of his firm Attachment to sd. Confession & c: in opposition to the new upstart Doctrines & Schemes, particularly such as we condemn'd in Mr. H-ll's Sermons.[67]

The remaining points required that no congregation present a call to such a minister until he had preached within the bounds of the Synod for a full six months, nor until members of the presbytery concur, that a student under care become well known to most of the ministers of the presbytery, and 'That the Synod would bear Testimony agst the late too common, and now altogether unnecessary Practice of some Presbrys in the north of Ireland *viz.* Their ordaining men to the Ministry *sine Titulo*, immediately before they come over hither....' Besides their presbyterial credentials, such candidates are to bring also private letters of recommendation 'from some Brethren there who are well known to some of our Brethren here to be firmly attached to our good old Principles and Schemes, inasmuch as the instance of Mr H-ll and some other Considerations to the same Purpose make us afraid lest we may again be imposed upon by men of his stamp, tho' furnished with all the Formalities of Presbyterial Credentials.'[68] Robert Cross, John Thomson, and Joseph Houston were assigned to communicate this action properly to the General Synod of Ireland.

The apparently stricter subscription described in the action of the Synod of 1736, no doubt influenced by the

---

67. Klett, *Minutes*, 132.
68. Ibid., 132-33.

experience with Hemphill, refers to offence 'with some Expressions or Distinctions in the first or preliminary act of our Synod, contained in the printed Paper, relating to our receiving or adopting the Westminster Confession & Catechisms & c.'[69] The printed paper referred to may indicate a version of the Adopting Act of 1729, which, like *A Vindication of the Reverend Commission and Remarks upon a Pamphlet*, contained only the morning or preliminary part of the action of September 19. The Synod of 1735 had ordered 'yt each Presbry have the whole adopting Act inserted in their Presbry Book', perhaps indicating that what had been commonly circulated was only the morning or preliminary part of the Adopting Act. Hence the Synod of 1736 felt the need to emphasize 'our firm attachment to our good old received Doctrines contained in sd. Confession without the least variation or alteration',[70] as indeed the Westminster doctrinal standards had been adopted in 1729.

But this did not change the method of subscribing, which must have remained as described in *A Vindication of the Reverend Commission*, with a minister or candidate declaring any exceptions and the judicatory rendering its judgment.[71] Such a principle was, after all, embodied in the original overture of 1727 from John Thomson that led to the Adopting Act: 'Fifthly, to enact, that if any

---

69. Ibid., 141.
70. Ibid., 142. Trinterud (*Forming*, 66) and Briggs (*American Presbyterianism*, 237-38) correctly point out that the stricter subscriptionists were disproportionately predominant in the attendance at the 1736 Synod. See the analysis in Barker, 'Subscription to the Westminster Confession,' 7-8. No doubt the lopsided representation contributed to the emphasis on the latter part of the Adopting Act by the Synod of 1736.
71. There is one clear instance in the Synod Minutes where a minister 'Proposed all the Scruples he had to make about any articles of the Confession and Catechisms & c: to the Satisfaction of the Synod' in his subscribing to the Westminster Standards. This was David Evans in 1730 (Klett, *Minutes*, 108.) We do not know what Evans' scruples were. It was not difficult for the Synod to unite against the deistical convictions of Hemphill. Whether it would have agreed in opposing some lesser deviations from the Confession in an area other than that of the civil magistrate is not clear.

minister within our bounds shall take upon him to teach or preach any thing contrary to any of the said articles, unless, first, he propose the said point to the Presbytery or Synod to be discussed by them, he shall be censured so and so.'[72] Such a procedure of declaring any exceptions would require serious study of the Westminster standards and would compel a candidate to be open about his differences. Thus Thomson and Dickinson, Cross and Andrews, could all join in screening out a deist like Hemphill, whose sermons 'were all of them as to their general Scope, opposed to the Necessity of our Interest in Christ's Satisfaction, and to our Justification thro' Faith in his Blood,'[73] and whose doctrines 'we are obliged to declare Unsound and Dangerous, contrary to the sacred Scriptures and our excellent Confession and Catechisms, having an unhappy tendency to corrupt the Faith once delivered to the Saints....'[74]

---

72. Quoted in Charles Hodge, *Constitutional History*, I, 141. See also Webster, *A History of the Presbyterian Church*, 103.
73. *A Vindication of the Reverend Commission*, 36.
74. *An Extract of the Minutes*, 12.

13

THE WESTMINSTER ASSEMBLY ON THE DAYS OF CREATION: A REPLY TO DAVID W. HALL*

Subscription to our doctrinal standards, the *Westminster Confession of Faith* and the *Larger* and *Shorter Catechisms*, is a matter to be taken seriously. The second ordination vow of the Presbyterian Church in America asks: 'Do you sincerely receive and adopt the *Confession of Faith* and the *Catechisms* of this Church, as containing the system of doctrine taught in the Holy Scriptures; and do you further promise that if at any time you find yourself out of accord with any of the fundamentals of this system of doctrine, you will on your own initiative, make known to your Presbytery [Session, in the case of ruling elders and deacons] the change which has taken place in your views since the assumption of this ordination vow?'

In the last few years the claim has been made by some that, if one does not hold to a view that the days of creation in Genesis 1 are six 24-hour days, then

---

*Rev. David W. Hall was pastor of Covenant Presbyterian Church (PCA) in Oak Ridge, Tennessee. His claims of twenty-one Westminster Divines who hold, explicitly or implicitly, to six 24-hour days of creation have been published electronically and in print and are being cited widely as having proven the position of the Westminster Assembly. The author, as a member of the PCA General Assembly's committee on the days of creation, has found it necessary to respond to these claims.

one should declare an exception to the Westminster Standards' language that God created the world 'in the space of six days' (*WCF,* IV. 1; cf. *LC,* Q. 15 and *SC,* Q. 9), and some presbyteries have indicated that they would not allow the teaching of any such exception. This claim has been bolstered by the evidence offered by David W. Hall that up to twenty-one Westminster Divines either explicitly or implicitly supported six 24-hour days, with at least nine of them explicitly advocating this view.[1] David Hall has done the church a service by gathering this evidence. It is my belief, however, that his conclusions go farther than the evidence allows.

In a brief four-page statement on the days of creation adopted by the faculty of Westminster Theological Seminary on March 1, 1999 the argument was made that the phrase 'in the space of six days', rather than simply 'in six days', was consciously adopted by the Westminster Assembly in order to disassociate itself from the view of instantaneous creation, as espoused by Augustine and others, just as John Calvin used the expression 'in the space of six days' in his Commentary on Genesis 1:5 in order to distance himself from Augustine's instantaneous view. The Westminster Seminary statement says:

> Even though Calvin, Ames, and the authors of the Westminster Standards, with few exceptions, if any, undoubtedly understood the days to be ordinary days, there is no ground for supposing that they intended to exclude any and all other views, in particular the view that the days may be longer. Such views are outside their purview; their concern, in fact, moves in the

---

1. David Hall's views were presented orally at the twenty-sixth General Assembly of the PCA in St. Louis in 1998 and now are published in two chapters of Joseph A. Pipa, Jr. and David W. Hall, eds., *Did God Create in Six Days?* (Taylors, S.C.: Southern Presbyterian Press and Oak Ridge, TN: The Covenant Foundation, 1999), 41-52 and 267-305, which is a collection of papers presented at a conference sponsored by the Greenville Presbyterian Theological Seminary in Greenville, SC, March 9–11, 1999.

opposite direction, against the instantaneous view that denies any length.

This point bears emphasizing within the context of the current debate about the days of Genesis. To establish that the Standards mandate the six 24-hour day view requires more than demonstrating that the Divines, perhaps even to a man, held that the days were ordinary days. To demonstrate that of itself establishes nothing. What needs also to be shown, which we believe cannot be shown, is that they intended to exclude the views that the days are longer in some respect or that they represent a literary framework.

David Hall has misunderstood this statement to mean that some Westminster Divines actually taught or entertained a view of long-age days or of a literary framework,[2] but all that the statement is claiming is that the language 'in the space of six days' does not exclude such possibilities, as further exegetical work might be pursued as to the nature of the six days of creation in Genesis 1. The issue is not whether any of the Westminster Divines held a view of long ages or of a literary framework, as Hall repeatedly claims, but whether the confessional language requires a view of six 24-hour days and nothing else.

The Westminster Divines were, of course, aware of Augustine's writings on the days of creation. Wrestling with the philosophic aspects of eternity and time, the

---

2. Ibid., 292-96. David Hall takes issue with the statement's claim that a six 24-hour day view 'never seems to have been regarded as a test of orthodoxy in the reformed churches' by asking on 293, 'What evidence to the contrary do they have to support their claim that the divines did not regard statements in the confession as tests of orthodoxy?' But the faculty's statement explained earlier, 'The Seminary has always held that an exegetical judgement on this precise issue [24-hour days of creation] has never of itself been regarded as a test of Christian orthodoxy or confessional fidelity, until some have sought to make it such in the modern period.' One can sincerely believe that God created all things out of nothing by the word of his power in the space of six days (as Genesis 1 says) without holding that these days are necessarily twenty-four hours long.

great North African theologian had commented in *The City of God,* 'What kind of days these were it is extremely difficult, or perhaps impossible for us to conceive.'³ Puzzled as to when God created time, with the sun (by which our normal days are measured) created only on the fourth day, Augustine opted for instantaneous creation, with the 'days' of Genesis 1 being treated as six repetitions of a single day or days of angelic knowledge or some other symbolic representation – a view which both Martin Luther and John Calvin rejected.

Such a view of instantaneous creation was, however, still current at the time of the Westminster Assembly, being advocated by Sir Thomas Browne, an Anglican physician, in his *Religio Medici,* published in 1643, the year of the Westminster Assembly's beginning.⁴ The Westminster Divines would have good reason, therefore, to stress the duration of time in the days of creation.

The understanding that the sun was created only on the fourth day lingered in the interpretation of the Reformers and Puritans. Calvin in his Commentary on Genesis 1:14 says of the fourth day:

> God had before created the light, but he now institutes a new order in nature, that the sun should be dispenser of diurnal light, and the moon and stars should shine by night. And he assigns them this office, to teach us

---

3. *City of God,* XI, 6. Augustine treats the subject of creation in several places, including two early anti-Manichean works: in the *Confessions,* Books XI-XIII; in *On Genesis Literally Interpreted;* and in *The City of God,* Books XI-XII. Understanding creation not to be in time, nor to take time, Augustine can nevertheless say that 'according to Scripture, less than 6000 years have elapsed since He [man] began to be' (*City of God,* XII, 12, ed., Whitney J. Oates, *Basic Writings of St. Augustine* [New York: Random House, 1948], II, 190) and yet can also say a few pages later, 'I own that I do not know what ages passed before the human race was created' (*City of God,* XII, 16, ed., Oates, II, 196).
4. Sir Thomas Browne, *Religio Medici,* in *The Consolation of Philosophy* (New York: Modern Library, 1943), 345, 358, 369. For a discussion of Browne (1605–1682), see Basil Willey, *The Seventeenth Century Background* (New York: Columbia University Press, 1933, 1967), 67-69. *Religio Medici* was probably written in 1635, first published by a friend in 1642, and then as authorized by Browne in 1643.

that all creatures are subject to his will, and execute what he enjoins upon them.[5]

Commenting on the creation of light on the first day in Genesis 1:3, Calvin pursues the same theme of God's sovereignty:

> It did not, however, happen from inconsideration or by accident, that the light preceded the sun and the moon. To nothing are we more prone than to tie down the power of God to those instruments, the agency of which he employs. The sun and moon supply us with light: and, according to our notions, we so include this power to give light in them, that if they were taken away from the world, it would seem impossible for any light to remain. Therefore the Lord, by the very order of the creation, bears witness that he holds in his hand the light, which he is able to impart to us without the sun and the moon.

Then he goes on to say:

> Further, it is certain, from the context, that the light was so created as to be interchanged with darkness. But it may be asked, whether light and darkness succeeded each other in turn through the whole circuit of the world; or whether the darkness occupied one half of the circle, while light shone in the other. There is, however, no doubt that the order of their succession was alternate, but whether it was everywhere day at the same time, and everywhere night also, I would rather leave undecided; nor is it very necessary to be known.

With the same characteristic reticence Calvin skirts the issue of the exact nature of the days of creation in the 1559 edition of his *Institutes*:

---

5. *Calvin's Commentaries*, 22 vols. (Grand Rapids, Mich.: Baker Book House, 1979 reprint). His Commentary on Genesis is Volume 1, translated by John King. It was originally published in Latin in 1554 and in French in 1563.

re, that we may apprehend with true faith what it profits us to know of God, it is important for us to grasp first the history of the creation of the universe, as it has been set forth briefly by Moses [Gen. chs. 1 and 2], and then has been more fully illustrated by saintly men, especially by Basil and Ambrose. From this history we shall learn that God by the power of his Word and Spirit created heaven and earth out of nothing; that thereupon he brought forth living beings and inanimate things of every kind, that in a wonderful series he distinguished an innumerable variety of things, that he endowed each kind with its own nature, assigned functions, appointed places and stations;... But since it is not my purpose to recount the creation of the universe, let it be enough for me to have touched upon these matters again in passing. For it is better, as I have already warned my readers, to seek a fuller understanding of the passage from Moses and from those others who have faithfully and diligently recorded the narrative of Creation [Gen. chs. 1 and 2].[6]

Discouraging speculation, Calvin thus refers his readers in a straightforward manner to the text of Genesis and to the help of such earlier commentaries as Basil's *Hexaemeron* and the *Hexameron* of Ambrose. Ambrose is explicit about 24-hour days, but both he and Basil clearly state that the sun is created only on the fourth day.[7]

The implication of the sun's being created on the fourth day apparently was lurking in the mind of the great Puritan theologian of the late Elizabethan period, William Perkins, who wrote in his *Exposition of... the Creede*:

---

6. Calvin, *Institutes of the Christian Religion*, I.xiv.20, 2 vols., ed., John T. McNeill, trans. Ford Lewis Battles, The Library of Christian Classics (Philadelphia: Westminster Press, 1960).
7. Basil, *Hexaemeron*, Homily VI, 2 (82-83 in the *Nicene and Post-Nicene Fathers*, 2nd Series, Vol. VIII); Ambrose's *Hexameron*, Book IV, Sixth Homily, Chap. 1 (125 in *Fathers of the Church*, Vol. 42). There is a large amount of 'hexaemeral' literature (writings about the six days of creation) from the pre-Reformation and Reformation eras. Some of this is described, with particular emphasis on the early thirteenth-

> ... *some may aske in what space of time did God make the world? I answer,* God could have made the world, and all things in it in one moment: but he beganne and finished the whole worke in sixe distinct daies. In the first day hee made the matter of all things and the light: ... in the fourth day hee made the Sunne, the Moone, and the Starres in heaven: ... and in the ende of the sixth day hee made man. Thus in sixe distinct spaces of time, the Lord did make all things.... [8]

Perkins' paraphrasing of 'six distinct days' with 'six distinct spaces of time' appears to be an acknowledgment that the nature of at least the first three days may not be clear. Whatever their length of time may have been, they were not solar days since the sun was created only on the fourth day.

With that background for the Westminster Assembly, whose members were well acquainted with the works of Calvin and of Perkins as well as of William Ames and their respected contemporary Anglican Archbishop of Ireland James Ussher, what are we to make of David Hall's claim of twenty-one of the Westminster Divines who either explicitly or implicitly supported a six 24-hour day view of the creation account? As Hall has indicated, I have been willing to grant that five of the Westminster Divines held to six 24-hour days: John Lightfoot, John White, John Ley, George Walker, and William Twisse – all prominent members of the Westminster Assembly. [9]

---

century Bishop of Lincoln, Robert Grossteste, in Robert Letham, ' "In the Space of Six Days": The Days of Creation from Origen to the Westminster Assembly,' *WTJ* 61 (1999) 149-74. In Frank Egleston Robbins, *The Hexaemeral Literature: A Study of the Greek and Latin Commentaries in Genesis* (Chicago: University of Chicago Press, 1912), an annotated 'Index of Names' describes 139 authors on hexaemeral literature (not including Grossteste) on 93-104.

8. William Perkins, *Works,* 3 vols. (London, 1612): Vol. 1, 143.

9. For biographical information on these and several other Westminster Divines, see William S. Barker, *Puritan Profiles: 54 Influential Puritans at the Time When the Westminster Confession of Faith Was Written* (Fearn: Ross-shire: Christian Focus Mentor, 1996).

First of all, it will not do to claim for the six 24-hour day view those who merely refer to six days of creation. This is to beg the very question of the nature of the six days spoken of in Genesis 1. This removes some of the Divines from Hall's list, including Stephen Marshall and John Wallis, and also the works by Thomas Vincent, *The Shorter Catechism Explained from Scripture* (1674) and by John Ball, *Short Treatise Containing All the Principle Grounds of Christian Religion* (1650), which were endorsed by some Westminster Divines.

Second, the mere support for the chronology of James Ussher of a date for the creation of man of around 4000 B.C. also does not serve to indicate a commitment to six 24-hour days of creation, for the estimate for the date of creation is derived from the genealogies in Genesis 5 and 11.[10]

This eliminates several more from Hall's list, including Thomas Goodwin[11] and Jeremiah Burroughes, plus such corroborative material as Zacharias Ursinus' *Commentary on the Heidelberg Catechism* (1616).[12]

Third, endorsement of another person's book does not mean support for every view expressed in that book. Hall adds to his list the names of Westminster Divines Joseph Caryl, Edmund Calamy, and Thomas Case because their names were included in a list of forty notable Puritans who endorsed Vincent's *The Shorter Catechism Explained from*

---

10. Peter Martyr Vermigli's sixteenth-century commentary on Genesis cautions that the date of the creation of Adam and Eve should not be estimated from the genealogies because, as Augustine commented, the sons listed might not be first-borns and also because the Hebrew manuscripts and the Septuagint do not agree on some of the numbers. (This reference has been provided by Westminster Ph.D. student Clark Stull, who is working on a translation of this Latin commentary by the Reformer, who taught at Oxford, 1548–53.)
11. It is interesting that Goodwin, in the same *Exposition of the Epistle to the Ephesians* that David Hall cites, makes an analogy between the days of creation and the 'days' of the new world since Christ has come, in which 'we are under the second day's work, if I may so express it' in the seventeenth century (*The Works of Thomas Goodwin* [Eureka, Calif.: Tanslic Publications, 1996], Vol. I, 520).
12. *Did God Create in Six Days?*, 289, note 45.

Scriptures (1674). Beside the fact that Vincent's language that God 'took six days' time' does not prove the necessary point, the endorsers give indication in their 'Epistle to the Reader' that some of them had not even read the entire book: 'And having, to our great satisfaction, perused it ourselves in whole *or in part*, do readily recommend it to others... .'[13] The basis for five others being included on Hall's list is similar endorsements of other writers' works: Simeon Ashe, Thomas Gataker, Daniel Cawdrey, Charles Herle, and Herbert Palmer.

Finally, the evidence offered for John Arrowsmith and Adoniram Byfield has to do with creation by God's direct word and not by natural processes, a subject that does not necessarily affect the nature of the days of creation in Genesis 1. As a result, Hall's list of twenty-one Westminster Divines is down to seven – the five whom I have acknowledged plus William Gouge and Thomas Gataker, whose additional material cited by Hall has not been available for me to examine in context.[14]

Of the remaining Westminster Divines who explicitly supported six 24-hour days of creation, some were very explicit on additional details, claiming more than the Scriptures make clear and certainly more than the Westminster Standards say. John Lightfoot, for example, deals with creation in a half-dozen very brief treatises or notes, making such assertions as that the first day was thirty-six hours long, that the creation took place on the autumnal equinox (rather than the vernal equinox, as George Walker affirmed), and that the fall of Adam and Eve occurred on the sixth day, Adam having been created around 9 a.m. and Eve having been tempted around 12 noon. Some of Lightfoot's reasons for his positions are fascinating – for example, he believes the creation took

---

13. Thomas Vincent, *The Shorter Catechism Explained from Scripture* (Edinburgh and Carlisle, Pa.: Banner of Truth, 1980), v, emphasis added.
14. *Did God Create in Six Days?*, 45 and 47.

place on the autumnal equinox because all things were 'created in their ripeness and maturity: apples ripe, and ready to eat, as is too sadly plain in Adam and Eve eating the forbidden fruit' – but they were merely his opinions and did not become the position of the Westminster Assembly as expressed in the *Confession of Faith* or *Catechisms*. Although Lightfoot said, 'That the world was made at equinox, all grant, – but differ at which, whether about the eleventh of March, or twelfth of September; to me, in September, without all doubt,' the Assembly did not see fit to require agreement to such speculation, which goes beyond what Scripture makes clear.[15]

A similar caution may have governed the Assembly with regard to any requirement of agreement to 24-hour days of creation. Consider the possibility of the following imaginary scenario:

George Walker: Mr. Assessor, I move that we describe the creation as taking place 'in the space of six 24-hour days'.

William Gouge: (occupying the chair in the absence of the ailing Dr. William Twisse): Is there a second to the motion?

John Ley: I second the motion, although I recognize that the Hebrew word for 'day' (*yom*) is not itself decisive.

John Lightfoot: I move an amendment that we add that the creation took place on the autumnal equinox, since God's creation would be in full ripeness.

Walker: I object to this amendment. It must have been at the vernal equinox, since God's creation would have the freshness of spring.

Gouge: The amendment is out of order because it goes beyond what Scripture clearly teaches or what might be drawn as a necessary inference.

Unidentified Divine No. 1: I have the same problem with the main motion. Since the sun is created by God

---

15. John Lightfoot, *Works* (1822), Vol. II, 71, 73, 74, 333-34, 335, 413; Vol. IV, 64; Vol. VII, 372, 373-76, 377-79.

on the fourth day, can we be sure about the nature of these creative days?

Unidentified Divine No. 2: We clearly want to express duration of time, in order to oppose the concept of instantaneous creation, as advocated by Augustine and so recently promoted by Sir Thomas Browne's *Religio Medici*.

Unidentified Divine No. 1: I therefore move an amendment that we strike the words '24-hour days' and merely employ the phrase 'in the space of six days'. That is the expression of John Calvin in his Commentary on Genesis and also of Archbishop Ussher in the Irish Articles of 1615, and William Perkins also wrote of creation 'in six distinct spaces of time'.

Unidentified Divine No. 2: I second the motion. The phrase 'in the space of six days' will express the description of duration of time in Genesis 1 and yet will not go beyond Scripture in deciding the exact nature of these creative days.

Gouge: All in favor of the amendment say aye. All in favor of the motion as amended say aye. The phrase 'in the space of six days' is adopted.

Admittedly, this scenario is imaginary. For one thing, the Assembly strove not to include references to theologians as authorities in order to focus only on Scripture. But could not the confessional phrase have been arrived at by such a thought process? I believe this is in accord with the available evidence.[16]

Because the phrase 'in the space of six days' does not necessarily mean six 24-hour days, it would not be necessary for a candidate for licensure or ordination to declare an exception if his only question concerns the length of the days of creation. As one who has publicly

---

16. We do not possess much in the way of commentaries on Genesis by the Westminster Divines or even by other contemporary Puritans. One by George Hughes (1603–1667), published posthumously in 1672 appears to support 24-hour days of creation. On the other hand, Thomas Burnet (1635–1715) in his *Telluris*

advocated honest subscription to the Westminster Standards, openly declaring one's exceptions to the appropriate church court (in a forum with Dr. Morton H. Smith at the Twentieth General Assembly of the PCA in Roanoke, Virginia in 1992 and also in various publications) and allowing that court to determine whether one is still faithful to the second ordination vow, and as one who has conscientiously expressed exceptions in three areas of the Standards to three different presbyteries of the PCA of which I have been, and am, a member in good standing (whose teaching has not been restricted as a consequence), I do not regard it necessary for me to declare an exception to the phrase 'in the space of six days'. I believe that this is what Genesis 1 says, but the nature of those days of creation remains an open question for further exegetical study for Christians who adhere to the doctrine of creation *ex nihilo* and to the special creation of Adam and of Eve.

---

theoria sacra or the *Sacred Theology of the Earth* (Latin version 1681, English 1684), according to Stephen Jay Gould in his book *Rocks of Ages: Science and Religion in the Fullness of Life* (New York: Ballantine, 1999), 18, 'argued that God's six "days" might represent periods of undetermined length, not literal intervals of twenty-four hours or physical episodes of one full rotation about an axis.' Burnet was a chaplain to King William III, until dismissed for some of his views on Genesis, and also was a friend of Sir Isaac Newton, who praised his book.

Those who have worked with the Minutes of the Westminster Assembly know how frustratingly sketchy they can be. There is one instance where the question of including the phrase 'twenty-four hours' for the Sabbath came up and was rejected:

'*Resolved* upon the Q., "God in His word hath appointed one day in seven for a Sabbath to be kept holy unto Him."

'*Ordered* – "which from the beginning of the world to the resurrection of Christ was the last of the week, and … from the resurrection to the end of the world the first of the week."

'*Resolved* upon the Q., These words, "consisting of twenty-four hours," shall be waived in this place' (*Minutes of the Sessions of the Westminster Assembly of the Divines,* ed. Alex F. Mitchell and John Struthers, 1874, reprint by Still Waters Revival Books, Edmonton, Alberta, **1991– 216** for Session 615, April 6, 1646).

Part 3

The Word of God

The key doctrinal issue of the twentieth century was the authority of Scripture. Even in some evangelical circles the concept of the inerrancy of the Bible was questioned. It was claimed that the formula 'inerrant in the original autographs' was an invention of the Old Princeton theologians A. A. Hodge and B. B. Warfield, and was not the view of the Protestant Reformers or of historic Christianity. My Vanderbilt dissertation on the English Reformer John Bradford, sometimes called 'the first English Calvinist' and a forerunner of the Puritans, led me to the conclusion that this claim was not true. The authority of Scripture as the inerrant Word of God is not only an important theological doctrine, but also a concept of great practical significance for personal assurance of salvation.

14

INERRANCY AND THE ROLE OF THE BIBLE'S AUTHORITY: A REVIEW ARTICLE

Jack Rogers and Donald McKim have co-authored a book of special significance for several reasons. It is entitled *The Authority and Interpretation of the Bible: An Historical Approach*.[1] It is a critique in historical form of the Old Princeton formulations of the doctrine of inspiration of the Scriptures – specifically their assertion of plenary verbal inspiration and their restriction of inerrancy to the original autographs. Seeking to demonstrate that the position finally elaborated by A. A. Hodge and Benjamin B. Warfield was not that of the sixteenth-century Reformers or of the Westminster Divines, or of Augustine and the early church, it asks the historical question, from where did the Princeton formulations come? It is also clearly an effort to provide a timely response for the United Presbyterian task force established by the 1978 General Assembly to study the authority and interpretation of the Bible in the hope that by 1981 there might be clarification of that denomination's confessional position and use of Scripture in theological controversies.[2]

---

1. Jack B. Rogers and Donald McKim, *The Authority and Interpretation of the Bible: An Historical Approach* (San Francisco: Harper & Row, 1979).
2. Rogers and McKim, 441, note 252.

But beyond these central issues of the book it also raises a number of stimulating issues along the way. It asks various hermeneutical questions. How is the Bible to be handled by the church? Is it intended to provide answers to scientific questions? Or, is it mainly to reveal salvation through Jesus Christ? How is the human element in the writing of Scripture to be recognized? What of cultural conditioning?

It also raises questions concerning the form of theological expression and method. Should the Bible determine the outline for the church's theology, or should a systematic, logical outline be imposed upon the Scriptures? Is there a place in the church's theologizing for a natural theology or for deductive reasoning?

It also raises questions concerning apologetics. How does reason interact with faith? What is the best approach to contemporary thought?

A book that raises so many important issues in a stimulating fashion clearly commands attention. Although I differ with the major conclusion to which the authors are directing their readers, I would commend the reading of this book to evangelical Presbyterian ministers who are desirous of exploring their theological heritage. The lines of connection are accurately drawn, and the biographical data are often interestingly presented while also difficult to find elsewhere assembled in one place. Sometimes, however, there are misinterpretations of the Old Princeton theologians that I feel exaggerate their alleged differences from the Reformers and Westminster Divines, and hence prejudice the argument against inerrancy in the current evangelical controversy over scriptural authority.

Jack Rogers and Donald McKim are United Presbyterian ministers who were reared in an evangelical environment that included the Princeton formulations concerning Scripture. As they testify in their preface,[3] it was not until graduate study got them into the source materials of the Reformed tradition that they came to believe that verbal inerrancy of the original autographs, as taught to them by godly pastors and professors, was not the traditional doctrine of Scripture in the church. Rogers, who is now a professor of philosophical theology at Fuller Theological Seminary, came to his conclusion while studying the Westminster Divines and nineteenth-century Dutch Calvinism, and McKim, who is presently a Visiting Faculty Member in Religion at Westminster College in New Wilmington, Pennsylvania, did so while studying Calvin and John Owen. In recent years Rogers has become a main spokesman for the Fuller Seminary position of limiting inerrancy to matters of the Bible's salvation message. As in the case of *The Authority and Interpretation of the Bible*, so his doctoral dissertation at the Free University of Amsterdam, *Scripture in the Westminster Confession of Faith: A Problem of Historical Interpretation For American Presbyterianism* (Grand Rapids: Eerdmans, 1967), as its subtitle indicates, was a lengthy tract for the times, supportive of the ultimate version of the United Presbyterian Confession of 1967 as being consistent with the Reformational concept of Scripture represented in the Westminster Confession. His argument in that work was that Warfield had read his own views on the inerrancy of Scripture back into the Westminster Divines and that a careful reading of the particular Divines who drafted the Confession of Faith showed that, like Calvin, they had not been concerned about errors in historical or scientific detail in the Bible, but sought only to deny any intention to deceive or any error in the redemptive message.

Now in *The Authority and Interpretation of the Bible* Rogers and McKim's thesis is that with regard to

---

3. Rogers and McKim, xi-xii.

the status and use of Scripture, 'A particular post-reformation scholastic tradition that has prevailed in much of American Protestant thought and church life has succeeded in obscuring our awareness of the central church tradition and its Reformation expression.'[4] This post-reformation scholasticism had roots in some of the contemporaries of Luther and Calvin, such as Philipp Melanchthon and Peter Martyr Vermigli, and in some of their successors, such as Girolami Zanchi and Theodore Beza. It came into full development in the Reformed camp in the late seventeenth-century Swiss theologian Francis Turretin. Characteristics of this scholasticism include such things as structuring theology 'as logical system of belief in reliance on Aristotelian syllogistic reasoning', the assumption that 'reason had at least equal standing with faith in religious matters, with the consequence that revelation was often relegated to a secondary position', the definition of faith 'first as an act of assent by the mind to the deposit of truths in Scripture and only secondarily as a relationship of personal trust in Christ wrought by the Holy Spirit', and the interpretation of Scripture 'as a nonhistorical body of propositions that offered a base of inerrant information on which to construct a universal philosophy'. Despite their intentions Reformed scholastics like Turretin 'departed significantly from the stance of Calvin'.[5] Unfortunately for American Christianity it was Francis Turretin's theology that was made the textbook for the newly founded Princeton Seminary in 1812. Combined with the prevalent philosophy of Scottish Common Sense Realism, Turretin's scholasticism was passed from Archibald Alexander to Charles Hodge to A. A. Hodge to Benjamin B. Warfield to J. Gresham Machen, all of whom

---

4. Rogers and McKim, xi.
5. Rogers and McKim, 185-86.

– and especially Warfield – are found to depart from the Augustinian tradition of faith seeking understanding and from the concept of accommodation in Augustine, Luther, and Calvin – that is, the concept that God conveys his meaning to man in human language and hence imperfectly. This Princeton scholastic approach was criticized by T. M. Lindsay and James Orr in Scotland and by Abraham Kuyper and Herman Bavinck in the Netherlands. They remained open to scholarly scientific investigation of the human element in Scripture in the conviction that the 'central saving message of Scripture could be received in faith without waiting for scholarly reasons'.[6] These evangelical theologians, along with P. T. Forsyth, reacted against scholasticism in a way that foreshadowed Karl Barth's position and also the Reformational position of G. C. Berkouwer and of the Confession of 1967.

My assessment of Rogers and McKim's case is that they score several points against Protestant scholasticism of the post-Reformation period, they score a few points against the Old Princeton theologians, but they fail to make their case against inerrancy of the Scriptures as the conviction of the church through its history.

To take the final and main point first, it is interesting that Rogers and McKim commend the article by Geoffrey W. Bromiley, 'The Church Doctrine of Inspiration,' in *Revelation and the Bible*, as 'still perhaps the best brief overview of the history of the doctrine of inspiration'[7] and yet Bromiley, Rogers' colleague at Fuller Seminary, supports the use of the term inerrancy, based upon inspiration, as they themselves acknowledge.[8] Bromiley's article says of the Reformers: 'The high inspiration of the

---

6. Rogers and McKim, 393.
7. *Revelation and the Bible*, edited by Carl F. H. Henry (Grand Rapids, Baker, 1958), 55, note 5.
8. Rogers and McKim, 198, note 252.

Bible; the fact that God himself is the Author of Scripture; the divine origin of even the detailed wording – these are matters which are not disputed.'[9] To make their case that Calvin did not hold to inerrancy, Rogers and McKim would have to prove that he believed there was an error in the Bible that could not be explained by transmission of the text, translation, or interpretation, the criteria that Augustine listed in his *Reply to Faustus* XI,5 and in his *Epistle 82* to Jerome.[10] Among the examples they cite is his comment on Matthew 27:9 that 'Zechariah' should be read instead of 'Jeremiah': 'How the name of Jeremiah crept in, I confess that I do not know, nor do I give myself much trouble to inquire.'[11] But the words 'crept in' indicate that Calvin felt the error here was a result of textual corruption in transmission. Calvin's comment on Acts 7:16, cited by Rogers and McKim on the same page, is more telling for their point, but whether Calvin is ascribing an error to Luke or to Stephen or to a copyist is not entirely clear in the context of his comment. (Calvin's words are: 'But when he goes on to say that they were buried in the sepulchre which Abraham had bought from the sons of Hamor, it is obvious that an error has been made in the name Abraham. For Abraham bought a double cave to bury his wife, from Ephraim the Hittite [Gen. 23:9], but Joseph was buried elsewhere, namely in the field which his father Jacob had bought from the sons of Hamor for a hundred lambs. This verse must be amended accordingly.' Edward A. Dowey, Jr., no friend of inerrancy, believes that Calvin ascribed all such errors to copyists' blunders and held to verbal inspiration.[12] Rogers and McKim's other citations of Calvin do not

---

9. Bromiley, 210.
10. Rogers and McKim, 28. note 128.
11. Rogers and McKim, 110.
12. Edward A. Dowey, Jr.,*The Knowledge of God in Calvin's Theology* (New York: Columbia University Press, 1952), 103-04.

accomplish more than to display an attitude of no great concern for trivial discrepancies, for, as Bromiley pointed out, the matter of Scripture's authority was not in dispute in the sixteenth-century controversies of the Reformers.

The same point may be made concerning Rogers and McKim's handling of the Westminster Assembly. Although they demonstrate that the Westminster Divines' concern was with the central saving message of the Scriptures, they do not show that any of them believed there was an error in the Bible that could not be explained by transmission of text, translation, or interpretation. With regard to Rogers' earlier study of the Westminster Confession on Scripture, Roger R. Nicole has remarked: 'Nowhere in his entire thesis, as far as we are aware, did he advance even one text from a Westminster divine in which it is stated that a passage of Scripture is actually in error.'

> ...Is it likely that there are ready and convincing statements of biblical errancy made by the Westminster men and that neither Briggs nor Rogers found any of them? Is it likely that having found them, they failed to quote them? The presumption must remain that unless clearcut evidence to the contrary is adduced, the Westminster divines held that the canonical Scriptures, being 'the Word of God written' (1.2), reflect the character of God 'the author thereof,' 'who is truth itself' (1.4), so that 'by…faith a Christian believeth to be true whatsoever is revealed in the Word, for the authority of God Himself speaking therein' (14.2).[13]

The main points that Rogers and McKim rightly make concerning Calvin and the Westminster Divines are that

---

13. Appendix 6 in A. A. Hodge and Benjamin B. Warfield, *Inspiration*, with Introduction by Roger R. Nicole (Grand Rapids: Baker, 1979), 99, 100.

they did focus on the redemptive message of the Bible and the faith and life resulting from it, and they did give priority to faith over reason, the 'inward work of the Holy Spirit, bearing witness by and with the Word in our hearts' being the source of 'our full persuasion and assurance of the infallible truth and divine authority' of the Scriptures, notwithstanding all the arguments 'whereby it doth abundantly evidence itself to be the Word of God' (*Westminster Confession of Faith* I. v). And this is where their criticism of Protestant scholasticism needs to be heard by those of us who adhere to inerrancy. The attitude of the Lutheran Abraham Calovius and the Reformed Gisbert Voetius toward the scientific discoveries of the seventeenth century illustrates the difficulties that can result from a rationalized theological system being imposed on the Scriptures. Rogers and McKim comment: 'Voetius declared that if the Holy Ghost had accommodated Himself to the common people of the biblical writer's day then the Holy Ghost would have been telling a lie.'[14] Francis Turretin is not faulted by Rogers and McKim for failing to focus on the redemptive message of Scripture, but he is criticized for basing belief in the Scriptures not on the witness of the Spirit, but on rational proofs of their inspiration and inerrancy:

> Turretin followed the Aristotelian-Thomistic method of placing reason before faith. He claimed: 'Before faith can believe, it must have the divinity of the witness, to whom faith is to be given, clearly established, from certain marks which are apprehended in it, otherwise it cannot believe.' Turretin placed proofs first, whereas for Calvin they were never anything more than 'secondary aids to our feebleness' to give comfort to those who had already believed through the witness of the Spirit.[15]

---

14. Rogers and McKim, 167.
15. Rogers and McKim, 176-77.

Rogers and McKim are almost totally negative toward this sort of Protestant scholasticism – indeed, Turretin is practically the villain in the historical plot. A more balanced historical assessment of Protestant scholasticism, however, is to be found in John H. Leith, who states that 'by the seventh decade of the sixteenth century, the critical issues of Protestant faith had been fought through'.

> After the 1560's Protestant theology faced a new task, namely one of consolidation, clarification, and elaboration. The necessity of this task arose out of the nature of theology itself. During the initial religious experience, words may be used loosely and without careful definition, but if a movement is to survive, it must sooner or later formulate precisely what it is saying or believing. It must ask how one affirmation fits with other affirmations, how the total experience holds together. There are dangers in this process, for when any great experience in life is analyzed, precisely defined, and described, there is the risk that the living reality will be destroyed. But in many areas of life, as psychology demonstrates, this process is necessary for the sake of the health of living experience itself. The new task that theology faced after 1560 was inevitable and ought not to be judged as good or bad in itself, but as a necessary stage in the development of any community or theology.[16]

Protestant scholasticism of the late sixteenth and seventeenth centuries thus was doing necessary work in responding to questions raised by the Catholic Counter-Reformation and by new thought. We do well, however, to take heed to the warning of dangers inherent in the process of systematizing the understanding of faith. Although Rogers and McKim defend the Westminster

---

16. John H. Leith, *Assembly at Westminster* (Richmond: John Knox, 1973), 65.

Assembly from charges of scholasticism, one can sense the movement toward precision and systematizing in the seventeenth-century Westminster Standards from the fresh, personal tenor of the sixteenth-century Scots Confession and Heidelberg Catechism.

It is the old Princeton Theology, however, that Rogers and McKim are most concerned to discredit. They call upon the present-day United Presbyterian Church to correct 'the decision of 1927 which left the Princeton Theology's interpretation of history unchallenged'.[17] That decision was the one that reserved the right to judge what was necessary for ordination to the ordaining body, the presbytery, and left the General Assembly with no means to declare doctrinal requirements other than to quote the confessional standards.[18] This eliminated the authority of the five fundamental points adopted by the General Assembly in 1910, 1916, and 1923, but it also voided the possibility of refuting the old Princeton position that inerrancy was the historic position of the church. The main contention of Rogers and McKim's book is that the Princeton position is not the historic position of the church on Scripture, but rather represents an aberration, in some respects a restoration of Thomistic scholasticism that places reason before faith, and in some respects an innovation that responded to scientific criticism by elaborating the new formula on inerrancy in the original autographs.

Having already indicated my shared concern over such rationalism as appeared in Turretin's scholasticism, I would acknowledge that a confidence in human reason's capacity to comprehend the Christian faith continued to manifest itself in the Princeton theologians. There is certainly a tendency in Charles Hodge to emphasize

---

17. Rogers and McKim, 459.
18. Rogers and McKim, 367, 368.

the common qualities of human nature and not to recognize or else to minimize the historical and cultural conditioning of different places and times.[19] This may reflect a failure of the Princeton theologians, under the influence of Scottish Common Sense philosophy, to recognize adequately the noetic effects of the fall,[20] whereas they did recognize the effect of sin on the emotions.[21]

The elaboration of the formula 'inerrant in the original autographs' was, however, not an innovation in substance so much as it was a new expression for a long-held belief. Augustine's recognition of the possibility of error in a corrupted text or translation or interpretation of Scripture points to the original writings as the inspired ones. The same is true of the Westminster Confession's statement:

> The Old Testament in Hebrew (which was the native language of the people of God of old), and the New Testament in Greek (which at the time of the writing of it was most generally known to the nations), being immediately inspired by God, and by his singular care and providence kept pure in all the ages, are therefore authentical; so as in all controversies of religion the Church is finally to appeal unto them (I. viii).

The Princeton theologians were by no means closed to scholarly biblical investigation, as Rogers and McKim

---

19. Rogers and McKim, 292, provides some examples of this in Charles and A. A. Hodge.
20. Cf. Charles Hodge, *Systematic Theology*, I, 9-15 on the inductive method; I, 633-35 on human testimony; and II, 129 on the effects of the first sin and 125-27 on the tree of knowledge. It is apparent that Hodge shared his age's optimism concerning the possibility for objective knowledge of truth if only the facts were known. The brief section on the effects of Adam's fall does not mention any epistemological consequence although the discussion of the tree of knowledge of good and evil suggests that Adam knew less of the difference between right and wrong after the fall than he did before.
21. Rogers and McKim, 290.

repeatedly claim, but rather they emphasized the value of textual or lower criticism, in order to arrive as close as possible to the original text, while rejecting the anti-supernatural presuppositions of much of higher criticism in its examination of such questions as authorship or time of origin. Almost invariably when referring to such expressions as 'the autographs' or 'the original manuscripts', Rogers and McKim insert 'non-existent' or 'lost'. This is misleading. As even liberal Roman Catholic Hans Küng has said:

> Despite the lack of original manuscripts and the fact that in many cases authentic readings were not fixed until a late date, textual criticism has succeeded in establishing, with the greatest possible certainty and exactitude, the original wording of biblical writings in the earliest form available to us.[22]

In describing Warfield's confidence that, although the original manuscripts may not exist, the autographic text is largely available to us, Rogers and McKim neglect Warfield's own expertise in New Testament textual criticism except for a brief reference to his *An Introduction to Textual Criticism of the New Testament*.[23] Roger and McKim go to great lengths to point out a shift between A. A. Hodge's first edition of *Outlines in Theology* in 1860 and the revised edition of 1879. No doubt the incursion of higher criticism in America after the Civil War was forcing a new articulation of the old doctrine of Scripture in order to meet new questions. It is interesting, however, that Charles Hodge's stable expression of the doctrine of Scripture was published in 1872–73 in his *Systematic Theology*, which then replaced Turretin as the Princeton textbook for the next two generations. It is easy for historians

---

22. Hans Küng, *The Church*, trans. Ray and Rosaleen Ockenden, (New York: Sheed & Ward, 1967), 2.
23. Rogers and McKim, as cited by John Gerstner, 375, note 149.

Inerrancy and the Role of the Bible's Authority

to read too much significance into slight shifts. While Rogers and McKim avoid the more extreme judgements of Ernest Sandeen's *The Roots of Fundamentalism*,[24] though they quote one such statement of his favorably,[25] they are mistaken when they see the Princeton formulation of 'inerrancy in the original autographs' as an innovation. The classic statement of this Princeton formulation, in the April 1881 *Presbyterian Review* article by A. A. Hodge and Warfield, dealt with by Rogers and McKim in little more than one page,[26] ironically includes many of the points that they are most concerned to safeguard as part of the central Christian tradition:

> It must be remembered that it is not claimed that the Scriptures, any more than their authors, are omniscient. The information they convey is in the forms of human thought, and limited on all sides. They were not designed to teach philosophy, science or human history as such. They were not designed to furnish an infallible system of speculative theology. They are written in human languages, whose words, inflections, constructions and idioms bear everywhere indelible traces of human error. The record itself furnishes evidence that the writers were in large measure dependent for their knowledge upon sources and methods in themselves fallible, and that their personal knowledge and judgments were in many matters hesitating and defective, or even wrong. Nevertheless, the historical faith of the Church has always been that all the affirmations of Scripture of all kinds, whether of spiritual doctrine or duty, or of physical or historical fact, or psychological or philosophical principle, are without any error when the *ipsissima verba* of the original autographs are ascertained and interpreted in their natural and

---

24. Ernest Sandeen, *The Roots of Fundamentalism* (University of Chicago, 1970).
25. Rogers and McKim, 375-76, note 157.
26. Rogers and McKim, 349-51.

intended sense. There is a vast difference between exactness of statement, which includes an exhaustive rendering of details, an absolute literalness, which the Scriptures never profess, and accuracy, on the other hand, which secures a correct statement of facts and principles intended to be affirmed. It is this accuracy, and this alone, as distinct from exactness, which the Church doctrine maintains of every affirmation in the original text of Scripture without exception. Every statement accurately corresponds to truth just as far forth as affirmed.[27]

Not surprisingly in a book so large there are numerous smaller things to criticize. Rogers and McKim's interpretation of Charles Hodge on page 296 appears to contradict their own quotation from Hodge, which says that it is the renewed soul which has saving faith based upon the testimony of the Holy Spirit. Right on the preceding and following pages of his *Systematic Theology*, Hodge discusses faith and the testimony of the Spirit in ways that counter Rogers and McKim's claims.[28] Other instances of incomplete understanding of the Princeton theologian's positions could be cited.

Although a massive amount of research lies behind the book, there is a tendency to rely on monographs rather than on source materials. This is admitted by the authors in their preface and is acknowledged by Ford Lewis Battles in his foreword, yet when Turretin plays such an important part in their thesis, it is unfortunate that they are dependent on citations from Turretin's *Institutio Theologiae Elencticae* contained in twenty-five pages of a Th.M. thesis.[29]

---

27. A. A. Hodge and Benjamin B. Warfield, *Inspiration*, 27-29.
28. Charles Hodge, *Systematic Theology*, III, 67, 69.
29. Rogers and McKim, 196, note 170, and 196-97, notes 180 through 239. Incidentally, the birth dates for Francis Turretin and for his son, Jean-Alphonse Turretin, on page 172 should be corrected from 1632 and 1648 to 1623 and 1674 respectively.

More distressing is the general support given to Charles Augustus Briggs in his controversy with Benjamin B. Warfield. More than once the authors state it as fact that Briggs was historically correct in his interpretation of the Westminster Divines' doctrine of Scripture and Warfield therefore was wrong. Perhaps this assurance stems from Rogers' earlier research on the Westminster Assembly, but not everyone agrees with the conclusions he has drawn there.[30] It seems strange for professing evangelical Presbyterians to sound so sure of Brigg's interpretation when he went on to claim that his questions about the traditional doctrine of original sin and his espousal of progressing sanctification after death were not at variance with the Westminster Confession.[31] Indeed, Rogers and McKim's book ultimately becomes an apology for the position of the Auburn Affirmation of 1923–24, that such points as the virgin birth of Christ, His miracles, His vicarious atonement, His bodily resurrection and second coming are only possible interpretations of Christ's incarnation and redemptive work and that the inerrancy of Scripture is a harmful doctrine. Machen is misrepresented as having 'inherited an ambivalence from his predecessor Princeton theologians. With them, he acknowledged that only faith in Christ was necessary in order to be a Christian. But the Princeton theologians had so built their apologetic approach on biblical inerrancy that it now had to be treated as essential'.[32] The 'essential and necessary doctrines' adopted in five points of the 1910 General Assembly were to be affirmed by all ordination candidates, not all members of the church.[33]

---

30. For example, Roger R. Nicole's 'Appendix 6: The Westminster Confession and Inerrancy' in A. A. Hodge and Warfield, *Inspiration*, 97-100.
31. Rogers and McKim, 359.
32. Rogers and McKim, 365.
33. Rogers and McKim, 362.

The discussion of Machen is disappointingly brief. Only a small section of his *Christianity and Liberalism* is discussed.[34] Further exposition of his doctrine of Scripture would have revealed that he related the authority of the Bible to the authority of Jesus Christ and to the saving purpose of His vicarious death.[35] This was the traditional position of the Princeton theologians:

> It is also a well-known fact that Christ himself is the ultimate witness on whose testimony the Scriptures, as well as their doctrinal content, rests. We receive the Old Testament just as Christ handed it to us, and on his authority. And we receive as belonging to the New Testament all, and only those, books which an apostolically instructed age testifies to have been produced by the apostles or their companions – i.e. by the men whom Christ commissioned, and to whom he promised infallibility in teaching.[36]

It is ultimately this faith commitment to Christ that precedes and underlines all the reasoning of the inerrancy position of the old Princeton theologians.

Despite these several serious criticisms there are many things to commend in the book. The work is impressive in its very size of almost 500 pages. Not quite one-fourth of the whole is composed of footnotes, many of which contain very helpful information. Those that are not merely bibliographical in nature are indicated in bold type. There are convenient summaries at the conclusion of each chapter as well as at the end of the book. An overview of the entire thesis can be gained from these summaries, but much of the essential argument is to be gathered only from the full text. In addition to particular

---

34. Rogers and McKim, 363-64.
35. J. Gresham Machen (1923), *Christianity and Liberalism* (Grand Rapids: Eerdmans), 76-79.
36. A. A. Hodge and Benjamin B. Warfield, *Inspiration*, 24.

sections already commended, I would point out the section discussing Calvin on the inner testimony of the Holy Spirit, where Rogers and McKim stress that Calvin rejected the necessity of rational proofs for the divinity of Scripture and also opposed a position of blind faith alone.[37] It is also encouraging that United Presbyterians opposing scholasticism should be harking back to the Westminster Confession as identifiable with the views of the Reformers. Although this is based on a differing interpretation of the Westminster Confession, it can only be hoped that renewed attention to the traditional doctrinal standards of Presbyterianism will help to draw United Presbyterians back to the Scriptures themselves and to an orthodox theology.

Meanwhile, what does a book like *The Authority and Interpretation of the Bible* have to say to those of us who adhere to inerrancy?

It suggests to me that we should explore more fully the writings of Calvin and other sixteenth-century Reformers such as John Knox, Martin Bucer, Ulrich Zwingli, Heinrich Bullinger, John Bradford, Richard Sibbes, and William Perkins, and the sixteenth-century confessional statements. (An appendix in Rogers and McKim includes selections from various Reformed confessions of the sixteenth century and the Westminster Confession, plus the Confession of 1967, on the doctrine of Scripture.) We should explore more fully the Westminster Divines and other seventeenth-century Puritans and such eighteenth-century figures as Jonathan Edwards and George Whitefield. And also the Princeton theologians themselves, including the original teachers, Archibald Alexander and Samuel Miller. We should also explore more fully such earlier figures as Irenaeus, Athanasius, Chrysostom, Augustine, and Anselm. My own study

---

37. Rogers and McKim, 103-06.

into the writings of these men – some of them only quite selective – has proven very rewarding and only confirmatory of the doctrine of inerrancy I was taught by godly pastors and professors.

We should also look closely at the argument that the human and divine elements in Scripture are analogous to the human and divine in the incarnation of Christ. While Whitefield rejected at least some aspects of this analogy,[38] it seems to me that the sinlessness of Christ's humanity properly parallels the inerrancy of the God-breathed writings of the human authors of Scripture. At least incarnational analogy as Luther and Calvin taught it need not lead to the absurd conclusion of P. T. Forsyth: 'If the *act* of salvation was bound up with a crime, need we be startled if its *Word* is mingled with error?'[39]

Rogers and McKim's work also constrains us to answer again the question of whether there is a conflict between faith and the use of evidences and reason. It seems to me that their description of Archibald Alexander's emphasis on both internal and external evidence represents the right kind of balance.[40]

Their book also should remind us of the danger of allowing apologetics to govern our theological study. Princeton Seminary was designed originally to combat deism.[41] When the culture had moved on to different challenges to the faith, the curriculum was still oriented to a particular kind of problem. The gospel itself must be the core of our theological reflection, and the Bible itself must shape our theological questions rather than a philosophical system shaping our approach to the Bible.

We must also recognize more fully the human element of Scripture along with the divine. We need to stress more

---

38. Rogers and McKim, 337.
39. Rogers and McKim, 404, note 102.
40. Rogers and McKim, 273.
41. Rogers and McKim, 269.

the historical aspect of grammatico-historical exegesis and be more aware of when cultural conditioning limits the universal applicability of certain passages.

We should also be willing to re-examine the epistemological base of our approach to religious knowledge. If the old Scottish Common Sense philosophy is defective, what is to replace it? What is the Bible's own epistemology? Rogers and McKim describe favorably Berkouwer's conclusion to his *Holy Scripture* in which he cites the statement of the disciples with whom the Lord walked on the way to Emmaus in Luke 24:32: 'Did not our hearts burn within us while he talked to us on the road, while he opened to us the Scriptures?' This correlation of the divine message of Scripture with human faith in it is offered as 'a third alternative' between scholastic rationalism and liberal subjectivism. But it is later in this same chapter of Luke 24 that the risen Jesus appears to the disciples gathered in Jerusalem, and He invites them to consider the evidences: 'Look at my hands and my feet.... Touch me and see.' He reasons with them: '...a ghost does not have flesh and bones, as you see I have,' and He eats a piece of fish in their presence. And ultimately He opened their minds so they could understand the Scriptures: 'This is what I told you while I was still with you: Everything must be fulfilled that is written about me in the Law of Moses, the Prophets and the Psalms.' Experience, reason, and the authority of Scripture can all be valid means of religious knowledge, but ultimately it is the Scriptures which testify to the Messiah, and He testifies to them in their entirety.

Let us constantly re-examine the Bible's own testimony to itself and ultimately Jesus' own testimony to Scripture's authority, and let us not fall short of that nor go beyond it.

15

The Authority of Scripture and Assurance of Salvation

Essential Qualities of Reformation Piety as Illustrated in the Life and Writings of John Bradford

The contemporary controversy over the inerrancy of the Scriptures is not just an abstract doctrinal issue. It relates directly to the very concrete practical matter of assurance of salvation. This was at the heart of the concerns of the Protestant Reformers and the Puritans of England and America.

The roots of Puritanism are to be found in the second-generation development of Protestantism on the European continent which can in a general way be termed 'Calvinism', and its first flowering may be seen in the reign of King Edward VI of England (1547–53). Its essential spirit was the sense of God's sovereignty as experienced in His gracious salvation and as expressed in His authoritative Word, the Bible. Because of the peculiar circumstances of the Reformation in England, its having arisen over Henry VIII's marriage and desire for a male heir and its having focused on the mass and the Prayer Book, the main issues of the controversy revolved around worship and the authority of the state in matters of religion. But the motivating forces for the genuine Protestant spirit of the Edwardian period –and hence of eventual Puritanism – were assurance of salvation and the authority of Scripture.

It is difficult for the twenty-first-century mind to appreciate these convictions fully without an effort of the imagination to put oneself in the shoes of these sixteenth-century Reformers. With regard to assurance of salvation Lacey Baldwin Smith put it this way:

> If the Reformation is viewed as a part of the closing years of the Middle Ages and as a solution to problems caused by the decay of medieval ideals and institutions, then the speed with which the revolt gained momentum becomes understandable, its European and international aspect becomes fully recognizable; and finally the conviction and courage of the martyrs becomes comprehensible since they now have something worth dying for: they had found 'marvellous comfort and quietness' in the intimate knowledge of a God both more merciful and more powerful than the visible church.[1]

This intimate knowledge of God had come through the Scriptures, which were rediscovered with freshness as read now in the vernacular and as expounded from the pulpit, so that people felt they were confronted by God with a new kind of immediacy. This dynamic impact of Scripture was to last through the Puritanism of most of the seventeenth century and would still be a key to the vitality of the spirituality of Jonathan Edwards and some of his contemporaries in the eighteenth century.

It is because of the importance of these two elements of Protestantism that lie behind the Puritan spirit – assurance of salvation and the authority of Scripture –

---

1. Lacey Baldwin Smith, 'The Reformation and the Decay of Medieval Ideals,' *Church History* (September, 1955), 219-20.

that I should like to present a case study of the piety of the Edwardian Reformation in the person of John Bradford, whom Gordon Rupp has termed both 'perhaps the first Calvinist among the Reformers' and 'in some ways the first great English Puritan'.[2]

1. The Career of John Bradford (c. 1510 or '20–1555)

John Bradford is not so significant for himself as he is for the influences he reflects and for his example of Reformation piety as it was conveyed to the common people. It must be remembered that Henry VIII's break with Rome had not encouraged a wide spreading of Protestant beliefs, and by the time Edward came to the throne in 1547 the people were still mostly ignorant of the Bible and committed to the Roman mass. In addition to the translation of Scripture, which figures like William Tyndale and Miles Coverdale provided, and reform of the worship services, which became Thomas Cranmer's major contribution, there was need for preaching the Protestant message into the corners of the realm, and John Bradford was to become one of the most effective of such preachers, probably second only to Hugh Latimer. It was the preaching of Latimer, in fact, which was to mark the turning point for Bradford from a career as a lawyer to service as a minister.

Born sometime between 1510 and 1520, Bradford grew up in the vicinity of Manchester, served in the army of Henry VIII in France as a paymaster from 1544 to 1546, and entered the Inner Court of the Temple to study law in 1547. It was here that he and his companion, the later Puritan Thomas Sampson, underwent conversion experiences. In Lent of 1548 Bradford heard Latimer, who had been restored by Edward after an eight-

---

2. Gordon Rupp, 'John Bradford, Martyr,' *London Quarterly and Holburn Review*, CLXXXVII (January, 1963), 51-52 and 53.

year silence imposed by Henry, preach on the subject of restitution, and he was conscience-stricken about a sizeable embezzlement in the army. Over a two-year period, at great sacrifice, he made restitution to the government, meanwhile entering Cambridge to study theology. Receiving his M.A. in October of 1549, he became a fellow of Pembroke Hall, Cambridge. At the end of 1549 Martin Bucer, the Strassburg Reformer who had accepted Cranmer's invitation to come to England, took up duties as Regius Professor of Divinity at Cambridge, and we can be sure that Bradford was among those who heard him lecture on John 6 and on Ephesians, using Calvin's commentary on the epistle. It was Bucer who encouraged Bradford when he had doubts as to his call to preach: 'If thou have not fine manchet bread, yet give the poor people barley bread, or whatsoever else the Lord hath committed to thee.'

Bradford was ordained deacon in August of 1550 and licensed to preach by Ridley, then Bishop of London. Bradford preached effectively in the vicinity of Cambridge, where he attended Bucer at his death at the end of February 1551. In August of 1551 Ridley had him appointed a prebendary of St. Paul's, which allowed him to preach in and about London. In 1552 he was active in preaching in his native county of Lancashire, where Romanism remained prevalent. During Lent of 1553 he preached at Court in a way that left an impression on both Ridley and John Knox.

When Mary came to the throne in July of 1553, Bradford was arrested on the pretext of having preached without permission, thus having stirred up a riot, when actually he had spoken to help put down an uproar at Paul's Cross over the restoration of certain Roman practices. He was imprisoned first in the Tower, where his jailers unwisely placed him eventually in the same cell with Cranmer, Ridley, and Latimer, who helped themselves prepare for a common defense. Bradford, however, was moved to other prisons, where he helped to organize an underground movement along with Ridley to keep the Protestants faithful to their principles both inside and outside the prison walls. Some ninety-five of Bradford's letters have been preserved, many of his writings furnishing a major portion of the first edition of Foxe's *Book of Martyrs*. He helped frame some 'prison articles' of the faith, which anticipate parts of the Puritan Westminster Confession of the 1640s, and he engaged in debate on predestination with some 'freewillers' who had been arrested under Mary. Tried for heresy in January of 1555, after almost a year and a half in prison while Parliament was reviving the laws for burning of heretics, his execution was postponed for another five months, after the first burnings in February, during which time he was plied with blandishments from bishops, chaplains, old friends, and Spanish friars in order to get him to recant, all to no avail. On July 1, 1555, he was burned at the stake in Smithfield.

Bradford's writings, which comprise two volumes of the Parker Society collection of English Reformers, bear the mark of Luther's beliefs, and he did translate a work of Melanchthon's. But Bucer was clearly his 'father in the faith'. He nevertheless deserves to be called the first English Calvinist, for he reflects several of the distinctives of Calvin and evidently had read several of his works. In turn, his life and writings had an influence on several later Puritans, such as Thomas Sampson his contemporary, William Perkins, Richard Greenham, John Dod, and some of the Westminster Divines.

2. *The Piety of the Christian's Inner Life*
Bradford's piety has assurance as its pivot point. Assurance is for him both the fruit of godly exercises in prayer and meditation in one's private life and the

root of godly activity in one's public life. With regard to the Christian's inner, private life Bradford outlined a piety that includes four distinct concepts resulting in assurance: repentance and faith, peace of conscience, a feeling of God's grace, and union with Christ.

1. Repentance and Faith

His most famous sermon, a 'Sermon on Repentance' which he preached in Lancashire in the summer of 1552 and which he was requested to publish, reveals his starting point of repentance, which Sampson regarded as the keynote of his friend's life and message. For Bradford repentance meant sorrow for sin, trust of pardon, and a purpose to amend, or conversion to a new life – these in contrast to the three points of Romanist penance – contrition, confession, and satisfaction – which, he says, because God's standards are too high, no one can really accomplish. In this sermon he prescribes five parallel steps for both the Christian's sorrowing for sin and his good hope for God's pardon, the third point of newness of life flowing from these first two.

In the first place Bradford stresses that sorrow for sin cannot be produced by man of his own free will. It can only be a gift of God's grace. Repentance must begin, therefore, in prayer to God for this gift. This is the first step. The second step is to 'get thee God's law as a glass to toot in; for in it and by it cometh the true knowledge of sin, without which knowledge there can be no sorrow.' One must look in this mirror of the Law not merely corporally or carnally, but spiritually, examining in it the inner man after the manner of Christ in the Sermon on the Mount.[3] The third step is to 'look upon the tag tied to God's law' – that is, the penalty or curse connected

---

3. John Bradford, *The Writings of John Bradford*, ed. Aubrey Townsend for the Parker Society (Cambridge University Press, 1848, 1853), I, 54.

with it.[4] Then, in the fourth step, one is to bring to mind examples of God's judgement, both from Biblical and contemporary history. Finally, step five is to consider the death of Christ, who became man and suffered for the sins of His people. When these steps have resulted in some feeling of hearty sorrow for sin, then one may proceed to the second part, of trust or good hope for God's mercy.

The second part follows the same pattern as the first. The first step is to recognize that faith comes not by man's free will and therefore must be implored of God in prayer. Secondly, one goes again to God's Word, but this time to His word of mercy, the gospel, and one meditates then upon the free and unconditional promises of the gospel. The third step is to contemplate the benefits God has bestowed in making one a man or woman rather than a toad or a dog, or a Christian man or woman rather than a Turk or a pagan. The fourth step is to review the examples of God's love in the Bible. And finally, the fifth step is once again to regard the death of Christ, this time as the culminating example of God's mercy and forgiveness.

In Bradford's view repentance and faith are thus bound together, with the inevitable consequence being newness of life. Two elements noteworthy in Bradford's development of repentance and faith are man's total dependence on the authority of God's Word, whether it be law or gospel. Repentance and faith, thus construed, are not just the beginning of the Christian's life, but are to be continually practiced, or else one will fall into either hardening of heart or despair. These dire pitfalls pointed up the need for tender regard of one's conscience.

---

4. Ibid., I, 57.

2. Peace of Conscience

The second important concept of Bradford's piety of the inner life is peace of conscience. As for Luther, the conscience for Bradford is essentially the inner conviction of right and wrong. He warns against the peril of wounding the conscience by proceeding to do what this inner conviction testifies is wrong or by neglecting to do what this inner conviction testifies is right. There were people with over-active consciences entertaining all sorts of doubts and there were people with sleepy consciences insensitive to sin. In either case the conscience is not the final authority, but must be informed by the Word of God. This was particularly important for those who struggled with doubts as to their salvation, as was true of Mistress Mary Honywood, one of Bradford's correspondents who experienced continued depression. She it was who had her glass rebound when she told Foxe some years later, 'I am as surely damned as the glass is broken.'[5] She evidently continued to experience depression in spite of, or perhaps because of, the fact that she lived 92 years and saw 367 descendants by her death in 1620! In such a case Bradford reminded her that the conscience is only the accuser, not the judge; God and His Word alone can and must govern the conscience.

Complete peace of conscience is not a constant experience of the Christian's life, for there is a spiritual warfare taking place within each individual Christian between the old man and the new, the flesh and the Spirit. This strife is but a proof that one is among the elect, and the conflict should cause one to have recourse to the law to keep the old man from carnal carelessness and to the gospel to keep the new man from despair.

---

5. Thomas Fuller, *The History of the Worthies of England* (New York: AMS Press), II, 158-59.

3. The Feeling of God's Grace

Of great help in this conflict, according to Bradford, is the actual experience, or feeling, of God's grace, and this is the third important concept of his piety of the inner life. He tends to describe this in almost sensuous terms, as though the presence of God were tangible to him. It was his own practice to employ a spiritual diary – that which would become the Puritan's substitute for the confessional – for the sake of exercising his conscience until, as Sampson described it, 'he had felt inwardly some smiting of heart for sin and some healing of that wound by faith, feeling the saving health of Christ'.[6] To one of his correspondents he urged meditation in the Word in hope of gaining that assurance 'whereof the Holy Ghost doth now and then give us some taste and smell, to our eternal joy'.

But Bradford avoids religious subjectivism and pure emotionalism by giving priority to the Word. One is to believe and obey the Word whether it produces any feeling or not. 'First must faith go before, and then feeling will follow.'[7] Nevertheless he maintains the importance of feeling, which he associates with the inward working of the Holy Spirit. It is Word and Spirit combined which is the ideal experience for the Christian, which will bring with it that chief blessing to be obtained in this life, assurance of union with Christ.

4. Union with Christ

Union with Christ, the fourth important concept of Bradford's piety of the inner life, does not entail a mystical losing of one's identity, but rather a joining or linking of the new man with Christ, an analogy with the marriage relationship. It is a matter of God condescending by

---

6. Thomas Sampson, 'To the Christian Reader,' in Bradford, *Writings*, I, 33.
7. Bradford, *Writings*, II, 152.

grace to dwell in each believer rather than a matter of the individual believer rising to be absorbed into God. Especially under persecution this sense of union with Christ was real to Bradford. He felt He was being persecuted in him. At the head of his letters, as death drew near, he frequently wrote 'Jesus Immanuel' – 'God with us'.

Union with Christ was a very practical reality, then, for the ordinary Christian to experience here and now. According to Bradford it is already a reality for all genuine Christians and has been signified for them in their baptism. Union with Christ is not merely the ultimate goal of the Christian's life, even more it is the beginning of the Christian's life, stemming from his election by God before creation. A sense of the reality of this union, however, is to be desired for the assurance which would result during this life.

The sovereignty of God and the authority of His Word run through all of Bradford's account of the Christian's inner life. The covenant is not a prominent term in his writings, but it is present, and the concept if not the term looms large in the background of his thought. Again to Mrs. Honywood he wrote:

> ...as Satan laboureth to loosen our faith, so we must labour to fasten it, by thinking on the promises and covenant of God in Christ's blood; namely, that God is 'our God' with all that ever he hath. Which covenant dependeth and hangeth upon God's own goodness, mercy, and truth only, and not on our obedience and worthiness in any point, for these should we never be certain. Indeed God requireth of us obedience and worthiness, but not that thereby we might be his children and he our Father; but, because he is our Father and we his children, through his own goodness in Christ, therefore requireth he faith and obedience.[8]

On the basis of this concept of the relationship between the believer and his God, Bradford urged a practice of prayerful meditation on the Scriptures which would have impact on the whole man, convincing the mind, affecting the emotions, and producing action, all in accord with and governed by the authoritative Word of God.

3. *The Piety of the Christian's External Activity*
The Elizabethan Puritans were certainly as active as they were contemplative. John Bradford likewise sought to see his piety put into action. He opposed those who held that religion was a purely spiritual, or inner matter. He also opposed those, like the freewillers in prison, who deplored his teaching of assurance because they felt it would lead to a careless and worldly life. Quite the contrary, said Bradford; it was doubt and insecurity that led to weakness and compromise with evil. Assurance, on the basis of God's gracious election, is the very fountainhead of godly living.

1. Body and Soul
From prison Bradford repeatedly urged Protestants outside the walls to avoid attendance at mass. As the First Commandment forbids all inward idolatry, so the Second forbids all outward idolatry. One must either reprove the mass when present or else separate from it entirely. Bradford called for purity in word and deed as well as in thought. At times his concern for the body as well as soul approached the rigors of asceticism.

2. Discipline
The Christian life, according to Bradford, required discipline. The true church in his day he discerned by

---

8. Ibid. II, 153.

'the Word of God truly preached, the sacraments purely ministered, and some discipline nothing so much as hath been, might be, and should be'.[9] True Christians are to 'keep company with disciples', for public use of the means of grace is important along with private meditation.[10] Using the term 'regeneration' to describe the process of spiritual development flowing from justification, Bradford measures this development by the Ten Commandments. In his expositions of the law he sees the Sabbath commandment as a moral law still in force, not only requiring worship but also ruling out legitimate work on Sunday.

3. The Commonwealth

Bradford's concern for the public observance of the Sabbath principle is but one example of his community-consciousness. He evidently belonged to a circle known as the 'commonwealth men' in Edward's reign, a group concerned to stop the enclosure movement and restore the fortunes of the common yeomen in England. Latimer had preached on behalf of social justice for the poorer classes, and Bucer's teaching and writing in England had stressed social ethics. Bradford himself denounced the oppression by the magistrates in his preaching at Court. He sensed a corporate responsibility for God's judgement on England following the failure to respond to the gospel in Edward's reign. With regard to the authority of the government Bradford opposed rebellion but taught that there is a higher authority in the person of God, whom one must obey rather than man. He did not have the same qualms of conscience that Cranmer had concerning the royal authority. But his hope was to persuade a contrary magistracy by constancy in passive resistance.

---

9. Ibid. II, 346.
10. Ibid. I, 72.

For Bradford, then, the Christian's outward piety is consistent with his inward piety. Governing both is a sense of the sovereignty of God and the authority of His Word. Internal spiritual devotion has its corresponding external activity. As communion with God produces assurance, so assurance produces obedience.

4. Love In Action
The crowning virtue for Bradford is love. He was distressed when fellowship with the freewillers in prison was severed. Accused of withholding from them a fair share of the Protestants' funds in prison, he sent a special gift, urging the freewillers, 'Though in some things we agree not, yet let love bear the bell away' – let love override all other considerations.[11] Here love is expressed not merely in sentiment but in action, it is not merely a private matter but a public matter, it involves not only individuals but the unity of the corporate whole.

Conclusion
How, finally, is Bradford's piety to be characterized? Although it emphasizes the role of the Holy Spirit in the individual's soul, it cannot be called mystical, for the basis is the objective Word of God, and the result of its union with Christ is not a flight from the world but rather a living of Christ's life in this world. Neither may his piety be described as rationalistic, because he stresses both the authority of God's Word and also the role of feeling in producing assurance. At the same time it cannot be regarded as primarily emotional, for the feelings are to be subsidiary to reasoned acceptance of and obedience to God's Word. Although obedience to God's law and purity of life are stressed in Bradford, his

---

11. Ibid. II, 180.

piety is not legalistic since there is no sense of reward or of merit, righteousness being the result of God's grace. Bradford gives some prominence to the sacraments and the institutional church, but his piety cannot be described as sacerdotal. It is probably best to characterize his piety as evangelical. It stressed above all the grace of God, ministered by the Holy Spirit from the Scriptures to the individual, who through a reasoned faith in what God has revealed experiences union with Christ, the assurance of which results in obedience to God's will out of love for God and one's fellow men. Founded on the grace of God at every point, Bradford's piety thus moves from the Word to the mind to the emotions and finally to action, with assurance being the pivot point between the inner spiritual life and the external activity of the Christian.

If we wish to understand the motivating spirit of the Puritans, we would do well to comprehend this sort of piety which manifested itself in the English Reformation of Edward's reign. The assurance that gave such earnest conviction to Bradford and the other Protestant martyrs and Reformers, and which would characterize the later Puritans, is based on a sense of authority of Scripture. Bradford's doctrine of Scripture – upholding the Bible's unique authority, its infallibility as inspired by the Holy Spirit, its interpretation by itself through comparison of passages in the original languages and according to the 'plain' sense of their contexts, and its sufficiency for all matters of faith and life as the Word of God written – is not a static view, but a dynamic one, for the very reason that the Scriptures are identified with the Word of God. It is this view that provided the impulse for Bradford's assurance, which is the essential feature of his piety. God has spoken and is still speaking to His people through the Scriptures. And what God is saying includes more than just that which is necessary to salvation; it includes also how He wants His church to serve Him in worship and in life. Until one can enter sympathetically into this sort of mentality, one cannot fully comprehend the Puritan spirit or epistemology. And it is this Puritan and Reformation quality of spirituality, understanding, and life that the evangelical church so urgently needs today.

Subject Index

abolitionism 65, 81, 84, 92
abolitionists 80-2
abortion 121, 145
Adopting Act 1729 208, 210, 212-16, 219-21, 230-3, 248, 250, 252, 254, 256
adoption 172, 199, 203
America 21, 24, 29, 32, 36-7, 39, 41, 68, 75, 77, 86-8, 96, 107, 114, 118-19, 124, 127-9, 131, 147, 156, 198, 210, 213-14, 236, 284, 293
    American Bill of Rights 128
        Civil War 88-9, 92, 99, 117, 284
        Congress 128
        Constitution 128, 147
        Declaration of Independence 128, 226
        First Amendment 115, 128
American Presbyterian Church *See under* Presbyterian church
Amsterdam 182, 275
Anabaptists 20, 26, 135, 181 202
anarchy 52
Anglicanism 126
Antinomians 182, 202 *See also* irresponsibility, Antinomian
apologetics 274, 290
Arianism 244
Arminianism 176, 202, 218, 220 *See also* moralism, Arminian
ascension 24, 53
Assessor 36-7, 40
assurance 24, 29, 41, 173, 199, 202, 272, 293-4, 297-8, 301-3, 305-6
atheism 96
    atheists 133
atonement 14, 287
Auburn Affirmation (1923-4) 287
Augustinianism 219, 221
authority, civil 20, 30, 90, 109, 113, 116, 120-1, 127, 131-5, 137-8, 142-6, 163-4, 182, 293, 304
    of Jesus /God 12-3, 16, 19, 52, 54, 110, 128, 148-9, 279, 288, 304
    religious 52, 136, 184
    of Scripture 14, 24, 81-4, 104, 126, 216, 272-4, 279-80, 288-9, 291, 293, 294, 299, 302, 305-6 *See also* Word of God
    spiritual 125-7, 134
    of Synod 229, 238 *See also* synod
Authority and Interpretation of the Bible (Rogers and McKim) 273, 275, 289
Awakening, Great 43

baptism 12, 14, 55, 188, 199, 302
Baptists 112, 155-6, 165, 183, 198 *See also* confessions of faith; London, Baptists
bishops 23, 107-8, 134, 167, 177-8, 186, 297 *See also* episcopacy
blasphemy 12, 115-16
Body of Divinity (Watson) 193, 197-8, 200, 202-3, 205-6
Boston (Lincolnshire) 37, 39
Boston (U.S.) 37, 41, 241
Brazil 35
British Empire 65
Bury St. Edmunds 176

Caesar 31, 70, 91, 124, 138-43, 147-9
    caesaropapism 30, 125
calling, effectual 16, 199, 202, 205
Calvinism 20, 24, 73-6, 88, 97, 101-2, 105, 156, 192, 202, 218-19, 221, 223, 225, 272, 275, 293, 297
Cambridge University 25-6, 38, 156, 189, 296
    Christ's College 26
    Emmanuel College 37, 39, 159, 193, 200
    Pembroke Hall 176, 189, 296
    Queen's College 26
Canterbury 40
catechism 35, 40, 191, 207
    Heidelberg 282
    Westminster Assembly, Larger 28, 39, 43, 49, 70, 152, 154, 156, 191, 198, 204, 209, 224-6, 250-1, 259
    Westminster Assembly, Shorter 39, 69, 114, 116-17, 152-4, 197-9, 200, 266-7
    Westminster Catechisms 35, 41, 156, 202-3, 208-12, 214-15, 220, 224, 230-3, 236, 254-7, 268
celibacy 62
Channel Islands 156
chiliasm 25-6
    chiliasts 162
China 124, 128
Christian Reformed Church (US) 207
church 12-15, 19-33, 39, 44-5, 49-51, 57-71, 79, 81, 83, 91-2, 94-6, 99, 101, 107, 110-12, 116, 118, 122, 124-8, 132-6, 142, 149, 154, 162, 167, 173, 178, 182, 184, 189-92, 205-7, 209, 222, 226, 250, 260, 274-7, 282, 294, 303, 306-7
    church growth 68
    church-state relations 29, 39,123, 131, 133-5, 138-9

Subject Index

early 55, 68, 121, 273
established 23-4, 126, 135
evangelical 36, 307
government *See* government, church
membership of 20, 23, 81
power of 111
Presbyterian *See* Presbyterian church
reformed 19, 22
Reformed 33, 127, 131, 220, 222
Prussian Church 94
Scottish church 164, 198
state church 134, 184
See also purity of church; unity of church
citizenship 20, 32, 52-4, 59, 70-1, 121, 147
Civil War (American*) See* America
Civil War (English) 37, 154, 170, 181-2, 193-4
class (social) 14, 49, 60, 67-8, 79, 92-4, 96, 103-4
clergy 93, 134, 162, 184, 186
  London 40, 152, 180, 185
commandment 47-9, 54, 60, 70-1, 96, 114, 116, 127, 135, 137-8, 140-1, 143-6, 203, 225-6, 303
  the Ten Commandments 39, 50, 116, 128, 144, 154, 191, 199, 204, 304
  Ten Commandments (Watson) 197, 200-1
Commission, Great 12-13, 15, 17, 35, 45, 64, 71, 148
Common Sense Realism 276, 283, 291
Commonwealth 193, 195, 304
communism 96, 115, 124, 128
community 19-20, 32, 49, 59-60, 67-9, 74, 87, 90, 99, 112, 122, 304
condemnation 64, 80-1, 172
confessions of faith 207-8, 210-12, 215, 217, 236, 248, 250, 289
  Baptist Confession 1742 156
  Scots Confession 1560 23, 282
  United Presbyterian Confession 1967 275, 277
  Westminster Confession of Faith 35, 45, 144, 152, 154-6, 168, 172, 191, 198, 202-3, 207-16, 218-25, 228, 230-4, 236, 247-52, 254-7, 259, 268, 275, 279-80, 283, 287, 289, 297
congregationalism 23-4, 155, 164, 183
  congregationalists 20, 156, 198, 228
conscience 41, 56-7, 67, 81, 90-1, 104, 113-14, 117, 135-6, 144-6, 159, 175, 186-7, 191, 202-3, 216, 222, 296, 298-301, 304
conservatism 73-5, 77-80, 83, 88-9, 92-3, 100, 104
Constantinople 111, 125-6, 134
conventicles 107, 196
conversion 25-7, 30, 39, 102, 134, 202, 246, 295, 298
  See also Indians; Jews, conversion of
corruption in society 28, 44, 49, 67
Counter-Reformation 35, 281
covenant 13, 32, 121, 136, 138, 145, 173, 180, 182, 188, 202, 302
  Ark of the, 110, 188

Covenant Seminary 12-13
Half-Way Covenant 1662 32
National Covenant 154, 154, 163-5, 182
Solemn League and Covenant 164-5, 182
theology 13, 203
  of grace 172, 199, 203
  of works 199, 203
creation 63, 198, 201, 259-62, 263-70, 302
creeds 22, 207, 220, 222, 225, 247
criticism of Scripture, higher 284
  textual 284
cross 11, 14, 47, 51-2, 71
crucifixion 24, 138
crusades 112, 126, 135
Cuba 124, 128
culture 14, 16, 50, 52, 54, 61, 65-6, 73, 92, 112, 115-17, 128, 132, 290

death 12, 108-9, 172-3, 199, 287, 302
  Christ's 14, 47, 53, 246, 288, 299
deism 214, 235, 238, 244, 246, 257, 290
democracy 85-8, 114
desegregation 66
determinism 103
diary, spiritual 173-4, 301
disciples 12-16, 47, 64, 67, 71, 109-10, 139, 148, 291, 304
discipleship 13-14
discipline 21-4, 108, 164, 210, 236, 303-4
doctrine 22, 24, 27, 35, 39, 55, 58-9, 63-4, 73, 77, 79, 97, 114, 132, 134-5, 144, 146, 152, 155-6, 172, 198-9, 201, 203, 205, 208-12, 215-16, 218-24, 227-8, 231, 236, 247-8, 251, 255-7, 259, 272-3, 275, 277, 284-8
  Arminian 154
  Puritan 179
  Reformed 152
  system of 210, 222-5
Donatists 31, 111
Dorchester 36-7
Dort, Synod of 26, 176

Eastern Orthodoxy 123
Eastern Roman Empire 125
'ecclesiocracy' 126, 134
ecclesiology 32
  Reformed 21
economics 80, 93
Edgehill, Battle of 170
edification 55, 57
Ejection, Great 193, 195, 204
elders 104, 178, 191, 209, 225-6, 259
election 24, 29, 172, 302-3
emancipation 80, 89, 92-3
enemies 51, 59, 119, 121, 139
England 19-21, 25-6, 29, 35, 37, 41-2, 88, 126, 154-5, 178, 182, 198, 214, 249, 293, 296, 304
Ephesus, Council of 431 25
episcopacy 40, 154, 160, 177-8 *See also* bishops

309

episcopalians 185
epistemology 291, 307
equality 85-7
Erastians 183, 192
eschatology 24-5, 27, 69
Essenes 141
established religion 20-1
eternal life 13, 15, 47
eternity 205-6, 262
ethics 84, 131, 191-2, 205, 304
evangelicals 65, 123, 131, 213, 274, 277
evangelism 43, 63-4, 122, 136, 192, 227
evil 24, 51-2, 56, 69, 81, 84, 99, 113, 179, 303
evolution 63
exaltation (of Christ) 199
excommunication 111, 229-30
Exodus 110

faith 12, 14-16, 43, 55-7, 64, 70, 73, 79-80, 101-2, 107-9, 112-15, 122, 125, 128, 131, 135-6, 138, 143-4, 147-8, 155, 199, 201-3, 207, 209-12, 219, 222, 226-7, 231, 236, 246, 251, 257, 264, 274, 276-7, 279-82, 285-6, 288-91, 297-9, 301-2, 306
    Reformed 35, 219
faithfulness 48, 61
fall 66, 199, 267, 283
family 49, 60
    God's 173
fast days 36-7, 157-8, 160-2, 170, 178-9, 181-3
Fatherhood of God 172
feeling 81, 161, 301, 305
fellowship 27, 58, 71, 81, 174, 206, 298, 305
Fifth Monarchy 26-7
forgiveness 12, 71, 119-20, 298, 299
France 41, 87, 295
Free Church of Scotland 93-4
free will 179, 298-9
    freewillers 297, 303, 305
freedom *See* liberty
Fuller Theological Seminary 275, 277
fundamentalists (Christian) 131

General Assembly (Presbyterian church) 76-7, 91, 93-4, 114, 209 *See also* United Presbyterian Church
Geneva 20-1, 23, 112
    Bible 25
gentiles 28, 31, 44, 58, 64, 113, 142, 144-5
Germany 20, 76, 126
gifts (from God) 14, 50-2, 100, 192, 298
gospel 22, 28, 35, 39, 44-5, 47-52, 54, 58-60, 63-6, 68-70, 93-6, 100, 109, 113, 136, 142, 144-5, 148, 192, 219-22, 228, 247, 290, 299, 304
    social gospel 96-7, 103, 104
government 28-9, 32, 50, 52-3 , 70-1, 75, 79, 84-5, 90, 100, 110, 114, 131-4, 140, 142-3, 145-6, 148-9, 185, 296, 304
    church 23, 104, 180, 185, 191, 210-12, 215, 227, 251

form of 114, 191
grace 14, 23, 47-8, 50-1, 58, 62, 64, 70, 111, 114, 117, 128, 136, 172-3, 179, 199, 201, 204, 206, 227, 298, 301-2, 304, 306
guilt, corporate 67, 248
    personal 107, 121, 172

heresy 107, 152, 181, 208, 213-14, 229-30, 297
Herodians 31-2, 70, 124, 127, 138-42
Holland 20, 185, 195
Holy Spirit 13, 15, 17, 33, 51-2, 57-8, 62, 69, 110, 144, 174, 202-3, 264, 276, 280, 286, 289, 301, 305-6
hope 12, 24-6, 29, 57, 121, 227, 298-9, 301 *See also* millennium
    millennial hope
Huguenots 111, 176
human nature, fallen 16, 62
human rights 66, 114
    See also rights (of man)
humanism 115-16
    humanists 133
humiliation (of Christ) 199
    (of soul) 179, 202

idolatry 107, 115, 147, 200, 205, 303
incarnation 287, 290
Independency 158-9
    Independents 159, 162, 164-5, 167, 178, 181-2, 185, 192, 194
Indians, conversion of 39
    mission to 37, 39-40, 43, 192
individualism 75, 79, 83, 102
Indulgence, Declaration of 1672 196
inerrancy (of scripture) 14, 207, 272-5, 277-8, 280, 282, 285, 287-90, 306
infralapsarianism 172, 192
injustice 91, 119
inspiration of Scripture 273, 277-8, 280, 306
Investiture Controversy 30, 126
Ireland 154, 235-6, 249-51
    Northern 214-15, 254-5
    See also synod
irresponsibility, Antinomian 179
Israel 27, 29, 31, 110, 119, 132-3, 136-7, 145, 169
Islam 123, 202

Jamaica 245, 253
Japan 35
Jerusalem 58, 110-11, 138, 291
Jesuits 35
Jews 25-8, 31, 35, 44, 48, 58, 64, 110, 124, 138, 140, 146
    conversion of 25-7
joy 57
Judea 54, 110
judgment 55, 57, 64, 81, 90, 100-1, 114, 118, 135, 179, 216, 219, 251-2, 256, 299, 304
    day of 27
justice 48-9, 66, 97, 99-100, 108-9, 127-9, 136, 142, 145, 153, 195, 246, 304

Subject Index

justification by faith 32, 192, 199, 203, 247, 257, 304

kingdom (of God) 27, 37, 44, 54, 70, 108-12, 114, 122, 142, 148-9, 163, 201, 204

Lancashire 296, 298
Lapps 44
law 47-9, 82, 87, 90-2, 108, 111, 115, 128, 134, 143, 145, 147-8, 169, 185, 196, 199, 203, 205, 291, 295, 297-9, 300, 304
    God's 131-3, 136-8, 143-6, 305
    of Nature 246
    Roman 125, 134
leadership 63, 65, 71, 137
liberalism, Victorian 100
liberation theology 68
Liberia 89
liberty 87-8, 91-2, 145-6, 148, 216
    Christian 54-7
    of conscience 104, 113-14, 145, 249, 251
    religious 36, 88, 113-16, 127-9, 133, 138, 143-4, 161
liturgy (Anglican) 154, 166, 177
London 37, 40, 152, 156, 162, 165, 170-1, 175-8, 180, 182-5, 190-1, 193-4, 196, 198, 296
    Baptists 155
    Great Fire of 189, 196
Lord's Supper 47, 71, 108, 135, 191, 199, 203
lordship (of Christ) 11-17, 24, 54-5, 59, 62, 122
love 47-62, 68-9, 71, 109, 111, 116, 128, 137, 143, 195-6, 199, 203, 299, 305-6
Lutheranism 126, 220
    Swedish Lutherans 44

magistrate, civil 20, 28, 44, 111, 134-7, 144, 209-10, 212, 214, 216, 221, 225, 231-2, 252, 254, 304
Manchester 295
marriage 29, 49, 60-2, 65, 97, 221, 225, 293, 301
martyrs 294, 306
Marxism 68
mass 293, 295, 303
Massachusetts 23-4, 36
    Company 37
meditation 206, 297, 301, 303-4
membership, church 20, 23
mercy 48, 51, 179, 299, 302
Methodists 94
millennium 25-7, 45, 111, 192
    millenarianism 162-3
        millennial hope 24-6
    See also postmillennialism; premillennialism; second coming
ministers 40, 58, 94-6, 104, 154, 169, 175, 177, 183, 185-7, 190, 193, 195, 201, 211-15, 218-20, 225-8, 232, 238-9, 251, 254-7, 274, 295
ministry 38, 41-2, 76, 97, 164, 169, 187, 195-6, 210, 214, 221, 236, 242, 251-2, 255

candidates for 93, 209, 211, 214-17, 221, 226, 232, 236, 251, 256, 270, 287
miracles 30, 110, 287
mission 12, 35, 37, 43-4, 58, 63-4, 88, 93, 120, 192
    See also Indians, mission to
moderation 77-8, 80, 84, 88, 104
monarchy 23, 86, 185
    Restoration of (England) 190, 193, 195
    Stuart 154
monasticism 45
monotheism 12, 147
moralism, Arminian 179, 214
morality 85, 115
Muslims 146

Nantes, Edict of 111
naturalists 133
neighbour 48-50, 52-4, 57, 59-60, 69, 116, 119, 128, 137, 143, 205
Netherlands 24, 41, 127, 193, 297
New England 19, 21, 25, 29, 32, 39-43, 102, 112
New England Way 19
New School (Presbyterians) 210, 220, 222
New Side (Presbyterians) 208-10, 226-7
New Haven (USA) 41
Nicaea, Council of 325 30, 125
Ninety-five Theses 35, 45
North Korea 124, 128
nonconformists 36, 189-90, 193, 196
    nonconformity 190, 193

obedience 14, 17, 32, 47, 70, 90, 124, 127, 146, 192, 199, 227, 302, 305-6
Old Princeton Seminary 208, 222
    Old Princeton theologians 272, 274, 277, 288
        theology 273
    See also under Princeton Seminary
Old School (Presbyterians) 210, 220, 222
Old Side (Presbyterians) 208-10, 226
ordinances 28, 44, 90, 173, 200, 206
ordination 164, 214-15, 236, 270, 282, 287
    vows 152, 208-9, 216-18, 222-3, 259, 270
origins, human 146
Oxford university 156, 169-70
    Magdalen Hall 168
    Trinity College 168, 174

pagan religion 140
    ritual 125
    society 137
papacy 111-12, 126, 134-5, 225
pardon *See* forgiveness
Parker Society 297
parish 62, 181, 183, 195
Parliament 40-1, 154, 156, 158, 160-1, 163-5, 167, 178-9, 181, 194-5, 198, 297
    Long 29, 157-8, 160, 162-3, 170, 178, 185, 187

311

Rump 158, 185, 194
    Short 154, 160
patience 101
patriotism 115
peace 55, 57, 107-10, 113, 118, 199, 217, 250, 298, 300
Pelagianism 218
penance 108, 298
persecution 20, 30-1, 41, 52, 109, 112, 124-5, 127, 133-4, 205, 302
perseverance 199
Pharisees 31, 48, 70, 124, 127, 138-43, 148
Philadelphia 237, 243
    First Presbyterian Church of Philadelphia 235, 237
piety 33, 36, 198, 200, 205, 292, 295, 297-8, 300-1, 303, 305-6
pluralism, religious 113-14, 131-3
    social 115
politics 14, 80, 87, 91, 93, 131-2
    pornography 145
Portugal 44
postmillennialism 26 *See also* millennium; premillennialism; second coming
poverty 68, 96-101, 108
power, civil / state 19, 31-2, 53, 90, 112, 114, 120, 125-6, 128, 134-5, 141, 147, 149, 212
    of God 12, 16, 28, 44, 65, 69-70, 110, 153, 179 201, 263-4
prayer 36, 43, 58, 107, 109, 118-21, 145, 166, 169, 192, 194, 196, 199, 201-2, 206, 222, 227, 297, 299
    Prayer Book 293
    Lord's 28, 43, 70, 118, 154, 199, 204, 225
    Lord's Prayer (Watson) 197, 201
preaching 15, 22-3, 32, 37-41, 94-6, 157, 161-3, 169, 171, 174,194, 196-7, 200, 227, 237, 295-6, 304
predestination 172, 297
prejudice, racial 63
premillennialism 26-7, 224-5 *See also* millennialism; postmillennialism; second coming
presbyter 20, 177-8
Presbyterian church 76, 93, 95, 104, 114, 222, 226, 234-5, 247, 249-50
    American Presbyterian Church (1729) 210, 225, 228 *See also below*
        Presbyterian Church in America
    Irish Presbyterian Church 236
    Orthodox Presbyterian Church 208
    Presbyterian Church in America 210, 232-3, 247, 249-59, 259
    Presbyterian Church in America (PCA) 208, 214, 232, 270
    Presbyterian Church of America (now OPC) 135, 224-5, 228 *See also above*
        Orthodox Presbyterian Church
    See also Philadelphia, First Presbyterian Church of;
        United Presbyterian Church

Presbyterians 40, 92, 94, 102, 114, 152, 155-6, 165, 167, 175, 178, 182, 184, 186, 189, 192, 194-5, 198, 219, 284, 289
    English 158, 196
    Scottish 135
Presbyterianism 13, 23, 74, 127, 158-60, 164-5, 180, 182, 185, 191, 217, 289
    American 152, 208, 216, 224, 230, 275
    Scottish 13, 224
presbytery 164, 208, 211-17, 219, 221, 232, 236-7, 251, 254-7, 259-60, 270, 282
priesthood (of believers) 55
priests 20, 125, 136, 142, 200
Princeton Theological Seminary 76-8, 246, 253, 276, 290
    Princeton theologians 282-3, 286-9
    theology 74, 76, 273, 277, 282
    See also under Old Princeton Seminary
Prolocutor 36
promises of God 16, 60, 205, 299, 302
prophecy 24-7
prophets 109, 137-8, 143
prosperity 97, 99-100, 108-10
Protestantism 20, 24, 35, 45, 123, 126, 220, 293-4
    American 135
    See also Reformation, Protestant
providence 24, 29-30, 45, 88-9, 93, 99-101, 103-5, 117, 128, 198, 236, 283
punishment 53, 97, 100-1
Puritanism 33, 102, 163, 182, 191, 293-4, 307
Puritans 19-21, 23-9, 31-3, 37, 41, 112, 153-4, 159, 162-3, 173, 180, 184, 186, 192-3, 262, 266, 272, 289, 293, 295, 297, 301, 303, 306
purity of church 15, 20-1, 24, 32, 59, 112, 144, 217
Quakers 112
quietism 120

race 14, 49, 60, 64, 91
    relations 62-3, 65-7
racism 64
reason 81, 112, 249, 274, 276-7, 280, 282, 290-1, 305
Rebellion, Puritan 32
redemption 13, 63-4, 142, 199, 201, 287
Reformation, English 31, 154-5, 161, 178, 198, 293-5, 306-7
    Protestant 20, 28, 35, 43-4, 55, 62, 123, 126, 135, 155, 276
    Swiss 20
Reformers, Protestant (of 16th century) 25-6, 30-1, 45, 126, 200, 262, 273-4, 277, 279, 289, 293-6, 297, 306
regeneration 49, 62-3, 67, 69, 102, 304
repentance 23, 63-4, 108, 120, 147-8, 179, 199, 202, 298-9
responsibility 55, 74, 96, 136, 138, 146, 162, 179, 217, 304

Subject Index

restitution 108, 296
resurrection 12, 15, 24, 27, 53, 110, 143, 199, 287
revelation 14, 112, 147, 202, 247, 276
revenge 51
revival 43, 102, 122
revolution 90
righteousness 48, 53-4, 57, 70, 109, 138, 146, 148, 248, 306
rights (of man) 82-3, 85, 92, 96-7, 132 *See also* human rights
Roman Catholic church 20, 22-4, 111, 127 *See also* schools
Roman Catholicism 123, 202-3
Roman Empire 54, 108, 111, 124-5, 146-7
Rome 54, 125, 134, 203, 295

Sabbath observance 146, 199, 206, 226, 304
sacraments 21-3, 32, 188, 200, 203, 206, 304, 306
sacrifice 11, 296
    living 51, 59
Sadducees 143
saints 27, 58, 73, 78, 166, 172-4, 202, 257
    visible 20, 23, 33
St Louis (USA) 66
salvation 12, 24, 32, 41, 53, 60, 64, 74, 102, 113, 122, 126, 128, 172-3, 179, 199, 202, 227, 247, 272, 274-5, 290, 293-4, 300, 306
sanctification 22, 63, 199, 203, 287
Savoy Declaration 155
Scandinavia 126
schism 22
scholasticism 112, 276-7, 280-2, 289
    Thomistic 282
schools 66, 145-6
Scotland 21, 25, 41, 112, 127, 154, 158, 164, 190-1, 198, 249, 223, 277
secessionists, Scottish 213
second coming 28, 44, 53, 287
    See also eschatology; millennialism; post-millennialism; premillennialism
sectarianism 184
secularism 147
segregation 64, 89, 119
self-sustentation 94-5, 104
Sermon on the Mount 50, 148, 298
service 68, 71, 74
sin 11-13, 28-9, 44, 49, 53, 56, 64, 66-7, 70, 84, 99, 101-2, 108, 110, 118, 121, 136, 145, 172, 174, 179, 187-8, 199, 201, 205, 225, 283, 287, 298-9, 300-1
Sion College, London 180
slavery 58, 65, 79-84, 88-9, 91-2, 105, 117, 119
society 31, 52, 54, 59-60, 63, 66-71, 75, 79-80, 83, 85, 87, 89, 91, 93, 97, 99, 105, 108, 115-16, 118, 122, 132-3, 137, 143, 146, 249

Socinianism 218, 246
    Socinians 202
Southern Baptist Convention 207
sovereignty of God 13, 29, 90, 99-100, 263, 293, 302, 305
Soviet Union 124 128, 147
Spain 44
Spanish Armada 29, 35
state 20, 27-33, 37-9, 52, 91-2, 108, 111-17, 123-8, 132-6, 144-5, 147
submission 61-2
subscription 152, 207-8, 218, 223-4, 229-30, 239, 254, 259, 270
    confessional 214, 216-17, 221, 232, 234, 242, 250, 252
subscriptionists, strict 210, 213, 223, 231, 233-4, 252-3
suffering 97-8, 100-1, 186, 196, 205
suffrage, universal 86
superstition 203
supralapsarianism 192
supremacy, racial 63-4
Switzerland 127
synod 207, 211-15, 232, 247, 250-1, 255, 257
Synod, Commission of 214, 229, 238-43, 245-6, 249-50, 252, 256
    General 238
    General Synod of Ireland 255
    National 179
    of 1729 210-12, 231-4, 250, 252, 254, 256
    of 1730 213-16, 231-3
    of 1734 236, 253
    of 1735 240, 242-9, 252, 254, 256
    of 1736 232-4, 256
    of Boston 1680 155
    of Cambridge, Mass. 1648 (Congregational) 155
    of Saybrook 1708 (Congregational) 155
    of New York and Philadelphia 209-10, 226, 228-30, 236
    See also Dort

temperance 79, 84
temple 110, 203
theism 96
    theists 133
theocracy 29, 31, 109, 132, 142-3, 145
theology 73, 78, 98, 102-3, 118, 154, 198, 274, 276, 281, 285, 289, 296,
    Protestant 155, 281
    Puritan 33, 191, 199
    Reformation 44
    systematic 205, 284
    See also Old Princeton, theology; Princeton, theology

theonomy 131-2, 136, 145
Thirty Years' War 24
toleration (religious) 181-2, 189, 249
tradition 73, 207, 276, 285
    Augustinian 112, 277
    Protestant evangelical 123
    Puritan 177
    Reformed 20, 49, 69, 105, 221, 275
    Scottish Presbyterian 13
transubstantiation 203
Trinity 12, 14, 198
trust 12, 14, 60, 102, 112, 276, 298-9
truth 23, 38, 56-7, 59, 68, 78, 81, 91, 95, 102, 104, 113, 121, 136, 138, 153, 183, 186, 191, 205-6, 222, 228, 276, 279, 286, 302
Uniformity, Act of 187, 189, 195
union with Christ /God 14, 64, 298, 301-2, 305-6
Unitarians 190, 214
United Presbyterian Church 273-4, 282
    General Assembly 273, 282, 287
    See also under confessions of faith
United Presbyterians 274, 289
U.S.A./United States *See* America
unity (of believers / church) 15, 23, 54, 57, 59, 64-5, 104
    of man 63
universities 112
utopianism 30

virgin birth 287
virtue 83, 85, 87

wealth 75, 111-12, 118, 120
Westminster Assembly 26, 28, 36-41, 43, 152, 154-6, 158, 160, 164-5, 168-9, 171, 174-5, 178, 180-1, 190-3, 197-8, 204, 211-12, 215, 251, 259-60, 262, 265, 268-9, 279, 282, 287

Directory of Worship 165-6, 191, 210, 233, 236
Divines 27, 35-7, 40, 43, 152, 154, 158, 181, 260-2, 265-7, 273-5, 279, 287, 289, 297
Standards 152, 191, 202, 209-10, 213, 215-22, 224-7, 229, 248, 256-7, 260-1, 267, 270, 282
See also catechisms; confessions
Westminster College, Pennsylvania 275
Westminster Theological Seminary 260
Westphalia, Peace of (1648) 45
wickedness 53, 70, 109, 145
will of God 28, 32, 49, 53, 56, 62, 69-70, 90-1, 101, 117-18, 121, 134, 263, 306
See also freewill
wisdom 48, 87, 100, 110, 139, 153, 201
witness 68, 122, 137, 222, 227, 280, 288
Word of God 16, 21, 23-4, 32-3, 67, 78-9, 81, 83, 101, 144, 153, 187, 192, 199-203, 206, 210, 217, 221, 264, 267, 279-80, 290, 293, 299-306
See also authority of Scripture
worship 12, 17, 42, 63, 68, 114, 127, 129, 135, 137, 141-5, 149, 166, 191, 196, 199-200, 203, 206, 210-12, 215, 227, 251, 293, 295, 304, 307
See also under Westminster, Directory for Worship
wrath (of God) 100, 199

Yale College 13

Zealots 31, 127, 139-40
Zurich 20

Scripture Index

Genesis
1................ 259, 261, 262, 264, 266-7, 269-70
1:3.................... 263
1:5.................... 260
1:14.................. 262
2....................... 264
5,11.................. 266
23:9.................. 278

Exodus
33:15................ 16

Leviticus
10:1.................. 203
19:18............ 48, 51

Deuteronomy
15:11.................. 67
31:6.................... 16

Joshua
1:5...................... 16
24:15................ 180

Judges
5:23.................. 161
21:25................ 110

1 Samuel
4:13.................. 188

2 Samuel
24:14................ 187

2 Chronicles
6:22-39............ 119
7:14.................. 118
19:11................ 136

Psalms
2:10-12............ 148
8:3.................... 201
118:22.............. 142
148:5................ 201

Isaiah
3:10-11............ 195
6:1, 5-8............ 121
57:1.................. 188
61:1.................... 67

Jeremiah
2, 3.................... 60
9:24.................. 48
18:7-10............ 178
29:7............ 109, 118

Ezekiel
16...................... 60
36:32................ 179

Daniel
2:44-5.............. 149
4:2, 8, 37.......... 137
6:26.................. 137

Micah
6:8...................... 48

Zechariah
7:9-10................ 48

Matthew
11:5.................... 67
12:25................ 182
21:33-46............ 31
21:45................ 142
22:15-22.... 31, 70, 138
22:37-40............ 48
23:23.................. 48
24:9-14............ 109
25:23.................. 17
26:11.................. 67
27:9.................. 278
28:18.................. 12
28:19-20............ 14
28:20............ 15, 71

Mark
2:23-3:6............ 226
9:24.................. 16
12:12................ 142
12:13-17........ 138-9
12:28................ 143
14:7.................... 67

Luke
1:51.................. 201
4:18.................... 67
12:48................ 186
14:23................ 111
20:16-17, 19.... 142
20:20-6.......... 138-9
24:32, 39.......... 291

John
3:16.................... 47
6...................... 296
6:60-4, 67-9..... 15
12:8.................... 67
13-16.................. 47
13:34................ 195
13:34-5.......... 48, 71
13:35.................. 16
14:15, 21, 23-4, 31...... 48
15:10, 12, 14, 17...... 48
19:10-11............ 53
20:21.................. 17
20:28.................. 16

Acts
4:12.................... 12
4:18-20............ 124
5:29............ 53, 124
5:41.................... 53
7:16.................. 278
7:60.................... 51
9:15-16.............. 58
10:38.................. 69
17:26.................. 63
17:30................ 181
22:14-15............ 58
26:16-20............ 58

Romans
1-11.................. 59
1:4.................... 12
1:11-12, 15........ 58
1:18-20............ 146
2:14-15............ 146
5:15-19.............. 63
8:16.................. 203
8:28.................... 53
10:1.................. 169
11................ 25, 27
12-16.......... 49-50, 59, 61
12:1.................... 59
12:1-9................ 50
12:9-21.............. 51
12:21.................. 52
13................ 90, 139
13:1-7.......... 124, 134

Word to the World

Romans (cont.)
13:1-14 52
13:3-14 53
13:8-10 48
13:8-14 53
13:5 144
14:1-15:6 54
14:1-15:13 .... 55, 57
14:5-8 56
14:13-15:6 56
15:15-16, 23-32. 58
16:5-15 58
16:2-3, 16-24 ... 59

1 Corinthians
4:7 51
9:14 93
11:2 73
12-13, 14 50
15:14, 17 15

2 Corinthians
7:1 195

Galatians
5:14 48
6:10 69

Ephesians
2:11-22 64
4:5 14
4:25-6:9 50
5:21 52
5:22-33 60-1

Colossians
3:3 201
3:18ff 61

2 Thessalonians
2:15 73
3:6 73

1 Timothy
1:17 13
2:1-2 109
2:1-5 121
2:1-6 124
2:1-7 134
2:2-7 .... 113, 118

2 Timothy
3:3 182
3:12 109

Hebrews
11 58
13:5 16

James
2:1-4 68
2:8 48
5:12 171

1 Peter
1:19 201
2 139
2:13-17 .... 124, 134
3:1ff 61

1 John
4:19 48

Revelation
1:10-16 225
15:2-4 162
20 25-6

PERSONS INDEX

Abraham 12, 278
Adam 63-4, 199, 201, 248, 267-8, 270
Agrippa, King 15
Alexander, Archibald 175, 276, 289-90
Alsted, Johann Heinrich 26
Ambrose, Bishop of Milan 108, 111, 200, 264
Ames, William 23-4, 191, 260, 265
Anderson, James 239
Andrew (disciple) 16
Andrews, Jedidiah 235, 237, 239, 241-2, 257
Anselm 200, 290
Antoninus Pius, Emperor 120, 148
Aquila 59
Aquinas, Thomas 176, 200
Archbold, Andrew 239
Aristotle 112, 200
Arrowsmith, John 38, 267
Ashe, Simeon 186-8, 267
Athanasius 42, 200, 289
Augustine (of Hippo) 14, 25, 31, 111, 115, 126, 134, 176, 200, 260-2, 269, 273, 277-8, 283, 289
Augustus, Emperor 124, 140

Bahnsen, Greg L. 131-3, 136-7, 145-6
Baillie, Robert 162, 164-5
Ball, John 266
Bancroft, Richard 167-8
Bar Kochba 141
Barber, Edward 183
Barlow, William 168
Barth, Karl 277
Basil 200, 264
Battles, Ford Lewis 286
Bavinck, Herman 277
Baxter, Richard 152, 167, 186, 191
Beadle, Abigail 194
Bellarmine, Robert 176
Berkouwer, G. C. 277, 291
Bernard of Clairvaux 111-12, 200
Beza, Theodore 25, 200, 276

Boniface VIII, Pope 31, 126
Bosch, David J. 44
Bossuet, Bishop 111
Boyd, Adam 239
Bradford, John 272, 289, 293, 295-306
Brent, Sir Nathaniel 159
Bridge, William 26, 180
Briggs, Charles Augustus 233, 279, 287
Brightman, Thomas 26

Bromiley, Geoffrey W. 277, 279
Brooks, Thomas 194-5
Browne, Sir Thomas 262, 269
Bucer, Martin 21-2, 25, 289, 296-7, 304
Bullinger, Johann Heinrich 200, 289
Buren, Martin van 86
Burgess, Cornelius 158, 160-1, 168, 177, 181, 184
Burroughes, Jeremiah 26, 160, 167, 176, 266
Burton, Henry 183
Bushnell, Horace 102-3
Buxbaum, Melvin 238
Byfield, Adoniram 267

Calamy, Edmund (the Elder) 39-40, 160, 174-90, 192, 194, 266
Calamy, Edmund (the Younger) 189-90
  family descendants 190
Calvin, John 21-2, 24-5, 30, 32, 35, 112, 135-6, 168, 174, 200, 260, 262-5, 269, 275-80, 289-90, 296-7
Calovius, Abraham 280
Carlyle, Thomas 100
Cartwright, Thomas 29, 32
Caryl, Joseph 166, 191, 266
Case, Thomas 185, 266
Castell, Robert 167
Cathcart, Robert 239
Cawdrey, Daniel 267
Chalmers, Thomas 93-5
Channing, William Ellery 80
Charlemagne 20, 126
Charles I of England 154, 163, 166, 184, 194-5
Charles II of England 167, 185-7, 195
Charnock, Stephen 196
Chrysostom 200, 289
Clarendon, 1st Earl of (Edward Hyde) 158, 161
Clarke, Samuel 171, 244
Colman, Benjamin 241
Constantine, Emperor 30, 111, 125, 134
Cope, Sir Anthony 167, 169
Cotton, John 26, 37, 39, 41-2
Coverdale, Miles 295
Craig, John 156
Cranmer, Thomas 30, 295-6, 304
Creaghead, Thomas 239
Cromwell, Oliver 154, 159, 163, 165, 185, 193-5
Cromwell, Richard 185
Cross, Robert 239-41, 245, 253, 255, 257

317

Crow, Jim 119
Cyprian 200

Daniel 137, 149
Darius 137
Davenport, John 41
David 12, 107-8, 110, 136
Deborah 161
Decius, Emperor 125
Dickinson, Jonathan 213, 230, 234, 239, 242-3, 245-6, 252-4, 257
  See also 'Jenkins, Obadiah'
Diocletian, Emperor 30, 125, 134
Dod, John 167, 169, 297
Dowey, Edward A., Jnr. 278

Edward VI of England 25, 31, 154, 293, 295, 304, 306
Edwards, Jonathan 13, 43, 289, 294
Eliot, John 41-23
Elizabeth I of England 29, 31, 154
Ephraim 278
Eusebius 111
Evans, David 239
Evans, Thomas 239
Eve 63, 267-8, 270

Fagius, Paul 25
Felton, Nicholas 176
Firmin, Giles 163
Forsyth, P. T. 277, 290
Foster, James 244
Foxe, John 29, 297, 300
Franklin, Benjamin 214, 230, 234, 237-8, 240-1, 243-8
Fuller, Thomas 36, 157

Gataker, Thomas 168, 267
Gelasius I, Pope 31, 125, 134
Gillespie, George 239
Goodwin, Thomas 26, 266
Gordon, Alexander 160
Gouge, William 39-40, 192, 267-9
Greenham, Richard 297
Gregory VII, Pope 30 126, 134
Gregory the Great 200
Grotius, Hugo 200

Hall, David W. 259-61, 265-7
Hall, Joseph 160, 177
Haller, William 29, 162, 175
Ham 63
Hamor 278
Harris, Robert 167-74
Hemphill, Samuel 214-16, 229-30, 232, 234-9, 251-7
Henry IV, Emperor 126
Henry VIII of England 20, 154, 293, 295-6
Herle, Charles 168, 267
Hezekiah 136, 182
Hill, Anita 119

Hill, Christopher 183
Hill, Thomas 37-8, 192
Hippolytus 141
Hodge, A. A. 78, 272-3, 276, 284-5
Hodge, Charles 73-105, 208, 217-22, 226, 228, 276, 282, 284, 286
Honywood, Mary 300, 302
Hooker, Thomas 41-2
Hopkins, Charles Howard 102
Houston, Joseph 239, 255
Hoyle, Joshua 168, 180
Hubbel, Nathaniel 239
Hunt, Elizabeth 170
Hutchison, Alexander 239

Ibbot, Benjamin 244
Innocent III, Pope 31, 126, 134
Irenaeus 25, 200, 289
Isaac 11
Isaiah 121

Jacob 11, 278
Jacob, Henry 24
James (disciple) 16
James I of England 154
Jamison, Robert 239
Janaway, Andrew 180
Japheth 63
Jehoshaphat 136
'Jenkins, Obadiah' 245-6, 249 (alias for Dickinson. Jonathan)
Jeremiah 109, 278
Jerome 200, 278
Jewel, John 23
John (disciple) 16, 48
John the Baptist 67
John Paul II, Pope 113
Joseph 278
Joshua 16
Josiah 31, 136
Judas (Iscariot) 67
Julius Caesar 200
Justin Martyr 120, 148-9

Kilpatrick, J. 236
King, Rodney 119
Knollys, Hanserd 184
Knox, John 23, 30, 112, 156, 289, 296
Knyvett, Thomas 161
Küng, Hans 284
Kuyper, Abraham 277

Laud, William 41, 154, 159
Latimer, Hugh 295-6, 304
Leaver, Anne 190
Leith, John H. 155, 281
Ley, John 265, 268
Lightfoot, John 265, 267-8
Lincoln, Abraham 101, 117-18
Lindsay, T. M. 277
Little, David 32

Persons Index

Liu, Tai 175
Locke, John 249
Louis XIV of France 111
Loury, Glenn 121
Love, Christopher 195
Luke 278
Luther, Martin 14, 20, 25, 35, 45, 135, 200, 262, 276-7, 290, 297, 300

Machen, J. Gresham 224, 276, 287-8
Machin, John 38
McKim, Donald 273-5, 277-87, 289-91
Manton, Thomas 185
Marshall, Stephen 157-67, 175, 177-9, 181, 266
Marx, Karl 103
Mary (Queen of England) 31, 154, 296-7
Mather, Cotton 41, 43
Matthew (disciple) 12, 16, 148
Mede, Joseph 26, 162
Melanchthon, Philipp 200, 276, 287
Miller, Samuel 289
Milton, John 20, 30, 160
Mitchell, Alexander 166
Monck, General George 187
Morgan, Edmund 23
Moses 16, 264, 291
Murray, Iain 26

Nahum ben Simai of Tiberia 141
Napoleon, Louis 87
Nebuchadnezzar 137, 149
Nero, Emperor 52
Newcomen, Matthew 160, 177, 181
Nichols, James Hastings 233
Nicole, Roger R. 279
Noah 63, 172
Nye, John 165
Nye, Philip 164-5, 178

Oecolampadius 200
Orr, James 277
Owen, John 152, 275

Packer, J. I. 186
Paley, William 82
Palmer, Herbert 39-41, 162, 192, 267
Paul 12, 14-15, 48, 50-61, 63-4, 68, 73, 91, 109, 113, 146-7
Paul, Robert S. 184
Pemberton, Ebenezer 239-41, 246, 253
Pepys, Samuel 186
Perkins, William 25, 27, 32, 191, 200, 265, 269, 289, 297
Peter (disciple) 12, 15-16, 61, 69
Peter Martyr Vermigli 25, 27, 276
Philip (disciple) 16
Philip IV of France 126
Pierson, John 239
Pilate 32, 52-3, 138
Plato 200

Plutarch 200
Polec, Eddie 119
Prince, Thomas 241
Priscilla 59
Pym, John 158-9, 161

Reid, James 1160, 175, 187
Reynolds, Edward 168, 185-6
Rich, Robert (2nd Earl of Warwick) 158, 160, 176
Ridley, Nicholas 296-7
Robinson, John 24
Roborough, Henry 180
Rockwell, Norman 120
Rogers, George 197
Rogers, Jack 273-5, 277-87, 289-91
Rogers, Richard 159
Rooy, Sidney H. 27-8
Rossiter, Clinton 74-5
Rupert, Prince 37
Rupp, Gordon 295

Sadoleto, Jacopo 22
Sampson, Thomas 295, 297-8, 301
Samuel 110
Sandeen, Ernest 285
Saul 110
Satan 28, 44, 70, 100, 114, 201, 302
Scaliger, Joseph 200
Schafer, Thomas 233
Schaff, Philip 155-6
Scudder, Henry 169-70, 174
Seaver, Paul 161
Shem 63
Sibbes, Richard 289
Simpson, O. J. 119
Smith, Lacey Baldwin 294
Smith, Morton H. 270
Snelling, Mary 189
Socrates 200
Solomon 110, 119
Spurgeon, Charles Haddon 197-8
Spurstowe, William 160, 177, 181, 185
Stauffer, Ethelbert 141
Staunton, Edmund 174
Stephen 51, 278
Stubbs, John 29

Temple, Thomas 168
Tennent, Gilbert 227, 239
Tennent, William Snr. 239
Tennent, William Jnr. 239
Tertullian 149, 200
Theodosius the Great 108, 111, 134
Thomas (disciple) 16
Thomas, Clarence 119
Thompson, John 213
Thomson, John 239, 252, 254-7
Tiberius, Emperor 124, 140
Timothy 59, 109
Treat, Richard 239

319

Word to the World

Trevor-Roper, H. R. 158, 161
Tuckney, Anthony 39, 192
Turretin, Francis 276, 280-2, 284, 286
Twisse, William 26, 162, 265, 268
Tyndale, William 295

Ursinus, Zacharias 266
Ussher, James (archbishop) 167, 265-6, 269
Uzziah 121

Vance, Patrick 236
Vane, Henry Jnr. 164
Vere, Lady Mary 193
Vincent, Thomas 266-7
Voetius, Gisbert 280

Walker, George 265, 267-8
Warfield, B. B. 222-4, 272-3, 275-7, 284-5, 287
Wallis, John 185, 266
Watson, Thomas 152, 193-206
Weigel, Georg 113

Wendel, François 22
Whately, William 169-70
White, James 37
White, John 36-7, 177, 192, 265
Whitefield, George 43, 289-90
Wilberforce, William 65
Wilkinson, Elizabeth 173
Wilson, John F. 162, 179
Wilson, Woodrow 77
Winthrop, John 37
Wren, Matthew (bishop) 176

Xavier, Francis 35

Young, Thomas 160, 177
Yule, George 182

Zanchi, Girolami 276
Zechariah 278
Zwingli, Ulrich 289